THE
DICTIONARY
OF
INITIALS

D0582424

THE

DICTIONARY

OF

INITIALS

WHAT THEY MEAN

*A guide to initials, acronyms and abbreviations
compiled and edited by*

HARRIETTE LEWIS

PAPERFRONTS
ELLIOT RIGHT WAY BOOKS
KINGSWOOD, SURREY, U.K.

Made and Printed in Great Britain by Cox & Wyman Ltd., Reading

How To Use This Book

Most of the entries in the dictionary refer to British abbreviations, but many foreign ones are included. These are indicated by the name or initials of the foreign country (for example, USA). International organisations, which are usually in the French language, are not so designated. Latin abbreviations are preceded by the word "Latin" in brackets, and musical terms by the word "music" in brackets.

Where the words represented by the initials are not particularly meaningful, a brief explanation is given in brackets. An English translation is given for foreign abbreviations.

With relatively few exceptions pertaining to large enterprises commonly known by their initials, such as BA and BL, initials employed by commercial undertakings have not generally been included.

The initials are in alphabetical order, but where more than one meaning appears for an initial or initials, the order in which the different meanings are set out is not alphabetical as this would usually serve no purpose to the user. The meanings which are expected to be those more likely or more frequently sought by the user have been given precedence.

Many abbreviations are often found punctuated, usually with full stops. But for clarity and ease of reference, they are all printed in this dictionary in a non-punctuated form.

Foreword And Acknowledgements

As I indicated in the much more restricted edition which was published privately a few years ago, this Guide is designed to soothe the temper of everyone who suffers from the current world-wide initial mania, which is just about everybody including our children whose "General Knowledge" question papers are now plagued with them.

The ailment has in fact reached epidemic proportions. It is plainly incurable but it can be alleviated by having, in the office, in the home and in the schoolroom, a copy of the new edition which contains several thousand additional entries.

I express my most sincere thanks to the Bolivian, Dutch, French, German, Greek, Irish, South African, Spanish, Swedish and Turkish Embassies as well as to the Zimbabwe High Commission for their invaluable help. In particular, I must thank Mr. Knopfli of the Portuguese Embassy who so kindly assisted me on a number of occasions.

My gratitude is also due to Dr. Preston of Queen Mary College, University of London, and to Mr. Howard Fisher, Deputy Director of the National Institute of Adult Education, for their so very kind and repeated assistance; nor would these few words of appreciation be complete without including all those who wrote or telephoned with their helpful suggestions, among whom of course I include all my friends as well as those of my colleagues in the National Council of Women of Great Britain who gave me their most generous assistance with this difficult, and often perplexing, task.

Finally, but by no means least, my sincerest thanks to Janet Pusey who had the unenviable and complicated task not only of typing the script but of inserting the thousands of additional initials in alphabetical sequence and I am grateful to her for her most appropriate suggestions.

H.L.

A

A Austrian International Motor Vehicle Registration Letter; film censorship *classification (now PG, q.v.)*

A1 In first-rate condition

A1/2/3 etc. Size of paper; classification and number of road

AA Air Attaché; Alcoholics Anonymous *(see also Al-Anon)*; Automobile Association; Architectural Association; Anti-Aircraft; Area Administrator; Anglers' Association; *(Spain)* Apostolic Anti-Communist Alliance; film censorship classification *(now "18")*

AAA Amateur Athletics Association; Action on Alcohol Abuse; Action Against Allergy; American Automobile Association; Australian Automobile Association; American Accountancy Association; Arab Aid Agencies; *(Argentina)* Anti-Communist Alliance *(right-wing secret society)*; *(Romania)* Automobile Association

AAAA American Amateur Athletic Association; American Association of Advertising Agencies; Australian Association of Advertising Agencies

AAAl Associate of the Institute of Administrative Accounting and Processing Ltd

AAAL American Academy of Arts and Letters

AAAS American Association for the Advancement of Science *(also known as Triple AS)*; American Academy of Arts and Sciences

AAC Agricultural Advisory Council; Amateur Athletic Club

AACC All Africa Conference of Churches

AACCA Now ACCA, *q.v.*

AACE Association for Adult and Continuing Education

AACP Anglo-American Council on Productivity

AACR Anglo-American Cataloguing Rules

AAE Association for Adult Education; American Association of Engineers

AAeE Associate in Aeronautical Engineering

AAETP *(USA)* Area Alcohol Education and Training Program

AAF *(USA)* Army Air Force; Auxiliary Air Force *(now RAAF, q.v.)*

AAG Assistant Adjutant General

AAI Association of Art Institutions; Architectural Association of Ireland; Associate of Chartered Auctioneers & Estate Agents' Institute

AAIA Associate of the Association of International Accountants; Associate of

the Australian Institute of Advertising

AAL Academy of Art and Literature; Association of Assistant Librarians

AAM Association of Assistant Mistresses; Anti-Apartheid Movement

AAMC Australian Army Medical Corps; Association of American Medical Colleges

AAMS Associate Member of the Association of Medical Secretaries, Practice Administrators and Receptionists

AAMSS Association of Assistant Masters/Mistresses in Secondary Schools

A and AEE Aeroplane and Armament Experimental Establishment

A and SH Argyll and Southern Highlanders

AAP Australian Associated Press *(News Agency)*

AAPA Advertising Agency Production Association

AAPC All-African Peoples' Conference

AAPHI Associate of the Association of Public Health Inspectors

AAPO All-African Peoples' Organisation

AAPS American Association for the Promotion of Science

AAPSS American Academy of Political and Social Science

AAPSW Associate of the Association of Psychiatric Social Workers

AAQMG Assistant Adjutant and Quartermaster-General

AAS American Academy of Arts and Sciences; American Astronomical Society; American Astronautical Society; American Antiquarian Society; Australian Academy of Science

AASA Associate of the Australian Society of Accountants

AASI Associate of the Ambulance Service Institute

AASPE *(Greece)* Communist Party

AATA Anglo-American Tourist Association

AAU Amateur Athletic Union

AAUW American Association of University Women

AAY Age Action Year *(1976)*

AB Able-bodied *(seaman)*; *(USA)* Bachelor of Arts; *(Sweden)* Aktiebolaget *(Joint Stock Company)*

Ab Alabamine

ABA Association of British Archaeologists; Amateur Boxing Association; American Booksellers' Association; American Bar Association; Antiquarian Booksellers' Association

ABAA Associate of the British Association of Accountants and Auditors; Antiquarian Booksellers' Association of America

ABAFA Association of British Adoption and Fostering Agencies

ABAS Association of Broadcasting Staffs

ABBA Amateur Basket Ball Association

ABBO Associate of the British Ballet Organisation

ABC The English Alphabet; Alphabetical Railway Guide; Advance Booking Charters *(on airlines)*; American Broadcasting Corporation; Australian Broadcasting Commission

ABCA *(USA)* Army Bureau of Current Affairs

ABCC Association of British Chambers of Commerce; Atomic Bomb Casualty Commission

ABCFM American Board of Commissioners for Foreign Missions

ABCM Association of British Chemical Manufacturers

ABD Association of British Detectives

ABF Actors' Benevolent Fund

ABH Alpha-Benzene-Hexachloride

ABHA Associate of the British Hypnotherapy Association

ABI Association of British Investigators

ABID Associate of the British Institute of Interior Design

ABIM Associate of the British Institute of Management; Association of British Insecticide Manufacturers

ab init *(Latin)* ab initio *(from the beginning)*

ABIS Association of Burglary Insurance Surveyors

ABLC Association of British Launderers and Cleaners

ABM Anti-Ballistic Missile

ABMEWS Anti-Ballistic Missile Early Warning System

ABMEX Association of British Mining Equipment Exporters

ABMPM Association of British Manufacturers of Printers' Machinery

ABO Area Building Officer

ABOY *(Finland)* Aktiebolag *(Joint Stock Company)*

ABP Associated British Ports *(formerly British Transport Docks)*

ABPD Association of Private Detectives

ABPI Association of the British Pharmaceutical Industry

ABPsS Associate of the British Psychological Society

ABRC Advisory Board on Research Councils

ABRO Animal Breeding Research Organisation

ABS Associate of the Building Societies' Institute; Association of Broadcasting and Allied Staffs; African Broadcasting Service; American Bible Society

ABSA Association for Business Sponsorship of the Arts

ABSC Associate of the British Society of Commerce

ABSI Associate of the Boot and Shoe Institution

ABSM Associate of the Birmingham School of Music

ABSW Association of British Science Writers

ABT Association of Building Technicians; American Ballet Theatre; Associate of the Association of Beauty Teachers

ABTA Association of British Travel Agents; Allied Brewery Traders' Association; Australia-British Trade Association

ABTAPL Association of British Theological and Philosophical Libraries

ABTSA Association of British Tree Surgeons and Arborists

ABTT Association of British Theatre Technicians

ABUSE Action to Bar the Sexual Exploitation of Children

ABZ Association of British Zoologists

AC Appeal Court; Army Council; Ambulance Corps; Aircraftsman; Agricultural College; Arts Council *(see also CEMA)*; Assistant Commissioner; Appeal Cases *(House of Lords and Privy Council)*; *(Latin)* Ante Christum *(before Christ)*; Alternating Current *(electricity)*; Companion of the Order of Australia; *(France)* Appellation Controlée *(State-Controlled Wine Quality)*

Ac Actinium

A/c, a/c Account

ac Author's correction

ACA Associate of the Institute of Chartered Accountants; Advisory Committee on Alcoholism; Agile Combat Aircraft; Associate in Commercial Arts; Angler's Co-operative Association; Australian Council for Aeronautics

ACACE Advisory Council for Adult and Continuing Education

Acad Academy

ACAE Associated Corporate Accountancy Executive *(Association of International Accountants)*

ACARD Advisory Council for Applied Research and Development

ACAS Advisory Conciliation and Arbitration Service; Assistant Chief of the Air Staff

ACAST Advisory Committee on the Application of Science & Technology *(UN, q.v.)*

ACATS Association of Civil Aviation

Technical Staffs

ACBSI Associate of the Chartered Building Societies' Institute

ACC Association of County Councils; Association of Chambers of Commerce; Army Catering Corps; Administrative Committee on Co-ordination *(UN, q.v.)*

ACCA Associate of the Association of Certified Accountants

ACCC Area Chemist Contractors' Committee *(NHS, q.v.)*

ACCEd Associate of the College of Craft Education

ACCEPT Alcohol Community Centre for Education, Prevention and Treatment

ACCESS Automatic Computer Controlled Electronic Scanning System

ACCI Association of Chambers of Commerce of Ireland

ACCM Advisory Council for the Church's Ministry *(formerly CACTM, q.v.)*

ACCO Association of Child Care Officers

ACCS Associate of the Corporation of Secretaries *(formerly of Certified Secretaries)*

ACDA *(USA)* Arms Control and Disarmament Agency

ACDS Assistant Chief of Defence Staff

ACE Advisory Centre for Education; Association of Consulting Engineers; Allied Command Europe *(of NATO, q.v.)*; Association of Cultural Exchange; American Council of Education

ACEA Associate of the Association of Cost and Executive Accountants; *(Algeria)* Association Culturelle et Educative à Algérie *(Cultural and Educational Association of Algeria . . . White Fathers)*

ACEC Advisory Council on Energy Conservation

ACEM Assembly of the Council of European Municipalities *(see also CEM)*

ACERT Advisory Committee for the Education of Romanies and other Travellers

ACF Army Cadet Force; *(France)* Automobile Club de France *(Automobile Club)*

ACFHE Association of Colleges for Further and Higher Education

ACFI Associate of the Clothing and Footwear Institute

ACG Assistant Chaplain General

ACGB Arts Council of Great Britain

ACGI Associateship of the City and Guilds of London Institute

ACh Associate of the Institute of Chiropodists

ACHA *(Spain)* Alliance Cultural Hispano-Americano *(Society for the promotion of Spanish and South American Culture)*

ACHE *(Egypt)* Association Culturelle de la Haute Egypte pour les écoles et la promotion sociale *(Cultural Association)*

AChS Associate of the Chiropodists' Society

ACI Associate of the Institute of Commerce; *(Italy)* Automobile Club d'Italia *(Automobile Club)*

ACIA Association of the Corporation of Insurance Agents

ACIArb Associate of the Chartered Institute of Arbitrators

ACIB Associate of the Corporation of Insurance Brokers

ACII Associate of the Chartered Insurance Institute

ACILA Associate of the Chartered Institute of Loss Adjusters

ACIOB Associate of the Chartered Institute of Building

ACIS Associate of the Institute of Chartered Secretaries and Administrators

ACIT Associate of the Chartered Institute of Transport

ACL Atlantic Container Line; *(Brazil)* Academia Carioca de Létras *(Rio de Janeiro Academy of Literature)*; *(Chile)* Academia Chilena de la Lengua *(Academy of Languages)*; *(Portugal)* Academia das Ciencias de Lisboa *(Lisbon Academy of Science)*

ACLANT Allied Command Atlantic *(of NATO, q.v.)*

ACLD Association for Children with Learning Disabilities

ACLP Association of Contact-Lens Practitioners

ACLS Automatic Carrier Landing System; American Council of Learned Societies

ACLU American Civil Liberties Union

ACM Air Chief Marshal; Association for Computing Machines

ACMA Associate of the Institute of Cost and Management Accountants

ACMC Association of Canadian Medical Colleges

ACML Anti-Common Market League

ACMS Approved Coal Merchants' Scheme; Agricultural Co-operation and Marketing Services

ACNS Assistant Chief of Naval Staff

ACO Association of Children's Officers

ACOP Association of Chief Officers of Police

ACORD Advisory Council in Research and Development

ACOS Assistant Chief of Staff

ACP Association of Clinical Pathologists; Advisory Committee on Pesticides; Africa, Caribbean and Pacific Ocean Countries *(47 partners of the European Community)*; Associate of the College of

Preceptors; Association of Correctors of the Press

ACPO Association of Chief Police Officers; Association of Chief Probation Officers

ACR Annual Confidential Report

ACRA *(USA)* Associate of the Corporation of Registered Accountants

ACRE Automatic Call Recording Equipment *(British Telecommunications)*

ACRO Association for the Care and Resettlement of Offenders

ACROSS Catholic charity *(taking people to Lourdes)*

ACS Alcohol Counselling Service; Access Control System; Association of Commonwealth Students; Additional Curates' Society; American Chemical Society; American College of Surgeons; *(Switzerland)* Automobil Club der Schweiz *(Automobile Club)*

ACSEA Allied Command South East Asia

ACSET Advisory Committee on Supply and Education of Teachers

ACSIR Advisory Council for Scientific and Industrial Research

ACSN Association of Collegiate Schools of Nursing

ACSTI Advisory Committee for Scientific and Technical Information

ACSTT Advisory Committee for the Supply and Training of Teachers

ACSW *(Canada)* Advisory Council on the Status of Women

ACT Association of Career Teachers; Advance Corporation Tax; Associate of the College of Technology; Australian Capital Territory; Association of Christian Teachers; *(USA)* Action on Children's Television

ACTC Art Class Teachers' Certificate

ACTO Advisory Council on the Treatment of Offenders

ACTS Advisory Committee for Toxic Substances

ACTSS Association of Clerical, Technical and Supervisory Staffs

ACTT Association of Cinematograph, Television and Allied Technicians

ACTU Australian Council of Trade Unions

ACU Association of Commonwealth Universities; Auto Cycle Union

ACV Air Cushion Vehicle

ACW Association of Community Workers; Aircraft Woman

ACWF *(China)* All-China Women's Federation

ACWU *(USA)* Amalgamated Clothes Workers' Union

ACWW Association of Country Women of the World

AD *(Latin)* Anno Domini *(in the year*

of our Lord); Architectural Design

Ad Advertisement

ADA Agricultural Development Association; Action for Dysphasic Adults; Americans for Democratic Action; *(USA)* Atomic Development Authority

ADAC *(West Germany)* Allgemeiner Deutscher Automobil Club *(Automobile Club)*

ADARF *(Ontario, Canada)* Addiction Research Foundation

ADAS Agricultural Development and Advisory Service

ADAT Army Dependants' Assurance Trust

ADB Associate of the Drama Board; *(Afghanistan)* Agricultural Development Bank

ADB(Ed) Associate of the Drama Board (Education)

ADB(S) Associate of the Drama Board (Special)

ADBAG Anti-Discrimination Bill Action Group

ADC Association of District Councils; Area Dental Committee; Aide-de-Camp; Amateur Dramatic Club; Aid to Dependent Children; Automatic Digital Calculator; Advise Dialling Charge *(telephone)*

ADCM Archbishop *(of Canterbury's)* Diploma in Church Music

ADC(P) Personal Aide-de-Camp to Her/His Majesty

ADEA American Drugs Enforcement Administration

ADES Association of Directors of Education, Scotland

ADF Automatic Direction Finder; *(Switzerland)* Assocation pour les Droits de Femme *(Association for Women's Rights)*

ADFAED Abu Dhabi Fund for Arab Economic Development

ADFW Assistant Director of Fortifications and Works

ADG Assistant Director General

ADGB Air Defence of GB, *q.v.*

ADGMS Assistant Director General of Medical Services

ADH Association of Dental Hospitals; Assistant Director of Hygiene

ADI Approved Driving Instructor

ADJAG Assistant Deputy Judge Advocate General

Adjt Adjutant

Adjt-Gen Adjutant-General

ADLP Australian Democratic Labour Party

ADM Annual Delegates Meeting

Adm/Adml Admiral

ADMA *(USA)* Aviation Distributors and Manufacturers Association; American Drug Manufacturers' Association

Admin Administrator/Administration

ADMS Assistant Director of Medical Services; American Director of Medical Services

ADN *(East Germany)* News Agency; Yemen International Motor Vehicle Registration Letters

ADO Assistant District Officer; Air Defence Officer; Association of Dispensing Opticians; Advanced Development Objective *(of USAF, q.v.)*

ADOS Assistant Director of Ordnance Services

ADP Association of Directors and Producers; Automatic Data Processing *(computers)*

ADPP Assistant Director of Public Prosecutions

ADPR Assistant Director of Public Relations

ADR Accord Européen Relative au Transport International des Marchandises Dangereuses par Route *(European Agreement on the International Transport of Dangerous Goods by Road)*

ADRA Animal Diseases Research Association

ADS Arab Development Society *(West Bank)*

ADS and T Assistant Director of Supplies and Transport

ADSS Association of Directors of Social Services

ad val *(Latin)* ad valorem *(in proportion to the value)*

ADVS Assistant Director of Veterinary Services

AE Atomic Energy; Aeronautical Engineer; Agricultural Engineer; Area Engineer

AEA Atomic Energy Authority *(see also UKAEA)*; Agricultural Engineers' Association; Actors' Equity Association; Agricultural Educational Association

AEAF Allied Expeditionary Air Force

AEB Associated Examining Board *(GCE, q.v.)*

AEC Association of Education Committees; Alcohol Education Centre; Agricultural Executive Council; *(USA)* Atomic Energy Commission

AECI Associate Member of the Institute of Employment Consultants

AECILic Licentiate Associate Member of the Institute of Employment Consultants

AEE Atomic Energy Establishment

AEF Allied Expeditionary Force; Amalgamated Union of Engineering and Foundry Workers; American Expeditionary Force; Australian Expeditionary Force

AEGIS Aid for the Elderly in Government Institutions

AEI Associated Electrical Industries

AELTC All-England Lawn Tennis Club

AEM Air Efficiency Medal

AENA All-England Netball Association

AER Aer Lingus *(Eire airline)*; Army Emergency Reserve

AERE Atomic Energy Research Establishment *(Harwell)*

AERI Agricultural Economics Research Institute

AES Agricultural Economics Society; Alternative Economic Strategy

aet *(Latin)* aetatis *(of the age of)*

AEU Amalgamated Engineering Union

AEW Aircraft Early Warning *(RADAR, q.v.)*

AF Air Force; Anglo-French; Audio Frequency; American Forces; *(France)* Associations Familiales *(Family Associations)*; *(France)* Action Française *(Royalist Party)*

AF 39 Exocet Missile

af or a/f at fault; as found *(auctioneers' terminology)*

AFA Associate of the Faculty of Actuaries; Associate in Fine Arts; Associate of the Faculty of Auditors; Amateur Football Association/Alliance; Amateur Fencing Association

AFAIAA Associate Fellow of the American Institute of Aeronautics and Astronautics

AFAS Associate of the Faculty of Architects and Surveyors; *(France)* Association Française pour l'Avancement de Science *(Association for the Advancement of Science)*

AFASIC Association For All Speech-Impaired Children

AFBIS Associate Fellow of the British Interplanetary Society

AFBU Amalgamated Film and Broadcasting Union

AFC Air Force Cross; Association Football Club; Automatic Frequency Control

AFCAI Associate Fellow of the Canadian Aeronautical Institute

AFCL Associate of the Farriers Company of London

AFCS Associate of the Faculty of Secretaries

AFD *(USA)* Doctor of Fine Arts

AFDCS Association of First Division Civil Servants *(see also CSFDA and IPCS)*

AFFDU *(France)* Association Française des Femmes Diplomées des Universités *(University Women's Association)*

Affil SLAET Affiliate of the Society of Licensed Aircraft Engineers and Technologists

AffInstSM Affiliate of the Institute of Sales Management

AffIP Affiliate of the Institute of Plumbing

AFFIRM Now WMAG, *q.v.*

AffIWHTE Affiliate of the Institution of Works Highway Technician Engineers

AffRSH Affiliate of the Royal Society of Health

AFG Afghanistan International Motor Vehicle Registration Letters

AFHQ Allied Forces HQ, *q.v.*

AFI Association des Femmes Ivoriennes *(NCW, q.v. of the Ivory Coast)*; American Film Institute

AFICD Associate Fellow of the Institute of Civil Defence

AFIMA Associate Fellow of the Institute of Mathematics and its Applications

AFLA Association of Fire Loss Adjusters

AFLCIO American Federation of Labour and Congress of Industrial Organisation

AFM Air Force Medal; *(Portugal)* Armed Forces Movement *(see also MFA)*

AFNOR *(France)* L'Association Française de Normalization *(Standards Association)*

AFO Admiralty Fleet Order

AFOM Associate of the Faculty of Occupational Medicine

AFP Alpha-fetoprotein *(blood test on pregnant women)*; *(France)* Agence France-Presse *(News Agency)*

AFPA *(France)* L'Association pour la Formation Professionelle des Adultes *(Professional Association of Adults)*

AFRAeS Associate Fellow of the Royal Aeronautical Society

AFRC *(Ghana)* Armed Forces Revolutionary Council

AFS Associate of the Faculty of Architects and Surveyors; Auxiliary Fire Service; African Front Line States; American Field Service *(High School Pupils)*

AFSC American Friends Service Committee

AFSERT Associate Fellow of the Society of Electronic and Radio Technicians

AFSLAET Associate Fellow of the Society of Licensed Aircraft Engineers and Technologists

AFTCom Associate of the Faculty of Teachers in Commerce

AFTIM *(France)* Association Française des Ingénieurs, Techniciens de Securité et Médicins du Travail *(Association of Engineers, Security Technicians and Medical Staff for Workers)*

AFV Armoured Fighting Vehicle

AG Attorney General; Adjutant General; *(West Germany)* Aktiengesellschaft *(Limited Company)*

Ag *(Latin)* Argentum *(Silver)*

AGA Amateur Gymnastics Association

AGAA American Gay Artists' Association

AGARD Advisory Group for Aerospace Research and Development

AGC Automatic Gain Control

AGCL Associate Member of the Guild of Cleaners and Launderers

AGENOR Transnational Socialist Group

AGERPRES *(Romania)* News Agency

AGGIE Royal Agricultural Hall *(affectionate title)*

AGI Associate of the Greek Institute; Associate of the Institute of Certificated Grocers; Artistes Graphiques Internationales *(Association of International Graphic Artists)*; Année Géophysique Internationale *(International Geophysical Year)*

AGIN Action Group on Immigration and Nationality

AGM Annual General Meeting; Air-to-Ground Missile

AGR Advanced Gas-cooled Reactor

AGRA Army Group Royal Artillery

AGS American Geographical Society; American Gynaecological Society

AGSM Associate of the Guildhall School of Music

AH Association of Headmistresses *(now joined with Headmasters' Association to form SHA, q.v.)*

AHA Area Health Authority *(NHS, q.v., now DHA, q.v.)*; Associate of the Institute of Health Service Administrators; American Hospitals Association

AHA(T) Area Health Authority (Teaching, now *DHA(T), q.v.*

AHCIMA Associate of the Hotel Catering and Institutional Management Association

AHE Association of Home Economists

AHEO Area Health Education Officers *(NHS, q.v.)*

AHIC Authorised Home Improvement Centre

AHMC Association of Hospital Management Committees

AHPhC Area Hospital Pharmaceutical Committees *(NHS, q.v.)*

AHPS Association of Headmistresses in Preparatory Schools

AHQ Army Headquarters

AHS Arab Horse Society

AHWA Association of Hospital and Welfare Administrators

AHWC Associate of the Heriot/Watt College *(Edinburgh)*

AHY Architectural Heritage Year *(1975)*

AI⁻ Amnesty International; Artificial Insemination

AIA Associate of the Institute of Actuaries; American Institute of Architects

AIAA Architect Member of Incorporated Association of Architects and

Surveyors

AIAE Associate of the Institution of Automobile Engineers

AIAgrE Associate of the Institution of Agricultural Engineers

AIAL Associate Member of the International Institute of Arts and Letters

AIAS Associate Surveyor Member of the Incorporated Association of Architects and Surveyors

AIAT Associate of the Institute of Animal Technicians; Associate of the Institute of Asphalt Technology

AIB Associate of the Institute of Bankers

AIB (Scot) Associate of the Institute of Bankers (Scotland)

AIBA Associate of the Institution of Business Agents

AIBD Associate of the Incorporated Institute of British Decorators and Interior Designers

AIBICC Associate of the Incorporated British Institute of Certified Carpenters

AIBiol Associate Member of the Institute of Biology

AIBP Associate of the Institute of British Photographers

AIC Agricultural Improvement Council; Associate of the Institute of Chemistry; Association of Independent Cinemas

AICA Association Internationale des Critiques d'Arts *(Association of International Art Critics)*

AICC All-India Congress Committee

AICE Associate of the Institution of Civil Engineers

AICeram Associate of the Institute of Ceramics

AIChor Associate of the Benesh Institute of Choreology

AICS Associate of the Institute of Chartered Shipbrokers

AICTA Associate of the Institute of the Imperial College of Tropical Agriculture

AICW Associate of the Institute of Clerks of Works

AID Agency for International Development; Action in Distress; All-Ireland Distress; Automatic Incident Detector; Arts In Danger; Assistance in Divorce; Acute Infectious Disease; Artificial Insemination by Donor

AIDDA *(Italy)* Associazione Italiana Delle Donne Amministrative *(Association of Women Executives)*

AIDS Acquired Immune Deficiency Syndrome *(health disorder)*

AIDTA Associate of the International Dance Teachers' Association

AIEE Associate of the Institution of Electrical Engineers

AIEM Associate of the Institute of Executives and Managers *(in the service*

industries); Association Internationale des Employées Municipales *(International Association of Local Government Officials)*

AIESEC Association Internationale des Etudiants en Sciences Economiques et Commerciales *(International Association of Students of Economics and Commerce)*

AIExpE Associate of the Institute of Explosives Engineers

AIF Alliance Internationale des Femmes *(Women's International Alliance, see also IAW)*; Australian Imperial Forces

AIFA Associate of the Institute of the International Faculty of Arts

AIFireE Affiliate of the Institution of Fire Engineers

AIFM Associate of the Institute of Factory Managers

AIFST Associate of the Institute of Food Science and Technology

AIGM Associate of the Institute of General Managers

AIH Associate of the Institute of Housing; Artificial Insemination by Husband

AIHA Associate of the Institute of Hospital Administrators

AIHVE Associate of the Institution of Heating and Ventilating Engineers

AII All-India International *(Airline)*

AIIAL Associate of the International Institute of Arts and Letters

AIIM Associate of the Institution of Industrial Managers

AIInfSc Associate of the Institute of Information Scientists

AIIP Associate of the Institute of Incorporated Photographers

AIITech Associate of the Institute of Incorporated Technologists

AIJPF L'Association Internationale des Journalistes de la Presse Féminine *(Association of International Women Journalists)*

AIL Associate of the Institute of Linguists

AILA Associate of the Institute of Land Agents

AILGA Associate of the Institute of Local Government Administrators

AIM Associate of the Institution of Metallurgists; *(Mozambique)* Information Agency

AIMarE Associate of the Institute of Marine Engineers

AIMBI Associate Member of the Institute of Medical and Biological Illustration

AIME Associate of the Institution of Mining Engineers; American Institute of Mechanical Engineers

AIMIT Associate of the Institute of

Musical Instrument Technology

AIMLS Associate of the Institute of Medical Laboratory Sciences

AIMM Affiliate of the Institution of Mining and Metallurgy; Associate of the Institute of Male Masseurs

AIMO Association of Industrial and Medical Officers

AIMS Association and Improvement Service *(Birmingham Housing Association, see also PIMS)*; Association for Improvement in Maternity Service

AIMTA Associate of the Institute of Municipal Treasurers and Accountants

AInstAM Associate Member of the Institute of Administrative Management

AInstBB Associate of the Institute of British Bakers

AInstBCA Associate of the Institute of Burial and Cremation Administration

AInstFF Associate of the Institute of Freight Forwarders

AInstM Associate of the Institute of Marketing

AInstMO Associate of the Institute of Market Officers

AInstP Associate of the Institute of Physics

AInstPet Associate of the Institute of Petroleum

AInstPI Associate of the Institute of Patentees and Inventors

AInstPS Associate of the Institute of Purchasing and Supply

AInstTA Associate of the Institute of Traffic Administrators

AIOC Associate of the Institute of Carpenters

AIP Association of Independent Producers *(film)*; American Institute of Physics; Associate of the Institute of Plumbing; *(Portugal)* Associaçao Industrial Portuguesa *(Industrial Association)*

AIPA Associate Member of the Institute of Practitioners in Advertising

AIPE Associate of the Institution of Production Engineers

AIPHE Associate of the Institution of Public Health Engineers

AIPM Associate of the Institute of Personnel Management

AIQPS Associate of the Institute of Qualified Private Secretaries

AIQS Associate of the Institute of Quantity Surveyors

AIR All-India Radio

AIRC Association of Independent Radio Contractors

AIRTE Associate of the Institute of Road Transport Engineers

AISA Associate of the Incorporated Secretaries' Association

AISL International Association for the Treatment of Leprosy

AISOB Associate of the Incorproated Society of Organ Builders

AISS Association Internationale de la Science du Sol, *(International Society of Soil Science, see also ISSS)*

AIST Associate of the Institute of Science Technology

AISTD Associate of the Imperial Society of Teachers of Dancing

AISTM Associate of the Institute of Sales Technology and Management

AIStructE Associate of the Institution of Structural Engineers

AIT Associate of the Institute of Transport; Association of Investment Trusts; Association of Her/His Majesty's Inspectors of Taxes

AITO Association of Independent Tour Operators

AITSA Associate Member of the Institute of Trading Standards Administration

AIWC All-India Women's Conference

AIWES Associate of the Institution of Water Engineers and Scientists

AIWSc Associate Member of the Institute of Wood Science

AJAG Assistant Judge Advocate General

AJAX Association of Journalists against Extremism

AJEX Association of Jewish Ex-Servicemen

AJWO Association of Jewish Women's Organisations

AK Knight of the Order of Australia

AKC Associate of King's College *(London)*

AKEL *(Cyprus)* Anorthotike Komma Engazomenou Lao *(Communist Party of the Working People)*

AKIM *(Israel)* Association for the Rehabilitation of the Mentally Handicapped

AL Albanian International Motor Vehicle Registration Letters

Al Aluminium

ALA Associate of the Liberal Arts; Associate of the Library Association; American Library Association

Ala Alabama *(USA State)*

ALAA Associate of the Library Association of Australia

ALAC Artificial Limb and Appliance Centre

ALAM Associate of the London Academy of Music and Dramatic Art

Al-Anon Organisation to help the families of alcoholics *(see also AA)*

ALARM Air-Launched Anti-Radar Missile *(UK, q.v.)*

ALAS Associate of the Chartered Land Agents' Society

Alas Alaska *(USA State)*

Alba Alberta *(Province of Canada)*

ALBM Air-Launched Ballistic Missile

ALBSU Adult Literacy and Basic Skills Unit

ALC Agricultural Land Commission; Association of Local Councillors *(usually preceded by the first letter of the local Council)*; African Liberation Committee

ALCM Associate of the London College of Music *(Performers' Diploma)*

ALCS Authors' Lending and Copyright Society

ALD/Ald Alderman

ALDS Association of Licensed Dealers in Securities *(Now NASDIM, q.v.)*

ALE Association for Liberal Education

ALEC Adult Learners Enquiry Centre

A Level Advanced Level *(GCE, q.v.)*

ALF Animal Liberation Front; Automatic Letter Facer

ALFSEA Allied Land Forces South East Asia

ALGES Association of Local Government Engineers and Surveyors

ALGFO Association of Local Government Financial Officers

ALHE Association of London Housing Estates

ALI Associate of the Landscape Institute; Argyll Light Infantry; *(Italy)* Alitalia *(air line)*

ALIMUPER *(Peru)* Acción para la Liberación de la Mujer Peruana *(Action for the Liberation of Peruvian Women)*

ALIO Association of Life Insurance Offices

ALLC Association for Literacy and Linguistic Computing

AllER/AER All England *(Law)* Reports

ALM Master of the Liberal Arts

ALP Action for Lesbian Parents; Australian Labour Party; American Labour Party

ALPA *(USA)* Air Line Pilots' Association

ALPSP Association of Learned and Professional Society Publishers

ALRA Abortion Law Reform Association; Adult Literacy Resource Agency

ALS Associate of the Linnean Society

Alta Alberta *(Province of Canada)*

Al-Teen Organisation to help the children of alcoholics *(see also AA and Al-Anon)*

ALTU Association of Liberal Trade Unionists

ALU Adult Literacy Unit

ALUT Associateship of Loughborough University of Technology

AM Air Ministry; Air Marshal; Member of the Order of Australia; Albert Medal; *(USA)* Master of Arts; Amplitude Modulation; *(France)* Alpes Maritimes *(Maritime Alps, Department of France)*

Am Americium

am *(Latin)* ante meridiem *(before midday)*

AMA Association of Metropolitan Authorities; Assistant Masters' Association; Associate of the Museums Association; Australian Medical Association

AMAB Army Medical Advisory Board

AMBA Associate Member of the British Arts Association

AMBAC Associate Member of the British Association of Chemists

AMBCS Associate Member of the British Computer Society

AMBEI Associate Member of the Institution of Body Engineers

AMBIM Associate Member of the British Institute of Management

AMBOV Association of Members of Boards of Visitors *(prison)*

AMC Association of Municipal Corporations; Area Medical Committee *(NHS, q.v.)*

AMCIB Associate Member of the Corporation of Insurance Brokers

AMCIT Associate Member of the Chartered Institute of Transport

AMCSI Associate Member of the Construction Surveyors' Institute

AMDEA Association of Manufacturers of Domestic Electric Appliances

AMEME Association of Mining, Electrical and Mechanical Engineers

AMES Air Ministry Experimental Station

AMF Arab Monetary Fund; Australian Military Forces

AMGasE Associate Member of the Institution of Gas Engineers

AMGOT Allied Military Government of Occupied Territory

AMHTTA Associate Member of the Highway and Traffic Technicians' Association

AMI Associazione Montessori Internationale *(International Montessori Association)*

AMIAE Associate Member of the Institution of Automobile Engineers; Associate Member of the Institute of Aeronautical Engineers

AMIAgrE Associate Member of the Institution of Agricultural Engineers

AMICE Associate Member of the Institution of Civil Engineers

AMICEI Associate Member of the Institute of Engineers, Ireland

AMIChemE Associate Member of the Institution of Chemical Engineers

AMICorrT Associate Member of the Institution of Corrosion Science and Technology

AMICW Associate Member of the Institute of Clerks of Works

AMIEE Associate Member of the Institution of Electrical Engineers

AMIEnvSc Associate Member of the Institute of Environmental Scientists

AMIERE Associate Member of the Institution of Electronic and Radio Engineers

AMIEx Associate Member of the Institute of Export

AMIFireE Affiliate of the Institution of Fire Engineers

AMIGasE Associate Member of the Institution of Gas Engineers

AMIGeol Associate of the Geological Society

AMIH Associate Member of the Institute of Housing

AMIHVE Associate Member of the Institute of Heating and Ventilating Engineers

AMIIA Associate Member of the Institute of Industrial Administration

AMIISE Associate Member of the International Institute of Social Economics

AMIManf Associate Member of the Institute of Manufacturing

AMIMarE Associate Member of the Institute of Marine Engineers

AMIMechE Associate Member of the Institution of Mechanical Engineers

AMIMGTechE Associate Member of the Institution of Mechanical and General Technician Engineers

AMIMH Associate Member of the Institute of Materials Handling

AMIMI Associate Member of the Institute of the Motor Industry

AMIMinE Associate Member of the Institution of Mining Engineers

AMIMM Associate Member of the Institution of Mining and Metallurgy

AMIMS Associate Member of the Institute of Management Specialists

AMIMunE Associate Member of the Institution of Municipal Engineers

AMInstBE Associate Member of the Institution of British Engineers

AMInstCM Associate Member of the Institute of Commercial Management

AMInstPC Associate Member of the Institute of Public Cleansing

AMInstR Associate Member of the Institute of Refrigeration

AMInstSM Associate Member of the Institution of Sales Management

AMInstTA Associate Member of the Institute of Transport Administration

AMIPA Associate Member of the Institute of Practitioners in Advertising

AMIPC Associate Member of the Institute of Production Control

AMIPlantE Associate Member of the Institution of Plant Engineers

AMIPM Associate Member of the Institute of Personnel Management

AMIPRE Associate Member of the Incorporated Practitioners in Radio and Electronics

AMIProdE Associate Member of the Institution of Production Engineers

AMIQ Associate Member of the Institute of Quarrying

AMIRTE Associate Member of the Institute of Road Transport Engineers

AMISM Associate Member of the Institute of Supervisory Management

AMITD Associate Member of the Institute of Training and Development

AMIWES Associate Member of the Institution of Water Engineers and Scientists

AMIWHTE Associate Member of the Institution of Works and Highways Technician Engineers

AMIWO Associate Member of the Institute of Welfare Officers

AMM Anti-Missile Missile

AMMA Assistant Masters and Mistresses Association

AMNI Associate Member of the Nautical Institute

AMNLAE Nicaraguan Women's Movement

AMO Association of Magisterial Officers; Area Medical Officer

AMOS Associated Minibus Operators (Ltd.)

AMP Advanced Management Programme

amp ampere; amperage

AMPA Associate Member of the Master Photographers' Association

AMPAS Academy of Motion Picture Arts and Science

AMPRI Associate Member of the Plastics and Rubber Institute

AMR Associate of the Association of Health Care Information and Medical Records Officers *(NHS, q.v.)*

AMRINA Associate Member of the Royal Institution of Naval Architects

AMRSH Associate Member of the Royal Society of Health

AMRTS Associate Member of the Royal Television Society

AMS Additional Member System *(alternative to STV, q.v.)*; Ancient Monuments' Society; Army Medical Staff/Service; All Main Services; Association of Medical Secretaries, Practice Administrators and Receptionists

AMS(Aff) Affiliate of the Association of Medical Secretaries, Practice Administrators and Receptionists

AMSERT Associate Member of the Society of Electronic and Radio Technicians

AMSHAA Associate Member of the Society of Hearing Aid Audiologists

AMSLAET Associate Member of the Society of Licensed Aircraft Engineers and Technologists

AMSO Area Management Service Officer *(NHS, q.v.)*

AMSS Associate of the Finnish Sauna Society

AMT Master of Arts in Teaching; Air Mail Transfer

AMTC Academy Member of Trinity College of Music; Art Masters' Teaching Certificate

AMTE Admiralty Marine Technology Establishment

AMTPI Associate Member of the Town Planning Institute

AMusLCM Associate in Music of the London College of Music

AMusTCL Associate in Music of Trinity College of Music, London

AMWES Associate Member of the Women's Engineering Society

AN Nicaraguan Airline

ANA Athens News Agency; Arab News Agency; Australian National Airways; *(Japan)* All Nippon Airways

ANAEA Associate of the National Association of Estate Agents

ANAPO *(Colombia)* Allianzia Nacional Popular *(National Popular Alliance)*

ANC Army Nursing Corps; African National Council/Congress *(anti-apartheid organisation)*; Ante-Natal Clinic; Air Navigation Commission

ANCRT Associate of the National College of Rubber Technology

ANC(Z) African National Council (Zimbabwe)

AND Andorran International Motor Vehicle Registration Letters

and *(music)* andante *(moderately slow)*

ANDE *(Italy)* Associazione Nazionale Donne Electrice *(Women's National Electrical Association)*

ANEDA *(France)* Association Nationale d'Etudes pour la Documentation Automatique *(National Association for Automatic Documentation)*

ANEF American-Nepal Education Foundation; *(Chile)* Association of Fiscal Workers

ANERA American Near East Relief Aid

ANF Atlantic Nuclear Force

ANGOP Official Angolan News Agency

ANI *(Portugal)* Agência de Noticias de Informacões *(News Agency)*; *(Portugal)* Agência Nacional de Informacões *(National Information Agency)*

ANIH Associate of the National Institute of Hardware

anim *(music)* animato *(animated)*

ANK Address Not Known

ANL Anti-Nazi League

ANLA Azania National Liberation Army *(also known as POQO, q.v.)*

ANM Admiralty Notice to Mariners

ANMC Area Nursing & Midwifery Committee

ANO Area Nursing Officer *(NHS, q.v.)*

anon anonymous

ANOP *(Portugal)* Agência Portuguesa de Noticias *(News Agency)*

ANP Australian Nationalist Party

ANPE *(France)* L'Agence Nationale pour l'Emploi *(National Employment Agency, see also APE)*

ANRC American National Red Cross

ANS Army Nursing Service

ANSA *(Italy)* Agenzia Italiana Stampa Associata *(Press Agency)*

ANSI American National Standards Institute

ANSP Australian National Socialist Party

ANSVAR *(Sweden)* Responsibility *(mutual insurance company for tee-totallers)*

ANU African National Unity; Australian National University

ANVIL Action for Non-Violence in Learning *(Quaker organisation)*

ANZAC Australian and New Zealand Army Corps

ANZEFA Australian and New Zealand Emigrant Families' Association

ANZUS Australia, New Zealand and US Treaty Nations

AO Air Officer; Area Officer; Order of Australia

AOA Air Officer in Charge of Administration; American Overseas Airlines

AOB Any Other Business

AOC Area Optical Committee *(NHS, q.v.)*; Army/Air Officer Commanding

AOC-in-C Air Officer Commanding-in-Chief

AOD Army Ordnance Department; Ancient Order of Druids

AOER Army Officers' Emergency Reserve

AOF Ancient Order of Foresters

A of F Admiral of the Fleet

AOH Ancient Order of Hibernians

AOP Association of Optical Practitioners

AOSTRA *(Canada)* Alberta Oil Sands Technology and Research Association

AOSW Association of Official Shorthand Writers

AP Associated Press *(News Agency)*; Pakistan Airline

APA Association of Public Analysts; Association for the Prevention of Addiction

APAS Association of Personal Assistants and Secretaries

APC Area Pharmaceutical Committee

(NHS, q.v.); Automatic Picture Control; *(Corsica)* Association des Patriots de Corse *(Patriotic Organisation)*

APCA *(France)* L'Association Permanente des Chambres d'Agriculture *(Association of Permanent Agricultural Councils)*

APCS Associate of the Property Consultants' Society

APDE Association of Painters and Decorators' Employers

APE Automatic Photomapping Equipment; Amalgamated Power Engineering; *(France)* Assemblée Parliamentaire Européenne *(European Parliamentary Assembly); (France)* Agence pour l'Emploi *(Employment Agency, see also ANPE)*

APEC *(France)* Agence pour l'Emploi des Cadres *("white-collar" employment Agency)*

APEX Association of Professional, Executive, Clerical and Computer Staffs; Advance Purchase Excursion (on airlines); Advancing Prospects of Employment for Ex-Offenders

APG Artists' Placement Group

APH Association of Private Hospitals

APHI Association of Public Health Inspectors

API Association of Plastics Institutes; American Press Institute

APIE *(Mozambique)* Administracio do Parque e Imobiliaro do Estado *(Government Agency managing rented housing)*

APL Assistant Patrol Leader

APM Assistant Provost Marshal; Assistant Pay Master

APMG Assistant Postmaster General

APMI Associate of the Pensions Management Institute

APN *(USSR)* Agentstvo Pechati Novosti *(Press Agency)*

APO Army Post Office; Area Personnel Officer *(NHS, q.v.)*

Appro (on) Approval

Approx Approximately

APR Annual Percentage Rate *(interest)*

Apr April

APRA American Public Relations Association; *(Peru)* Alianza Popular Revolucionaria *(Popular Revolutionary Alliance)*

APRI Associate of the Plastics and Rubber Institute

APRT Advance *(payments of)* Petroleum Revenue Tax

APS Assisted Places Scheme; Aborigines' Protection Society

APSW Association of Psychiatric Social Workers

APT Advanced Passenger Train; Association of Polytechnic Teachers; Association of Printing Technologists;

Automatic Public Toilet

Apt Apartment

APTO *(USA)* Association for the Psychiatric Treatment of Offenders

APTS Association for the Prevention of Thefts in Shops

APU Assessment of Performance Unit *(DES, q.v.)*; Anti-Poaching Units *(wildlife)*

APUC Association for Promoting the Unity of Christendom

APWA All-Pakistan Women's Association *(Pakistan National Council of Women)*

AQC Associate of Queen's College *(London)*

AQMG Assistant Quartermaster General

A–R Rediffusion Television

AR Autonomous Region; Army Regulation; Aerolineas Argentinas *(Argentine Airline)*

Ar Argon

ARA Aircraft Research Association; Associate of the Royal Academy of Arts; *(Portugal)* Acçau Revolucionária Armada *(Armed Revolutionary Action)*

ARAD Associate of the Royal Academy of Dancing

ARAgS Associate of the Royal Agricultural Society

ARAL Associate of the Royal Academy of Literature

ARAM Associate of the Royal Academy of Music

ARBA Associate Member of the Royal Society of British Artists

ARBD Alcohol-Related Birth Defects

ARBS Associate Member of the Royal Society of British Sculptors

ARBSA Associate of the Royal Birmingham Society of Artists

ARC Architects' Registration Council; Agricultural Research Council; Aeronautical Research Council; Action Resource Centre; The Arthritis and Rheumatism Council *(for research);* American Red Cross; Accelerated Rare Calorimetry; *(Corsica)* Action pour la Renaissance de Corse *(Action for the re-birth of Corsica)*

ARC/CRA American Regional Council/ Consejo Regional de Las Americas *(ICW, q.v. Regional Latin American Council)*

ARCA Associate of the Royal College of Arts

ARCamA Associate of the Royal Cambrian Academy of Art

ARCC Action Resource Centre Council; Action Research for the Crippled Child

ARCE Academical Rank of Civil Engineer

ARCIC Anglo-Roman Catholic International Commission

ARCM Associate of the Royal College

of Music

ARCO Associate of the Royal College of Organists

ARCO (CHm) Associate of the Royal College of Organists *(Choir Training Diploma)*

ARCPsych Associate of the Royal College of Psychiatrists

ARCS Associateship of the Royal College of Science; Australian Red Cross Society

ARCUK Architects' Registration Council of the UK, *q.v.*

ARD Acute Respiratory Disease; *(West Germany)* Deutsches Fernsehen *(television)*

ARE Adoption Resource Exchange; Associate of the Royal Society of Painters, Etchers and Engravers; Association for Recurrent Education; Arab Republic of Egypt; *(Portugal)* Armed Revolutionary Action

ARELS Association of Recognised English Language Schools

ARENA *(Brazil)* Aliança Renovadora Nacional *(Government National Alliance)*

ARF *(Canada)* Addiction Research Foundation; Advertising Research Foundation; ACCEPT *(q.v.)* Research Foundation

ARFL *(Canada)* Addiction Research Foundation Library

Arg Argentina/Argentine

ARIAS Associate of the Royal Incorporation of Architects, Scotland

ARIBA Associate of the Royal Institute of British Architects

ARICS Associate of the Royal Institute of Chartered Surveyors

ARINA Associate of the Royal Institution of Naval Architects

ARIPHH Associate of the Royal Institute of Public Health and Hygiene

Ariz Arizona *(USA State)*

Ark Arkansas *(USA State)*

ARKIA *(Israel)* Internal Airways

ARL Admiralty Research Laboratory; Aeronautical Research Laboratory

ARM Anti-Radar Missile; Alliance of Radical Methodists; Animal Rights Militia

Arm Armenia

ARMC Anglian Regional Management Centre

ARMS Action for research into Multiple Sclerosis; Associate of the Royal Society of Miniature Painters; Association of Radical Midwives

ARN *(Italy)* Armata Revoluzione Nucleare *(Armed Revolutionary Nucleus)*

ARNA Arab Revolutionary News Agency

ARNO Association of Royal Naval Officers

ARP Air Raid Precautions *(Second World War)*

ARPS Associate of the Royal Photographic Society

ARR/arr Arrival

ARRC Associate of the Royal Red Cross

ARRG Association for Research into Restricted Growth

ARSA Associate of the Royal Society of Arts; Associate of the Royal Scottish Academy of Painting, Sculpture and Architecture

ARSCM Associate Member of the Royal School of Church Music

ARSE Animal Research Scientific and Experimental

ARSM Associateship of the Royal School of Mines

ARTC Air Route Traffic Control

ARTI Automatic Real Time

ARVA Associate of the Rating and Valuation Association

ARVIA Associate of the Royal Victorian Institute of Architects

ARWA Associate of the Royal West of England Academy

ARWS Associate of the Royal Society of Painters in Water Colours

AS Anglo-Saxon; Active Sampling *(work study)*

As Arsenic

ASA Advertising Standards Authority; Amateur Swimming Association; Atomic Scientists' Association; American Statistical Association; Associate Member of the Society of Actuaries; American Standards Association; Army Sailing Association

ASALA Secret Army for the Liberation of Armenia *(see also ASLA)*

ASAM Associate of the Society of Art Masters

ASAP As Soon As Possible

ASAT Anti-Satellite *(weapon testing and development)*

ASBAH Association for Spina Bifida and Hydrocephalus

ASBSBSW Amalgamated Society of Boilermakers, Shipwrights, Blacksmiths and Structural Workers *(now amalgamated to form GMBATU, q.v.)*

ASBTh Associate of the Society of Health and Beauty Therapists

ASBU Arab States Broadcasting Union

ASC Administrative Staff College; American Society of Cinematographers; Army Service Corps

ASCA Associate of the Society of Company and Commercial Accountants; American Senior Citizens Association

ASCAP American Society of Composers, Authors and Publishers

ASCT Associate Member of the Society of Cardiological Technicians; Associate of the Society of Commercial

Teachers

ASDC Associate of the Society of Dyers and Colourists

ASDIC Anti-Submarine Detection Investigation Committee

ASE Advancement of State Education; Associate of the Society of Executives; Engineering Associate of the Society of Engineers; American Stock Exchange

ASEAN Association of the South East Asian Nations

ASF Associate Member of the Society of Floristry

ASFS *(Switzerland)* Alliance de Sociétés Féminines Suisses *(Swiss National Council of Women)*

ASH Action on Smoking and Health

ASIA Associate of the Society of Investment Analysts

ASIAD Associate of the Society of Industrial Artists and Designers

ASIO Australian Security Intelligence Organisation

ASLA Armenian Secret Liberation Army *(see also ASALA)*

ASLC Advanced Secretarial Language Certificate

ASLEF Associated Society of Locomotive Engineers and Firemen

ASLIB Association of Special Libraries & Information Bureaux

ASLO Association of Scottish Life Offices

ASLP Amalgamated Society of Lithographic Printers

ASM Assistant Stage Manager

ASNE American Society of Newspaper Editors

ASPADS Associated Sheepdog Police and Army Dog Society

ASPCA American Society for the Prevention of Cruelty to Animals

ASPRO Associated Schools Project *(UN, q.v.)*

ASPS Anti-Saturday Parent Sentiments/Statements *(Association for one-parent families)*; Association of Supervisors in Purchasing and Supply

ASSC Accounting Standards Steering Committee

ASSET Association of Supervisory Staffs, Executives and Technicians

ASSF Associate of the Society of Shoe Fitters

Associate ITE Associate of the Institution of Electrical and Electronics Technician Engineers

AssocIPHE Associate of the Institution of Public Health Engineers

AssocIPRE Associate of the Incorporated Practitioners in Radio and Electronics Ltd

AssocMIAeE Associate Member of the Institute of Aeronautical Engineers

AssocRINA Associate of the Royal Institution of Naval Architects

AssocSE Associate of the Society of Engineers

AssocSLAET Associate of the Society of Licensed Aircraft Engineers and Technologists

ASSR Autonomous Soviet Socialist Republics

Assyr Assyria/Assyrian

AST Atlantic Standard Time

ASTA Associate Member of the Swimming Teachers' Association

ASTES *(Spain)* Agrupacion Parael Segura Turistico Español *(Consortium of Insurers to cover holiday makers up to 31 days)*

ASTM American Society of Tropical Medicine

ASTMS Association of Scientific, Technical & Managerial Staffs

ASTRO Air Space Travel Research Organisation

ASTUC Anglo-Soviet Trades Union Committee

ASVA Associate of the Incorporated Society of Valuers and Auctioneers

ASW Association of Scientific Workers; Anti-Submarine Warfare; Amalgamated Society of Woodworkers

AT Appropriate Technology

At Astatine

ATA Air Transport Association; Air Transport Auxiliary; Atlantic Treaty Association

ATAB Air Travel Advisory Bureau

ATAC Anti-Tritium Action Campaign

ATAE Association of Teachers in Adult Education

ATAF Allied Tactical Air Force

ATB Agricultural Training Board; Air Transportation Board

ATC Art Teacher's Certificate; Annotated Tax Cases *(Law Reports)*; Air Training Corps; Air Traffic Control

ATCA Air Traffic Control Assistant

ATCDE *(See ATTCDE)*

ATCL Associate of Trinity College of Music, London

ATCO Air Traffic Control Officer

ATD Art Teacher's Diploma

ATEE Association for Teacher Education in Europe *(EEC, q.v.)*

a tem *(music)* a tempo *(in time)*

ATFA Association of Technicians in Finance and Accounting

ATI Associate of the Textile Institute

ATII Associate of the Institute of Taxation

ATO Army Technical Officer

ATOL Air Travel Organisers' Licence

ATP Adenosine Triphosphate *(an ingredient of the nerve system)*

ATPA Association of Trade Protection Agents

ATPL Airline Transport Pilot's Licence

ATS Auxiliary Territorial Service *(Second World War Women's Army Corps, now WRAC, q.v.)*; Anti-Tetanus Serum

ATSC Associate in the Technology of Surface Coatings

ATT American Telephone and Telegraph

ATTCDE Association of Teacher Training Colleges and Department of Education *(amalgamated in 1976 with the ATTI, q.v., to become NATTHE, q.v.)*

ATTI Association of Teachers in Technical Institutions *(see ATTCDE and NATTHE)*

ATU Association of Telephone Users

ATUC Air Transport Users' Committee; African Trade Union Confederation

ATV Associated Television

ATWU Amalgamated Textile Workers' Union

Au *(Latin)* Aurum *(Gold)*

AUAW Amalgamated Union of Asphalt Workers

AUB *(Lebanon)* American University of Beirut

AUC Airline Users' Committee

AUCCTU *(USSR)* Soviet TUC, *q.v.*

AUEW Amalgamated Union of Engineering Workers

Aug August

AUH *(Lebanon)* American University Hospital

AUMIST Associateship of the University of Manchester Institute of Science and Technology

AURA Audience Research Assessment System *(IBA, q.v.)*

Aus Australia

AUT Association of University Teachers

AUT(S) Association of University Teachers (Scotland)

Aux Auxiliary

AVC Army Veterinary Corps

Ave Avenue

AVLA Audio Visual Language Association

AWA Anglian Water Authority

AWACS Airborne Warning and Control Systems *(aircrafts' Radar, q.v.)*

AWARE Advanced Warning Radar Equipment *(against nuclear weapons)*; Women's Research Group

AWCW Asian Women Community Workers

AWeldI Associate of the Welding Institute

AWG Association of Waterloo Groups

AWO Area Works Officer *(NHS, q.v.)*

AWOL Absent Without Official Leave

AWPR Association of Women in Public Relations

AWRE Atomic Weapons Research Establishment *(Aldermaston)*

AWT Animal Welfare Trust

AWUCOC Afro West Indian United Council of Churches

AYH American Youth Hostels

AZ Zimbabwe Airlines

AZAPO Azanian People's Organisation

AZW Association of Zaire Women

B

B Belgian International Motor Vehicle Registration Letter; Boron; Formosa Airline

BA British Airways; Bachelor of Arts; British Academy; Buenos Aires; Booksellers' Association; Board of Agriculture

BA(Econ) Bachelor of Arts in Economics and Social Studies

BA(Ed) Bachelor of Arts (Education)

BA(GB) Booksellers' Association (Great Britain)

BA(Law) Bachelor of Arts in Law

BA(Mus) Bachelor of Arts in Music

BA(OU) Bachelor of Arts (Open University)

Ba Barium

BAA British Airports Authority; British Acupuncture Association; British Astronomical Association; British Archaeological Association; British Association of Accountants and Auditors

BAAB British Athletic Association

Board; British Amateur Athletic Board

BAAF British Agencies for Adoption and Fostering

BAAS British Association for the Advancement of Science

BAB British Airways Board

BABP British Association of Behavioural Psychotherapy

BAC British Association for Counselling

BAc Bachelor of Acupuncture

BACAT Barge Aboard Catamaran *(Shipping)*

BAcc Bachelor of Accountancy

BACCC British Amateur Cinematographers' Central Council

BACIE British Association for Commercial and Industrial Education

BACM British Association of Colliery Management

BACR British Association for Cancer Research

BAD British Association of Dermatology; *(South Africa)* Bantu Administration Department

BADA British Antique Dealers' Association

BAdmin Bachelor of Administration

BAe British Aerospace

BA(Econ) Bachelor of Arts in Economics and Social Studies

BAEE British Army Equipment Exhibition

BAFS British Academy of Forensic Sciences

BAFTA British Academy of Film and Television Arts *(see also SFTA)*

BAG Business Art Galleries *(Royal Academy of Arts)*

BAGA British Amateur Gymnastics Association

BAGDA British Advertising Gift Distributors' Association

BAGMA British Agricultural & Gardening Machinery Association

BAgr Bachelor of Agriculture

Bah Bahamas

BAHOH British Association for the Hard of Hearing

BAI *(Latin)* Baccalaureus in Arte Ingeniaria *(Bachelor of Arts in Engineering)*

BAIE British Association of Industrial Editors

BALPA/BAPA British Airline Pilots' Association

B-ALPES Basses-Alpes *(Department of France)*

Balt Baltimore *(USA State)*

BAMA British Aerosol Manufacturers' Association

BAN British Association of Neurologists

b and b bed and breakfast

B and CE Building and Civil Engineering

B and FBS British and Foreign Bible Society

BANK International Bank for Reconstruction & Development *(relating to UN, q.v.)*

BAO Bachelor of Obstetrics

BAOR British Army of the Rhine

BAOS British Association of Oral Surgeons

BAPA See BALPA

BAPS British Association of Paediatric Surgeons; British Association of Plastic Surgeons

BARB British Association of Rose Breeders; Broadcasters' Audience Research Bureau/Board *(Television Research System, BBC and ITV q.v.)*

BARC British Automobile Racing Club; British American Repertory Company

BArch Bachelor of Architecture

BARP British Association of Retired Persons; British Association of Rehabilitated Psychotherapy

Bart Baronet *(Also Bt)*

BAS British Association for Settlements; Bachelor in Agricultural Science; British Antarctica Survey; British Acoustical Society

BASc Bachelor of Applied Science

BASE *(Portugal)* Ultra-leftist movement, close to anarcho-syndicalism

BASI British Association of Ski Instructors

BASIC Beginners All-purpose Symbolic Instruction Code *(computer)*

BASPCAN British Association for the Study and Prevention of Child Abuse and Neglect

BASSAC British Association of Settlements and Social Action Centres

BASW British Association of Social Workers

BAT British American Tobacco

BATS British Association of Traumatology in Sport

BAWA British American Wrestling Association

BAWE British Association of Women Executives

BB Boys' Brigade

BBA British Bankers' Association

BBBC/BBB of C British Boxing Board of Control

BBC British Broadcasting Corporation

BBFC British Board of Film Censors

BBTA British Bureau of Television Advertising

BC Before Christ; British Council; British Columbia *(province of Canada)*; Borough Council *(normally preceded by the initial letter of a County/Borough or Town)*; Bowling Club

BCA British College of Acupuncture; *(USA)* Bureau of Current Affairs

BCAPC British Code of Advertising Practice Committee

BCAR British Council for Aid to Refugees

BCC British Copyright Council; British Council of Churches

BCE Board of Customs and Excise

BCF British Chess Federation; British Cycling Federation

BCFI Bar Association for Commerce, Finance & Industry

BCG Bacillus Calmette Guérin *(anti-tuberculosis vaccine)*

BCh Bachelor of Surgery

BChD Bachelor of Dental Surgery

BChir Bachelor of Surgery

BCI Bureau Central International *(Central International Bureau)*

BCINA British Commonwealth International News Agency *(see also "Visnews")*

BCIRA British Cotton Industry Research Association

BCL Bachelor of Civil Law

BCMA British Colour Makers' Association; *(Canada)* British Columbia Medical Association

BCMS Bible Churchmen's Missionary Society

BCMSA *(South Africa)* Black Consciousness Movement

BCN Birmingham Canal Navigation

BCom Bachelor of Commerce

BComStuds Bachelor of Combined Studies

BCOO British College of Ophthalmic Opticians

BCP *(South Africa)* Basotho Congress Party; Burma Communist Party *(see also CPB)*

BCS British Computer Society; British Cardiac Society

BCT Bank Credit Transfer

BCURA British Coal Utilisation Research Association

BCYC British Corinthian Yacht Club

BD Bachelor of Divinity; Bangladesh International Motor Vehicle Registration Letters

BDA British Dental Association; British Deaf Association; British Diabetic Association; *(West Germany)* Bundesverband der Deutschen Anwender *(Employers' Federation)*

BDC Book Development Council

BDHF British Dental Health Foundation

BDHO British Dental Health Organisations

BDI British Dental Institute; *(West Germany)* Bundesverband der Deutschen Industrie *(National Industrial Federation)*

BDL British Drama League; *(India)* Bharatiya Lok Dal *(People's Political Party)*

BDM Brazil Democratic Movement

BDMAA British Direct Mail Advertising Association

BDS Bachelor of Dental Surgery; Barbados International Motor Vehicle Registration Letters; *(Latin)* bis in diem sumendus *(take twice daily)*

BDTC British Dependent Territories Citizenship

BDU Bomb Disposal Unit

Be Beryllium

BEA British Electricity Authority; British Epilepsy Association; British European Airways *(now BA, q.v.)*

BEAB British Electrotechnical Approvals Board *(for domestic appliances)*

BEAMA British Electrical and Allied Manufacturers' Association

BEC Business Education Council

BEcon Bachelor of Economics

BEd Bachelor of Education

BEDA British Electrical Development Association

Beds Bedfordshire

BEE Bachelor of Electrical Engineering

BEF British Expeditionary Force; British Equestrian Federation

BEIA Board of Education Inspectors' Association

BEIS British Egg Information Service

Belg Belgium

BEM British Empire Medal

BEMA British Electrical Manufacturers' Association

BEMB British Egg Marketing Board

B en Dr *(France)* Bachelier en Droit *(Bachelor of Laws)*

BENELUX Belgium, Netherlands and Luxembourg

Beng Bengal

BEng Bachelor of Engineering

BEng(Tech) Bachelor of Engineering (Technology)

BEPA British Egg Products Association

Berks Berkshire

BESA British Engineering Standards Association

B ès L *(France)* Bachelier ès Lettres *(Bachelor of Letters)*

B ès S *(France)* Bachelier ès Sciences *(Bachelor of Science)*

BEU Benelux *(q.v.)* Economic Union; British Empire Union

BEUC Bureau Européen des Unions de Consommateurs *(EEC, q.v., Consumer Lobby Group)*

BF Bloody Fool

b/f brought forward

BFA Bachelor of Fine Arts; British Film Academy

BFAG British Foods Action Group

BFAR British Foundation for Age Research

BFBS British Forces Broadcasting Service; British & Foreign Bible Society

BFFS British Federation of Film Societies

BFI British Film Institute

BFMIRA British Food Manufacturing Industries Research Association

BFN British Forces Network

BFPA British Film Producers' Association

BFPO British Forces Post Office

BFSS British Field Sports Society

BFTA British Fur Trade Association

BFUW British Federation of University Women

BG Board of Governors; Bulgarian International Motor Vehicle Registration Letters

BGA British Gliding Association

BGC British Gas Council

BGLA British Growers Look Ahead

BGS *(West Germany)* Bundesgrenzschutz *(Federal Frontier Forces)*

BH Bachelor of Humanities; Belize International Motor Vehicle Registration Letters

BHA British Humanist Association; British Hospitals Association; British Hotels Association; British Homeopathic Association; British Hypnotherapy Association

BHC British High Commissioner; Benzine Hexachloride

BHHI British Home and Hospital for Incurables

BHI British Horological Institute

BHL British Housewives' League

bhp brake horse power

BHRA British Hydraulics Research Association; British Hotels and Restaurants Association

BHPS British Hedgehog Preservation Society

BHRCA British Hotels Restaurants and Caterers Association

BHS British Horse Society

BHSI British Horse Society's Instructor's Certificate

BHT Butylated Hydroxytoluene *(antioxidant)*

Bi Bismuth

BIA British Insurance Association; British Island Airways

BIAC Business and Industry Advisory Committee *(OECD, q.v.)*

BIATA British Independent Air Transport Association

BIB Blocked Investment Balance

BIBA British Insurance Brokers' Association

BIBRA British Industrial Biological Research Association

BIC Butter Information Council

BICERI British Internal Combustion Engine Research Institute

BIET British Institute of Engineering Technology

BIF British Industries Fair

BIFA British Industries Film Association

BIFU British Insurance and Finance Union

BIHA British Ice Hockey Association

BIICL British Institute of International & Comparative Law

BILC British International Law Cases

BILD *(Canada)* Board of Industrial Leadership and Development

BILS British International Law Society

BIM British Institute of Management

BioTech Biotechnical Research and Development Services

BIR Board of Inland Revenue; British Institute of Radiology

BIRE British Institution of Radio Engineers

BIRS British Institute of Recorded Sound

BIS Bank for International Settlements; British Information Services *(Foreign Office)*

BISF British Iron and Steel Federation

BISFA British Industrial & Scientific Film Association

BISRA British Iron & Steel Research Association

BIT Binary Digit *(Computer Terminology)*; Bureau International du Travail *(International Labour Office, see also ILO)*

BITA British Industrial Truck Association

BIWF British-Israel World Federation

BJ Bachelor of Journalism

BJJA British Ju-Jitsu Association

BJSM British Joint Services Mission

Bk Berkelium

BKA *(West Germany)* Bundeskriminal Amt *(Federal Criminal Bureau)*

BKB British Karate Board

BKPA British Kidney Patient Association

BKSTS British Kinematograph Sound and Television Society

BL Bachelor of Law; British Library; British Leyland; British Legion

BLA British Legal Association

BLD Bachelor of Landscape Design; *(India)* Right-wing Political Party *(one of the four constituents of the Janata Alliance)*

Bldg Building

BLESMA British Limbless Ex-Servicemen's Association

BLib Bachelor of Librarianship

BLing Bachelor of Linguistics

BLISS Baby Life Support Systems

BLitt Bachelor of Letters

BLMAS Bible Lands Missions' Aid Society

BLP Barbados Labour Party

BLS Bachelor of Library Studies; *(USA)* Bureau of Labour Statistics

Blvd Boulevard

BM British Museum; British Medal; Bachelor of Medicine; *(Latin)* Bene Merenti *(to the well-deserving, a Papal Medal)*; Boatswain's Mate *(RN, q.v.)*

BMA British Medical Association; British Majorettes' Association

BMAA British Microlight Aircraft Association

BM,BCh Bachelor of Medicine, Bachelor of Surgery

BM,BS Bachelor of Medicine, Bachelor of Surgery

BMC British Medical Council; Book Marketing Council

BMedBiol Bachelor of Medical Biology

BMedSci Bachelor of Medical Sciences

BMedSci (Speech) Bachelor of Medical Sciences (Speech)

BMEF British Mechanical Engineering

Federation

BMet Bachelor of Metallurgy

BMEWS Ballistic Missile Early Warning System

BMF British Motorcycle Federation

BMJ British Medical Journal

BMK Benzyl methyl ketone

BMMA British Microcomputer Manufacturers Association

BMNatHist British Museum, Natural History

BMNH British Museum Natural History

BMPS British Medical Protection Society; British Musicians' Pension Society

BMRB British Marketing Research Bureau

BMS Baptists' Missionary Society

BMSc Bachelor of Medical Science

BMT Basic Military Training; Bachelor of Medical Technology

BMTA British Motor Trade Association

BMus Bachelor of Music; British Museum *(also BM, q.v.)*

BN Bachelor of Nursing

bn billion

BNA British Nursing Association; British North America Act

BNCSR British National Commission for Space Research

BND *(West Germany)* Bundesnachrichten Dienst *(Federal Intelligence Service)*

BNEC British Nuclear Energy Conference

BNF British Nuclear Fuels; British Nutrition Foundation

BNFC British National Film Catalogue

BN Nursing Studies Bachelor of Nursing, Nursing Studies

BNOC British National Oil Corporation; British National Opera Company

BNP Bangladesh Nationalist Party; British National Party *(see also NF)*

BNurs Bachelor of Nursing

BO Body Odour

BOA British Optical Association; British Orthopaedic Association; British Osteopathic Association; British Olympic Association

BOA(Disp) British Optical Association (Dispenser)

BOAC British Overseas Airways Corporation *(now BA, q.v.)*; Better-On-A-Camel *(Jocular title for BOAC)*

BOC British Oxygen Company; British Overseas Citizenship

BOCE Board of Customs and Excise

B of T See BOT

Bol Bolivia; Boliviano (Monetary unit of Venezuela and Bolivia)

BON-P British Organisation of Non-Parents

BOSS *(South Africa)* Bureau for State Security *(now DONS, q.v.)*

BOT Board of Trade

BOTB British Overseas Trade Board

BOTU Board of Trade Unit

BP British Public; British Pharmacopoeia; British Patent; British Petroleum

Bp Bishop

B-P Baden-Powell *(Boy Scout Movement)*

BPA British Pilots' Association; Bookmakers' Protection Association; British Paediatric Association

BPAS British Pregnancy Advisory Service

BPB British Plaster Board

BPC British Pharmaceutical Codex; British Productivity Council; British Pharmacopoeia Commission; *(South Africa)* Black People's Convention *(young militants)*; British Printing Corporation

BPCC British Printing and Communications Corporation

BPF British Philatelic Federation

BPG Broadcasting Press Guild

BPharm Bachelor of Pharmacy

BPhil Bachelor of Philosophy

BPhil(Ed) Bachelor of Philosophy (Education)

BPI Bachelor of Planning; British Phonographic Industry; Bits Per Inch *(Computer Terminology)*

BPIF British Printing Industries Federation

BPL Bachelor of Planning

BPO Berlin Philharmonic Orchestra

BPRA Book Publishers Representatives' Association

BPS British Pharmacological Society; British Phrenological Society; British Printing Society

BPsS British Psychological Society

bps bits per second *(units of speech/transmission speed)*

BPT British Philatelic Trust

B-Pyr Basses-Pyrénées *(Department of France)*

BR British Rail; Basic Rate; Brazilian International Motor Vehicle Registration Letters

Br British; Branch; Bromine

BRA British Rheumatism & Arthritis Association; Bayswater Road Association *(London Amateur Painters' Exhibition)*; Bee Research Association; Brigadier Royal Artillery

BRAC Bangladesh Rehabilitation Association Committee

BRAD Bradstreets *(street directory)*; Biochemical Research and Development; British Rates and Data *(advertising)*

Braz Brazil

BRC British Research Council

BRCS British Red Cross Society

BRD Building Regulations Decisions

BRDC British Research and Development Corporation; British Racing Drivers' Club

BRE Building Research Establishment *(Department of Environment)*

BREAK Organisation providing short-stay emergency care for handicapped and deprived children and young adults

BREMA British Radio and Electronic Equipment Manufacturers' Association

BRF British Roads Federation

BRhin Bas-Rhin *(Department of France)*

BRIC Bloodstock & Racehorse Industries Confederation

Brig Brigadier

BRIT *(Belgium)* Flemish-speaking Radio and Television

Brit British

BritMus See BM and BMus

BRN Bahrain International Motor Vehicle Registration Letters

BRNC Britannia Royal Naval College

Bros Brothers

BRS British Road Services

BRU Brunei International Motor Vehicle Registration Letters

BS Bachelor of Surgery; *(USA)* Bachelor of Science; British Standard; Bahamas International Motor Vehicle Registration Letters

BSA British Student Association; British School of Archaeology; British Sociological Association; Building Societies' Association

BSAD British Sports Association for the Disabled

BSAS British Ship Adoption Society

BSB British Standard Beam *(metal, formerly RSJ, q.v.)*

BSBI Botanical Society of the British Isles

BSC British Steel Corporation; British Society of Cinematographers; British Sugar Corporation; British Safety Council

BSc Bachelor of Science; Bachelor of Science in Polymer Science and Technology

BSc(Agr.) Bachelor of Science in Agriculture

BSc(Architecture) Bachelor of Science (Architecture)

BSc(Econ) Bachelor of Science in Economics

BSc(Eng) Bachelor of Science in Engineering

BSc(For) Bachelor of Science in Forestry

BSc(MedSci) Bachelor of Science (Medical Sciences)

BSc(MLS) Bachelor of Science in Medical Laboratory Sciences

BSc(Soc) Bachelor of Science (Sociology)

BSc(Social Science) Bachelor of Science (Social Science)

BSc(SocSc Nursing) Bachelor of Science

(Social-Science Nursing)

BSc(Tech) Bachelor of Science (Technology)

BSc (Town & Regional Planning) Bachelor of Science (Town & Regional Planning)

BScAgr Bachelor of Science in Agriculture

BScBCom Bachelor of Science and Bachelor of Commerce

BScDent Bachelor of Science in Dentistry

BScEcon Bachelor of Science in the Faculty of Economic and Social Studies

BScTech Bachelor of Technical Science

BSFA British Science Fiction Association

BSI British Standards Institution; Building Societies Institute

BSIA British Security Industry Association

BSIRA British Scientific Instruments Research Association

BSJA British Show Jumping Association

BSL British Sign Language

BSM British School of Motoring

BSO Bank Standing Order

BSocSc Bachelor of Social Science

BSPS British Show Pony Society

BSS British Standards Specification

BSSc Bachelor of Social Science

BSSG Member of the British Society of Scientific Glass Blowers

BST British Summer Time

BT British Telecommunications

Bt Baronet *(see also Bart)*

BTA British Tourist Authority; British Travel Association; British Tinnitus Association

BTC British Transport Commission

BTCV British Trust for Conservation Volunteers

BTech Bachelor of Technology

BTF British Trawler Federation

BTh Bachelor of Theology

BTHA British Tourist Hotels Association; British Toy and Hobby Manufacturers' Association

BTI British Telecommunications International

BTO British Trust for Ornithology

BTP Bachelor of Town and Country Planning

BTS Blood Transfusion Service

BTU British Thermal Unit

BTV Border Television

BU Bakers' Union

BUAV British Union for the Abolition of Vivisection

Bucks Buckinghamshire

BUDSU British Urban Development Services Unit *(Department of Environment)*

BUF British Union of Fascists

BUFC British Universities' Film Council

BUJ Bachelor of Canon Law

Bulg Bulgaria/Bulgarian

BUM *(South Africa)* Black Unity Movement

BUP British United Press

BUPA British United Provident Association

BUR Burma International Motor Vehicle Registration Letters

BVA British Veterinary Association

BVDU Bromovinyl deoxyuridine *(antivirus drug)*

BVetMed Bachelor of Veterinary Medicine

BVF British Volunteer Force *(extreme right-wing political party)*

BVJ British Veterinary Journal

BVM Blessed Virgin Mary

BVM&S Bachelor of Veterinary Medicine and Surgery

BVP British Volunteer Programme

BVSc Bachelor of Veterinary Science

BWAC *(USA)* Brooklyn Welfare Action Council

BWB British Waterways Board

BWC Beauty Without Cruelty

BWI British West Indies *(now WI, q.v.)*

BWIA British West Indian Airways

BWM British War Medal

BWNIC British Withdrawal from Northern Ireland Campaign

BWR Boiling Water Reactor

BWTA British Women's Temperance Association

BYC British Youth Council

BYIL British Yearbook of International Law

Byz Byzantine

Bz Benzene

C

C Century; Catholic; Celsius; Centigrade; Conservative; Carbon; Cuban International Motor Vehicle Registration Letter; 100 *(Roman numeral)*

c cent; centime; centimetre; carat; *(Latin)* circa *(about)*

CA Crown Agent; Civil Aviation; Community Association; Chief Accountant; Consumers' Association; Chartered Accountant *(Scotland and Canada)*; County Alderman; Central America; Court of Appeal; *(USA)* City Attorney; College of Agriculture; Contingency Allowance

Ca Calcium

C/A Current Account; Credit Account

CAA Campaign Against Arms *(Trade)*; Civil Aviation Authority

CAABU Council for the Advancement of Arab-British Understanding

CAAC China Civil Aviation Authority

CAACE Christian Association for Adult and Continuing Education

CAAT *(Canada)* College of Applied Arts and Technology

CAB Citizens' Advice Bureau; *(USA)* Civil Aeronautics Board

CABIN Campaign Against Building Industry Nationalisation

CABX Citizens' Advice Bureaux

CAC Central Arbitration Committee; County Agricultural Committee; Countryside Amenities Committee; Crafts Arts Council; *(USA)* Consumers' Advisory Council; Christian Affirmation Campaign

CACC Council for the Accreditation of Correspondence Colleges

CACM Conservatives Against the Common Market

CACTM Central Advisory Council of Training for the Ministry *(now ACCM)*

CAD Computer Aided Design

Cad *(music)* Cadenza *(final flourish)*

CAER Conservative Action for Electoral Reform

CAF Charities Aid Foundation; College of Agriculture and Forestry; *(Italy)* Comitati Associazioni Feminili *(Women's Right-wing Catholic Organisation)*; Central African Federation

CAFCA Campaign for the Abolition of Film Censorship for Adults

CAFE Comité d'Association Féminine Européene *(Committee of the Association of European Women)*

CAFRIC Campaign For Real Ice Cream

CAG Controller and Auditor General

CAH College of Agriculture and Horticulture

CAHID Committee of Experts for Identity Documents *(EEC, q.v.)*

CAITS Centre for Alternative Industrial and Technological Systems

Cal Caledonia; Calcutta

cal *(music)* calando *(gradually slower, with decreasing volume)*

Calif California *(USA State)*

CALIP Campaign Against Lead In Petrol

CALL Cancer Aid Listening Line

CALM Campaign Against the Lorry Menace

CALPA Canadian Air Line Pilots' Association

CAM Computer Aided Manufacture; Communication, Advertising and Marketing Education Foundation

Cambs Cambridgeshire

CAMRA Campaign for Real Ale

CAMRASO Cleaning and Maintenance Research and Service Organisation

CAMREB Campaign for Real Bread

CAMW Central Association for Mental Welfare

Can Canada

CANAL Campaign for Action on Navigation and Locks

CANCUN Mexican Conference on Third World *(1981)*

C and D Collection and Delivery *(British Rail Parcels Service, discontinued 1980)*

C and E Customs and Excise

C and G City and Guilds

CANDU Canadian Deuterium Uranium *(Canadian Atomic Nuclear Reactor)*

CANS Citizens' Advice Notes *(Public Library Reference Book)*

Cantab Cantabrian (of Cambridge University)

CANTAT Canada Transatlantic Telephones

CANTO Concern Against Nuclear Technology Organisations

CAO *(Netherlands)* Collectief Arbeids Overeenkomst *(Collective Labour Agreement)*

CAP Common Agricultural Policy *(of the EEC, q.v.)*; Combat Air Control; Code of Advertising Practice; *(Portugal)* Confederação dos Agricultores Portugueses *(Confederation of Farmers)*

CAPC Code of Advertising Practice Committee

CAPD Continuous Ambulatory Peritoneal Dialysis

CAPITAL Computer Assisted Placings in and around London

CAPS Captive Animals' Protection Society

Capt Captain

CAR Civil Air Regulations; Corsica Anti-Repression

car carat

CARAF Christians Against Racism and Fascism

CARD Campaign Against Racial Discrimination

CARE Council for Current Affairs, Research and Education; Cottage And Rural Enterprises; *(USA)* Co-operative for American Relief Everywhere

CARF Campaign Against Racism & Fascism

CARFF *(Africa)* Centre Africain de Recherche et de Formation pour la Femme *(Centre for Research into the Advancement of Women)*

CARICOM Caribbean Common Market

CARITAS Confédération Internationale d'Organismes Catholiques d'Action Charitable et Sociale *(International Confederation of Catholic Organisations for Charitable and Social Action, see also CICC)*

CARM Campaign Against Racism in the Media *(Group within the NUJ, q.v.)*

CARP Council for Alcohol-Related Problems

CART Computer-Assisted Railway Timetabling

CAS Children's Aid Society; Centre for Agricultural Strategy; Chief of the Air Staff

CASE Confederation for the Advancement of State Education; Centre for Advanced Studies in Environment

CAST The Creative and Supportive Trust *(charity run by and for prisoners)*

CAT College of Art and Technology; College of Advanced Technology; Civil Air Transport

CATCA Canada Air Traffic Control Association

CATITB Cotton and Allied Textiles Industrial Training Board

CATO Civil Air Traffic Operation

CAUN Club des Amis de l'Unesco *(friends of Unesco, q.v., Club)*

CAVU Ceiling and Visibility Unlimited

CAWP *(Philippines)* Civic Assembly of Women

CAWU Clerical and Administrative Workers' Union

CB Companion of the Order of the Bath; Confined to Barracks; County Borough; Conciliation Board; Citizen's Band *(private radio communication)*

CBA *(China)* Central Broadcasting Administration; Council for British Archaeology; *(USA)* Community Broadcasting Association

CBAEW Certificated Bailiffs Association of England & Wales

CBC County Borough Council; Canadian Broadcasting Corporation

CBE Commander of the Order of the British Empire

CBEVE Central Bureau for Educational Visits and Exchanges

CBF *(Eire)* Córas Beostoc Feola *(Irish Meat Board)*

CBI Confederation of British Industry; *(USA)* Central Bureau of Investigation

CBIM Companion of the British Institute of Management

CBM Chief Boatswain's Mate

CBMs *(USA)* Confidence Building Measures *(to reduce danger of war)*

CBRPT Confederation of British Road Passenger Transport *(formerly PVOA, q.v.)*

CBS Columbia Broadcasting System

CBSA Clay Bird Shooting Association

CC Cross Country *(horseriding)*; College of Commerce; County Court; County Council; City Council; Community Council; Cricket Club *(usually preceded by the name of the club)*; Cycling Club *(usually preceded by the name of the club)*; Chamber of Commerce, Consumer Council; 200 *(Roman numeral)*

CC(Scotland)A Chief Constables (Scotland) Association

cc copies; cubic centimetre

CCA Court of Criminal Appeal; County Councils' Association

CCAB Consultative Committee of Accountancy Bodies

CCACMF *(USA/Penn)* Concerned Citizens Against Centralia Mine Fires

CCBE Consultative Committee of the Bars and Law Societies of the European Community

CCBN Central Council for British Naturism

CCC Central Criminal Court; County Cricket Club; 300 *(Roman numeral)*; Consumers' Consultative Committee *(European Community)*

CCCC Charity Christmas Card Council

CCCI Conceal – Control – Command – Instruction *(NATO, q.v.)*

CCCP Childless by Choice – Curtail Pension; *(Russia/USSR)* Soyuz Sovietskikh Sotsialisticheskikh Respublik *(Trans-literal translation of USSR, Union of Soviet Socialist Republics)*

CCD Conference of the Committee on Disarmament; *(Belgium)* Conseil de Coopération Douanière *(Co-operation Council on Customs)*

CCE Campaign for Comprehensive Education

CCEO Community and Continuing Education Officer

CCETSW Central Council for Education and Training in Social Work

CCF Congress for Cultural Freedom; Combined Cadet Force; *(France)* Club Chrétien Français *(Christian Club)*

CCFA Combined Cadet Force Association

CCFM Combined Cadet Forces Medal

CCG Control Commission in Germany

CCHE Central Council for Health Education; Co-ordinating Council for Higher Education

CChem Chartered Chemist

CCHMS Central Committee for Hospital Medical Services

CCI Chambre de Commerce Internationale *(International Chamber of Commerce)*

CCIA Churches' Commission on International Affairs *(see also WCC)*

CCJ Council of Christians & Jews

CCL Commonwealth Countries League

CCLEPE Consultative Committee for Local Ecumenical Projects in England

CCM *(Zanzibar)* Revolutionary Party

CCMA Contract Cleaning and Maintenance Association

CCol Chartered Colourist

CCOO *(Spain)* Comisiones Obreras *(Workers' Commissions/ Trade Union)*

CCP Chinese Communist Party

CCPR Central Council of Physical Recreation

CCR County Court Rules; Common Centre of Research; *(USA)* Commission of Civil Rights

CCRST *(France)* Comité Consultatif de la Recherche Scientifique et Technique *(Consultative Committee for Scientific and Technical Research)*

CCS Casualty Clearing Station; Corporation of Certified Secretaries; Council for Science and Society

CCSU Council of the Civil Service Union

CCt County Court *(see also CC)*

CCTV Closed Circuit Television

CCU Civil Contingency Unit *(Cabinet Office)*; Coronary Care Unit

CD Civil Defence; Corps Diplomatique *(Diplomatic Corps)*; 400 *(Roman numeral)*

Cd Cadmium

CDA Comprehensive Development Area *(Borough Planning)*; College Diploma in Agriculture; *(Netherlands)* Christen Democratisch Appèl *(Christian Democratic Appeal)*; Co-operative Development Agency

CDC Commonwealth Development Corporation; *(USA)* Centre for Disease Control

CDDC(A) *(Argentina)* Comision de Documentacion Cientifica *(Science Documentation Centre)*

CDEE Chemical Defence Experimental Establishment

Cdre Commodore

CDF *(USA)* Children's Defense Fund

CDIIIU Central Drugs and Illegal Immigration Intelligence Unit

CDipAF Certified Diploma in Accounting and Finance

CDMD Campaign for Defence and Multilateral Disarmament

CDN Canadian International Motor Vehicle Registration Letters

Cdo Commando

CDOC Community Drying Out Centre *(for alcoholics)*

CDP Community Development Projects; Committee of Directors of Polytechnics; Christian Democratic Party

CDR *(Cuba)* Committee for the Defence of the Revolution

Cdr Commander

Cdre Commodore

CDS Chief of the Defence Staff; *(France)* Centre des Democrats Sociaux *(anti-De Gaulle political group)*; *(Portugal)* Centro

Democrático Social *(Christian Demo-cratic Party)*; *(Spain)* Centro Democrático y Social *(Democratic and Social Centre Party)*

CDSO Companion of the Distinguished Service Order

CDT Craft Design Technology

CDU *(West Germany)* Christliche Demokratische Union *(Christian Democratic Union)*

CE Council of Europe; Church of England; Civil Engineer; Communautés Européennes *(European Community)*

Ce Cerium

CEA Council for Educational Advancement; Central Electricity Authority; Cinematograph Exhibitors' Association of Great Britain; Community Education Association; Centre Européen des Assurances *(European Insurance Committee)*; Commission Economique des NU, *q.v.*, pour l'Afrique *(Economic Commission of the UN, q.v., for Africa)*

CEAC Commission Européenne de l'Aviation Civile *(European Commission for Civil Aviation)*

CEB Central Electricity Board; *(Belgium)* Comité Electrotechnique Belge *(Electrotechnical Committee)*

CEBEMO *(Netherlands)* Katholieke Organisatie voor Medefinanciering van Ontwikkelingsprogramma's *(Catholic Relief Agency)*

CEC Commission of the European Communities; Commonwealth Economic Committee

CECG Consumers in the European Community Group

CECIF Centre Européen du Conseil International des Femmes *(European Centre of the International Council of Women, see also ECICW)*

CED *(USA)* Campaign for Economic Democracy

CEDC Community Education Development Centre

CEDEFOP Centre Européen pour le Developpement de la Formation Professionnelle *(European Centre for the Development of Vocational Training EEC, q.v.)*

CEDO Centre for Educational Development Overseas

CEE Council for Environment Education; Certificate of Extended Education; Communauté Economique Européenne *(European Economic Community, see also EEC)*; Commission Economique des NU, *q.v.*, pour l'Europe *(Economic Commission for Europe, see also ECE)*

CEEC Council for European Economic Co-operation

CEEFAX see facts *(BBC, q.v., broad-casting system for information on television screens)*

CEF Canadian Expeditionary Force

CEGB Central Electricity Generating Board

CEHO Chief Environmental Health Officer *(Local Authority)*

CEI Council of Engineering Institutions

CEIR Corporation for Economic and Industries Research

CELAM *(Latin American)* Bishops' Conference

CELF *(France)* Collectif des Etudiants Libéraux de France *(Liberal Students Union)*

CEM Council of European Municipalities *(see also ACEM)*

CEMA Council for the Encouragement of Music & the Arts *(now Arts Council of Great Britain, see also AC)*

CEMS Church of England Men's Society

CEng Chartered Engineer

CENTO Central Treaty Organisation *(Military Alliance of Britain, Turkey, Iran and Pakistan with US as associate member, see also CTO)*

CEO Chief Education Officer *(Local Authority)*; Chief Executive Officer; Customs Enforcement Officer; Confederation of Employee Organisations

CEP Community Enterprise Programme *(now CP)*; Community Education Programme

CEPAL Conférence Economique pour l'Amérique Latine *(Economic Conference for Latin America, see also ECLA)*

CEPE *(Ecuador)* Coporacion Estatal Petrolena Ecuatoriana *(Government Oil Company)*

CERA Civil Engineering Research Association

CERD Committee for European Research and Development

CERES *(France)* Centre d'Assais et de Recherches d'Engins Speciaux *(Research Centre for Speciality Engines)*; *(France)* Comité d'Etudes Régionales Economiques et Sociales *(Regional Social and Economic Studies Group)*

CERL Central Electricity Research Laboratories

CERN *(France)* Conseil Européen pour la Recherche Nucléaire *(Now ORN, q.v.)*

CERP Centre Europeen des Relations Publiques *(European Centre for Public Relations)*

Cert Certificate

CertAIB Certificated Associate of the Institute of Bankers

CertCAM Certificate of the Communication Advertising and Marketing Education Foundation

CertEd Certificate in Education

CertHE Certificate of Health Education

CES Centre for Environmental Studies

CESAP Consultation Régionale de l'Aië pour l'Asie et le Pacifique *(Regional Consultation of the IYC, q.v., for Asia and the Pacific, see also ESCAP)*

CESI Centre for Economic and Social Information

CESRF Christian Economic and Social Research Foundation

CET Council for Educational Technology; Central European Time; Common External Tariff *(EEC, q.v.)*

CETS Church of England Temperance Society

CEWC Council for Education in World Citizenship

CF Chaplain to the Forces

Cf Californium

cf *(Latin)* confer *(compare)*

c†f carry forward

CFA Commonwealth Forestry Association; Committee on Food Aid *(FAO, q.v.)*;

CFCS Chlorofluorocarbons *(propellant gas used in aerosol spray cans)*

CFCYP Centre of Films for Children and Young People *(see also CIFEJ)*

CFD *(India)* Congress For Democracy

CFPT *(France)* Confédération Française Démocratique du Travail *(Socialist-led Trade Union)*

CFE College of Further Education

CFF Children's Film Foundation *(now CFTF, q.v.)*

CFI Chaplain to Foreign Immigrants

cfi cost, freight, insurance

CFM Cadet Forces Medal

cfm cubic feet per minute

CFP Common Fisheries Policy *(EEC, q.v., fishing regulations)*

CFR Commercial Fast Reactor

cfs cubic feet per second

CFT *(France)* Confédération Française du Travail *(Right-Wing Gaullist Trade Union)*

cft cubic foot/feet

CFTC Commonwealth Fund for Technical Co-operation; *(France)* Confédération Française des Travailleurs Chrétiens *(Confederation of Christian Workers)*

CFTF Children's Film and Television Foundation

CG Chaplain General; Consul General; Coast Guard

cg centigramme

CGA Country Gentlemen's Association

CGBR Central Government Borrowing Requirement

CGC *(France)* Confédération Générale des Cadres *(General Confederation of Supervisory Employees)*

CGIA City and Guilds of London Institute Insignia Award in Technology

CGIL *(Italy)* Confederazione Generale Italiana del Lavoro *(General Confederation of Labour)*

CGLI City and Guilds of London Institute

CGM Conspicuous Gallantry Medal

CGPME *(France)* Confédération Générale des Petites et Moyennes Entreprises *(General Confederation of Small and Medium-Sized Businesses)*

CGRM Commandant-General, Royal Marines

CGS Chief of the General Staff *(see also CIGS)*

CGT Capital Gains Tax; *(France)* Confédération Générale du Travail *(Communist-led Trade Union)*; *(Argentina)* General Labour Confederation

CGTO *(France)* Confédération Générale du Travail Force Ouvrière *(General Manual Workers' Union)*

CGTSF *(France)* Compagnie Générale de Télégraphie Sans Fils *(Radio & Industrial Corporation)*

CGTU *(France)* Confédération Générale de Travail Unitaire *(General Federation of United Labour)*

CH Companion of Honour; Swiss International Motor Vehicle Registration Letters; Central Heating; College of Horticulture

ch central heating

CHA Community Health Area

ChanCom Channel Committee

Chap Chaplain; Chapter

CHAR Campaign for the Homeless and Rootless

CHARM Scientific name for a minute particle of matter

CHAS Catholic Housing Aid Society

ChB Bachelor of Surgery

CHC Community Health Centre/Council

CHD Coronary Heart Disease

ChD Chancery Division *(of the High Court)*; Chancery Division *(Law Reports)*

CHE College of Higher Education; Campaign for Homosexual Equality

ChE Chief Engineer; Chemical Engineer

Chem Chemistry

CHERISH *(EIRE, Dublin)* Organisation for single mothers

CHE's Children's Community Homes

Ches Cheshire

Chm Chairman

ChM Master of Surgery

CHPDH Combined Heat and Power District Heating

CHSE Central Health Services Executive

CI Crime Intelligence; Commonwealth Institute; Ivory Coast International Motor Vehicle Registration Letters; Imperial Order of the Crown of India; Community Industry *(organisation to help young unemployed, DoE, q.v.)*;

Channel Islands

CIA Consumer Inducement Agency; Chemical Industries Association; Commonwealth Industries Association; *(USA)* Central Intelligence Agency

CIAD Central Institute of Art & Design

CIAG Centre of Information of Graphic Arts

CIAgrE Companion of the Institution of Agricultural Engineers

CIAL Corresponding Member of the International Institute of Arts & Letters

CIAS Conseil International de l'Action Sociale *(International Council for Social Action)*

CIB Chartered Institute of Building; Corporation of Insurance Brokers

CIBICC Craftsman of the Incorporated British Institute of Certified Carpenters

CIBS Coach & Independent Bus Sector of CBRPT, *q.v.*; Chartered Institute of Building Services

CIC Commonwealth Information Centre; Conseil International de la Chasse et de la Conservation du Gibier, FAO, *q.v.* *(International Hunting and Shooting Council)*

CICB Criminal Injuries Compensation Board

CICC Confédération Internationale des Charités Catholiques *(International Confederation of Catholic Charities, see also CARITAS)*

CICILS Confédération Internationale du Commerce et des Industries des Légumes Sec, *(FAO, q.v., International Pulse Trade and Industry Federation)*

CICPLB Comité International pour le Controle de la Productivité Laitière du Bétail, *(FAO, q.v.), (International Committee for Recording the Productivity of Milk Animals, see also ICRPMA)*

CICR Comité International de la Croix Rouge *(International Red Cross)*

CID Criminal Investigation Department; Committee for Imperial Defence; Council of Industrial Design

CIDA Canadian International Development Agency

CIDEC Conseil International pour le Developpement du Cuivre *(International Council for the Development of Copper)*

CIDR Compagnie Internationale de Developpement Rural *(International Rural Development Company)*

CIE *(Eire)* Córas Iompair Eireann *(State Rail and Road Transport Authority)*; Companion of the Order of the Indian Empire; Confédération Internationale des Etudiants *(International Confederation of Students)*

CIEC Commonwealth International Economic Council; Conference of International Economic Co-operation *(also known as North/South Dialogue)*

CIEE Conference of the Institution of Electrical Engineers

CIEO *(Belgium)* Catholic Education Office

CIF *(France)* Centre d'Information Féminin *(Women's Information Centre)*; Conseil International de Femmes *(ICW, q.v.)*; *(Italy)* Centro Italiano Feminile *(Women's Forum)*

cif cost, insurance, freight

CIFEJ Centre International du Film pour l'Enfance et la Jeunesse *(International Centre of Films for Children and Young People, see also ICFCYP)*

CIGR Commission Internationale du Génie Rural *(International Commission of Agricultural Engineering, FAO, q.v.)*

CIGS/CGS Chief of the Imperial General Staff

CIH Certificate in Industrial Health

CIHEAM Centre International de Hautes Etudes Agronomiques Méditerranéennes, *(FAO, q.v., International Centre for Advanced Mediterranean Agronomic Studies, see also ICAMAS)*

CII Chartered Insurance Institute; Cats In Industry

CIIA Commission Internationale des Industries Agricoles et Alimentaires *(FAO, q.v., International Commission for Agriculture and Food Industries, see also ICAI)*

CIIR Catholic Institute for International Relations

CILAF Comité International de Liaison des Associations Feminines *(International Liaison Committee of Women's Organisations)*

CILT Centre for Information on Language Teaching

CIMarE Companion of the Institute of Marine Engineers

CIMechE Companion of the Institution of Mechanical Engineers

CIMGTechE Companion of the Institution of Mechanical and General Technician Engineers

CIMRA Colonialism and Indigenous Minorities Research and Action

Cin Cincinnati

CINA Commission Internationale de la Navigation Aérienne *(International Commission on Air Navigation)*

C-in-C Commander-in-Chief

CINCLANT *(USA Navy)* Commander-in-Chief Atlantic Fleet

CIO *(USA)* Congress of Industrial Organisations

CIOB Chartered Institute of Building

CIOC Craftsman of the Institute of Carpenters

CIOSTA International Commission of Scientific Management in Agriculture,

(FAO, q.v.)
CIPA Chartered Institute of Patent Agents
CIPFA Chartered Institute of Public Finance and Accountancy
CIPQ Centre International pour la Promotion de Qualité *(International Centre for the Promotion of Quality)*
CIPRA Clothing Industry Productivity Resources Agency
CIQ International Association for Quality Research on Food Plants *(FAO, q.v.)*
CIRIA Construction Industry Research and Information Association
CIS Institute of Chartered Secretaries and Administrators; Counter-Information Services *(group of radical journalists)*
CISAC Confédération Internationale des Sociétés d'Auteurs et Compositeurs *(International Confederation of Author and Composer Societies)*
CISCO Civil Services Catering Organisation
CISF *(India)* Central Industrial Security Force
CISL *(Italy)* Confederazione Italiana di Sindicati Liberi *(Confederation of Free Workers)*; *(Italy)* Confederazione Italiana Sindicati Lavoratori *(Confederation of Labour Unions)*
CISNU *(Iran)* Confederation of Iranian Students
CISO Canadian Industrial Safety Organisation; *(Italy)* Centro Italiano Studi Aziendali *(Study Centre)*
CISOB Counsellor of the Incorporated Society of Organ Builders
CISSY Campaign to Impede Sex Stereotyping in the Young
CIT Central Independent Television; Chartered Institute of Transport; *(California)* Carnegie Institute of Technology; *(Italy)* Compagnia Italiana Turismo *(Largest travel agency)*
CITB Construction Industry Training Board
CITES *(USA)* Convention on International Trade in Endangered Species *(see also IUCN)*
CIU Club and Institute Union
CIUS Conseil International des Unions Scientifiques *(FAO, q.v., International Council of Scientific Unions, see ICSU and COGENE)*
CIWF Compassion in World Farming
CJ Circuit Judge; Chief Justice
CJCC Commonwealth Joint Communications Committee
CJD Campaign for Justice in Divorce
CJDE *(France)* Centre des Jeunes Dirigéants d'Entreprises *(Centre for Young Businessmen)*
CL Sri Lankan International Motor Vehicle Registration Letters; 150 *(Roman numeral)*
CL(ADO) Diploma in Contact Lens Fitting of the Association of Dispensing Opticians
Cl Chlorine
Cl/cl Clause
CLA Country Landowners' Association
CLAC Cost of Living Advisory Committee
CLAF Contingency Legal Aid Fund
CLAPA Cleft Lip and Palate Association
CLCB Committee of London Clearing Bankers
CLE Council of Legal Education
CLÉ *(Eire)* Cumann Leabharfhoilsitheoiri Eireann *(Irish Booksellers' Association)*
CLEA Council of Local Education Authorities
CLEAR Council for Lead-free Air
CLIC Cancer and Leukaemia in Children
clin clinical
CLit Companion of Literature *(Royal Society of Literature Award)*
Cllr Councillor
CLP Constituency Labour Party
CLPD Campaign for Labour Party Democracy
CLR Campaign for Labour Representation *(in Northern Ireland)*
CLRC Criminal Law Revision Committee
CLT Computer Language Translator
CLV Campaign for Labour Victory
CM Congregation of the Mission; Certificated Master; 900 *(Roman numeral)*
Cm Curium
cm centimetre
CMA Canadian Medical Association; Certificate in Management Accountancy; Certificate in Municipal Administration
CMAC Catholic Marriage Advisory Council
CMB Central Medical Board; *(Certified by)* Central Midwives' Board
CMBHI Craft Member of the British Horological Institute
Cmd Command Paper
Cmdr Commodore
CMEA Council for Mutual Economic Assistance *(see also COMECON)*
CMF Coal Merchants' Federation
CMG Companion of the Order of St. Michael and St. George
CMH Campaign for the Mentally Handicapped
CMIWHTE Companion Member of the Institution of Works and Highways Technician Engineers
CMIWSc Certified Member of the Insti-

tute of Wood Science

CMLR Common Market Law Reports

CMN Common Market Nations/Nationals

CMO Chief Medical Officer; Cabinet Ministers Only

CMRB Chemicals & Minerals Requirements Board

CMRST Committee on Manpower Resources for Science and Technology

CMRU Child Minder Research Unit

CMS Catholic Missionary Society; Church Missionary Society; Conservative Medical Society; Certificate in Management Studies

CMT Chinese Musical and Theatrical Association

CMV Cytogalovirus *(virus causing mental disability)*

CN Charge Nurse

CNA Commission de la Navigation Aérienne *(Air Navigation Commission)*

CNAA Council for National Academic Awards

CNAFM Conseil National des Associations de Femmes de Madagascar *(Council of Women's Associations of Madagascar)*

CND Campaign for Nuclear Disarmament

CNDCA *(France)* Comité National de Défence contre l'Alcoolisme *(Committee for Defence Against Alcoholism)*

CNDI *(Italy)* Consiglio Nationale delle Donne Italiane *(NCW, q.v.)*

CNES *(France)* Centre National d'Etudes Spatiales *(Centre for Space Studies)*

CNF *(France)* Comité National Féminin *(WNC, q.v.)*

CNFB *(Belgium)* Conseil National de Femmes Belges *(NCW, q.v.)*

CNFF *(France)* Conseil National des Femmes Françaises *(NCW, q.v.)*

CNIP *(France)* Centre National des Indépendants et Paysans *(National Centre of Independents & Countrymen)*

CNMG *(Guatemala)* Consejo Nacional de Mujeres de Guatemala *(NCW, q.v.)*

CNMU *(Uruguay)* Consejo Nacional de Musjeres *(NCW, q.v.)*

CNO Chief Nursing Officer

CNPF *(France)* Conseil National de Patronats Français *(National Council of Employers)*

CNR Canadian National Railways

CNT *(Spain)* Confederación Nacional del Trabajo *(National Confederation of Labour)*

CO County; Company; Colonial Officer; Commanding Officer; Commonwealth Office; Colonial Office; Conscientious Objector; Co-Action Programme *(Unesco, q.v., Gift Coupon Programme, see also GCP)*; Clerical Officer *(BBC, q.v., Staff Grade)*; Colombia International Motor Vehicle Registration Letters

Co Company; County; Cobalt

Co-Action See GCP *(Gift Coupon Programme, UNESCO q.v.)*

c/o care of

COASY Care of Animals Society

COB *(Bolivia)* Central Obrera Boliviana *(Central Workers' Confederation/ Central Workers' Union/Central Labour Organisation)*

COBOL Common Business Oriented Language *(Computer Terminology)*

COBRA Cabinet Office Briefing Room

COCSU Council of Civil Service Unions

COD Cash on Delivery; Concise Oxford Dictionary

Cod Codicil

CoEnCo Council for Environmental Conservation

C of A College of Arms; Certificate of Airworthiness

COFACE Committee of the EEC, *q.v. (Family Organisations)*

C of C Chamber of Commerce

C of E Council of Europe; Church of England

COFEPOSA *(India)* Conservation of Foreign Exchange & Prevention of Smuggling Act

C of I Church of Ireland

C of S Church of Scotland; Chief of Staff

COGENE Committee on Genetic Experiments

COHSE Confederation of Health Service Employees

COI Central Office of Information; Conseil Oleicole International *(International Olive Oil Council, FAO, q.v., see also IOOC)*

COID Council on International Development

COIT Council of Industrial Tribunals

COL Cost of Living; Computer Oriented Language *(Data Processing)*

Col Colonel; Columbia; Colorado *(USA State)*; Monetary unit of Costa Rica and El Salvador

COLA Cost of Living Allowances

Coll College; Collegiate

Colo Colorado *(USA State)*

Col-Sergt Colour Sergeant

CoM Committee of Management

Com Committee

COMA Government Committee of Experts on Diet

Comdr Commander

Comdt Commandant

COMEC Council of the Military Education Committees *(UK, q.v., Universities)*

COMECON Conseil pour l'Aide Mutuelle Economique *(Council for Mutual Economic Aid, see also CMEA)*

COMET Combined Organic Movement for Education and Training

COMEXO Committee for Oceanic Exploration

Comintern Communist International

Comm Commissioner; Commission

Commie/Commy Communist

COMP Council of Management and Professional Staffs *(TUC, q.v.)*

CompanionICE Companion of the Institution of Civil Engineers

CompanionIEE Companion of the Institution of Electrical Engineers

CompanionIGasE Companion of the Institution of Gas Engineers

CompanionIP Companion of the Institute of Plumbing

CompSLEAT Companion of the Society of Licensed Aircraft Engineers and Technologists

con*(Latin)* contra *(against)*

CONAD *(Bolivia)* Comité Nacional Para Defensa de la Democracia *(National Committee for the Defence of Democracy)*

CONE Creation of New Enterprises

Conf Conference

Cong Congress; Congregational§Congregation

CONGO Conference Of Non-Governmental Organisations

Cong Orat Congregation of the Oratory

CONI *(Dominican Republic)* Consejo Nacional para la Niñez *(National Council for Children)*

Conn Connecticut *(USA State)*

CONOCO Continental Oil Co. *(UK)*

Co-Ord Co-ordination of 25 organisations formed in defence of the 1967 Abortion Act

Cons Conservative

CONSOC Conservative Society

Consols Consolidated funds

Const Ct Consistory Court

Cont/cont Continued/continued

Contemp Contemporary

Co-Op Co-Operative

COPA Comité des Organisations Professionelles Agricoles *(Committee of Professional Agricultural Organisations, Committee of European Farmers' Unions, EEC, q.v.)*

COPCON *(Portugal)* Comando Operacional do Continente *(Operational Commandos – military security force)*

COPEC Conference on Politics, Economics and Christianity

COPEL Spanish Prisoners' Association

COPS Civilian Organisation of Protection Security (Ltd)

CORAD Committee on Restrictions Against the Disabled

CORE *(USA)* Congress of Racial Equality

CORESTA Co-operation Centre for Scientific Research Relative to Tobacco *(FAO, q.v.)*

CORGI Confederation of Registered Gas Installers

Coro Corsica *(Department of France)*

Corol Corollary

Corp Corporal; Corporation

CORT Cognitive Research Trust

COS Chief of Staff; Certificate in Office Studies

COSA Colliery Officials and Staffs Association *(section of NUM, q.v.)*

COSE Committee on Secondary Education *(Scotland)*

CoSIRA Council for Small Industries In Rural Areas

COSPAR Committee on Space Research

COSW Citizens' Organisation for a Sane World

COW Cinema of Women

Coy Company *(see also Co)*

COYOTE Call-Off-Your-Old-Tired-Ethics

CP College of Preceptors; Common Pleas *(Court of)*; Communist Party *(see also CPGB)*; Community Programme *(see also CEP)*; Bolivia Airline

cp compare

CPA Chartered Patent Agent; Calico Printers' Association; Canadian Pacific Airline; Commonwealth Parliamentary Association; Clyde Ports Authority; Commonwealth Producers' Association

CPAC Consumer Protection Advisory Committee

CPAG Child Poverty Action Group

CPAL Canadian Pacific Airlines *(see also CPA)*

CPAS Church Pastoral Aid Society

CPB Community Project Board; *(Burma)* Communist Party *(see also BCP)*

CPBF Campaign for Press and Broadcasting Freedom

CPC Clerk to the Privy Council; Conservative Political Centre; City Police Commissioner; Christian Peace Conference; Certificate of Professional Competence

CPD Community Project Development

CPF Community Projects Foundation

CPG *(Greece)* Ginaikion Prodeftiko Comma *(Women's Progressive Party)*; Communist Party of Greece

CPGB Communist Party of Great Britain

CPH Certificate of Public Health

CPI Consumer Price Index

CPI(M) Communist Party of India

CPL Commercial Pilot's Licence; Cats' Protection League

Cpl Corporal

CPM Commissioner of Police for the Metropolis

CPME Council for Postgraduate Medical Education

CPN Communist Party of the Netherlands

CPNA Council of Photographic News Agencies

CPO Compulsory Purchase Order; *(Yemen)* Central Planning Organisation; Chief Petty Officer; Cancel Previous Order

CPR Cardiopulmonary Resuscitation; Canadian Pacific Railway

CPRE Council for the Protection of Rural England

CPRS Central Policy Review Staff; *(Portugal)* Social Democratic Centre

CPRW Council for the Protection of Rural Wales

CPS Commons, Open Spaces and Footpaths Preservation Society; Centre for Policy Studies; *(Latin)* Custos Privati Sigilla *(Keeper of the Privy Seal)*

CPSA Civil & Public Services Association

CPSU Communist Party of the Soviet Union; *(Cuba)* Partido Socialista Popular *(Communist Party)*

CPU Commonwealth Press Union; Central Processing Unit *(Computer Terminology)*

CQEE *(Canada/Quebec)* Conseil du Québec de l'Enfance Exceptionelle *(Council for the Gifted Child)*

CQMS Company Quartermaster Sergeant

CQSS Certificate of Qualification in Social Science

CQSW Certificate of Qualification in Social Work

CR Community Relations *(now RRB, q.v.)*; Consciousness-Raising *(feminist pressure group)*; Costa Rican International Motor Vehicle Registration Letters

Cr Chromium

Cr/cr Credit/credit

CRA Commander Royal Artillery; Corporate Restructuring Agency

CRAC Central Religious Advisory Committee *(joint committee dealing with religious programmes for both BBC, q.v., and IBA, q.v.)*; Careers Research and Advisory Centre

CRACK Young section of the Multiple Sclerosis Society

CRAE Committee for the Reform of Animal Experimentation

CRAM Campaign against Racism in the Media

CRAPE Committee for the Restructuring and Progress of Equity *(Actors' Trade Union)*

CRASC Commander Royal Army Service Corps

CRC Cancer Research Campaign; Camera Ready Copy *(for printing)*

CRCCYP Certificate in the Residential Care of Children and Young People

Cr Ct Crown Court

CRD Campaign for Representative Democracy; Chronic Respiratory Disease; Conservative Research Department

CRDP *(France)* Centre de Recherche et Documentation Pédagogique *(Education Research Centre for Teachers, Regional Offices of the INRDP, q.v.)*

CRE Commission for Racial Equality *(now RRB, q.v.)*; Commander Royal Engineers; *(Standing)* Conference of Rectors *(Presidents and Vice-Chancellors of the European Universities, EEC, q.v.)*

CREEP *(USA)* Committee to Re-elect the President *(organisation formed to re-elect President Nixon for second term of office)*

Cres Crescent

cresc *(music)* crescendo *(increasing volume)*

CREW Centre for Research on European Women

CRF Citizens' Research Foundation; *(France)* Croix-Rouge Française *(French Red Cross)*; Cancer Research Fund; Conservation and Research Foundation

CRIF *(France)* Conseil Représentatif des Israélites de France *(Representative Council of French Jews)*

CRISTAL Contract Regarding an Interim Supplement on Tanker Liability for Oil Petroleum *(Cargo Owners' Insurance Scheme)*

CRMP Corps of Royal Military Police

CRO Community Relations Officer; Criminal Records Office; Citizens' Rights Office; Commonwealth Relations Office *(now CO, q.v.)*; Companies Registration Office

CRS Catholic Record Society; Cereals Research Station; Cold-Rolled Steel; *(USA)* Catholic Relief Services; *(France)* Compagnies Républicaines de Sécurité *(Security Companies)*

CRSW Certificate in Residential Social Work

CRT Cathode Ray Tube

CRTC Canada Radio and Television Company

Cruz Cruzeiro *(Monetary unit of Brazil)*

CS Civil Service; Civil Servant; Common Sergeant; Court of Sessions; City Surveyor; College of Science; Conservation Society; Christian Science; Clerk to the Signet; Crown Silvered *(electric light bulb)*; Czechoslovakian International Motor Vehicle Registration Letters; *(France)* Centre de Secours *(First Aid Centre)*

Cs Caesium

CSA Community Standards Association; Canadian Standards Association; Confederate States of America

CSAC Consumer Standards Advisory Committee

CSandEU See CSEU

CSB Bachelor of Christian Science

CSBF Civil Service Benevolent Fund

CSC Civil Service Commission; Conspicuous Service Cross

CSCA Civil Service Clerical Association, now CPSA, q.v.

CSCE Conference on Security & Co-operation in Europe

CSD Council for Social Democracy; Civil Service Department

CSE Certificate of Secondary Education; Combined Services Entertainment *(successor to ENSA, q.v.)*

CSERB Computer Systems & Electronic Requirements Board

CSEU/CS & EU Confederation of Ship building and Engineering Unions

CSFDA Civil Servants First Division Association *(see also AFDCS & IPCS)*

CSI Companion of the Order of the Star of India; Church of Southern India; Commission Séricole Internationale *(International Sericultural Commission, FAO, q.v., see also ISC)*

CSIR Commonwealth Council for Scientific and Industrial Research, *(now CSIRO, q.v.)*

CSIRO Commonwealth Scientific and Industrial Research Organisation

CSM Company Sergeant Major

CSMA Civil Service Motoring Association

CSO Community Service Order; Chief Scientific Officer; Chief Signal Officer; Chief Staff Officer; Central Selling Organisation *(diamonds)*; Central Statistical Office

CSP Chartered Society of Physiotherapy; Pakistan Civil Service

CSPI *(USA)* Center for Science in the Public Interest

CSS Certificate in Social Services; Council for Social Service

CSSB Civil Service Selection Board

CSSC Civil Service Sports Council

CSSD Central Sterile Supply Department *(NHS, q.v.)*

CSSP Centre for Studies in Social Policy

CSSS Civil Service *(and Post Office)* Sanatorium Society

CST College of Science and Technology

CSTI Council of Science and Technology Institutes

CStJ Commander of the Order of St. John of Jerusalem

CSU Civil Service Union; *(West Germany)* Christliche Soziale Union *(Christian Social Union)*

CSV Community Service Volunteers

CSYS Certificate of Sixth Year Studies

CT Civic Trust; College of Technology

Ct Court

ct carat

CTA California Teachers' Association

CTB Commonwealth Telecommunications Board

CTBF Cinema & Television Benevolent Fund

CTC Central Television Company; Cyclists' Touring Club

CTCC Central Transport Consultative Committee

CTCM and H Certificate in Tropical Community Medicine and Health

CTEB Council of Technical Examining Bodies

CTF *(France)* Comité du Travail Féminin *(Working Women's Joint Committee)*

CTIF *(Africa)* Centre de la Tribune Internationale de la Femme *(Centre of the International Tribune for Women)*

CTK *(Czechoslovakia)* Ceskoslovenska Tisková Kancelar *(Offical News Agency)*

CTN Confectioner, Tobacconist and Newsagent

CTO Central Treaty Organisation *(see also CENTO)*

CTR **(Harwell)** Controlled Thermonuclear Research *(Harwell)*

CTT Capital Transfer Tax

CTU Conservative Trade Unionist

CTUC Commonwealth Trade Union Council

CTV Channel Television

CTVC Centre for Television and Radio Communication

CU Cambridge University; *(USA)* Consumers' Union; Cuba Airline

Cu *(Latin)* Cuprum *(Copper)*

Cu/cu Cubic/cubic

CUA Computer Users' Association

CUAC Cambridge University Athletic Club

CUAFC Cambridge University Association Football Club

CUAS Cambridge University Air Squadron

CUBC Cambridge University Boat Club

CUC Coal Utilisation Council; Churches Unity Commission

CUCC Cambridge University Cricket Club

CUCO Conservative and Unionist Central Office

CUDS Cambridge University Dramatic Society

CUGC Cambridge University Golf Club

CUHC Cambridge University Hockey Club

CULGB Credit Union League of Great Britain

CULTC Cambridge University Lawn Tennis Club

CUMS Cambridge University Musical Society

CUOG Cambridge University Opera Group

CUP Cambridge University Press

CURB Campaign on Use and Restriction of Barbiturates

CURUFC Cambridge University Rugby Union Football Club

CUS *(France)* Centre des Démocrats Sociaux *(anti- De Gaulle political group)*

CUSA *(USA)* Christians and Jews United for Social Action; Cavitron Ultrasonic Aspirator

CV/cv *(Latin)* Curriculum Vitae *(life history)*

CVCP Committee of Vice-Chancellors/ Chairmen and Principals *(of Universities)*

CVF *(Argentina)* Centre of Volunteers for the Fatherland

CVO Commander of the Royal Victorian Order

CVS Community Volunteer Service; Council for Voluntary Service *(usually preceded by the initial of County or Borough)*

CWA Crime Writers' Association

CWDE Centre for World Development Education

CWL Catholic Women's League

CWO Cash With Order

CWOI *(Israel)* Council of Women's Organisations *(NCW, q.v.)*

CWS Chemical Warfare Service; Co-Operative Wholesale Society

cwt hundredweight

CX Uruguay Airline

CY Cyprian International Motor Vehicle Registration Letters

Cy Cyprus

CYDA Confederation of Yemeni Development Associations

cyl cylinder/cylindrical

CYO Catholic Youth Organisation

CYSA Community and Youth Service Association

CZ *(Panama)* Canal Zone; Cubic Zirconium *(synthetic diamond)*; Monaco Airline

Czech Czechoslovakia/Czechoslovakian

D

D Director; 500 *(Roman numeral)*; West German International Motor Vehicle Registration Letter

d dollar; dinar *(Monetary unit of Yugoslavia and other countries)*; drachma *(Monetary unit of Greece)*

DA Diploma in Anaesthetics; District Administrator *(NHS, q.v.)*; Deputy Assistant; Diploma in Art; Disability Allowance; Daughters of America; Doctor of Art *(Scotland)*; *(USA)* District Attorney; *(Denmark)* Employers' Federation; Deposit Account

DA(Edin) Diploma of Associate Edinburgh College of Art

D/A Deposit Account

DAA & QMG Deputy Assistant Adjutant and Quartermaster General

DAAG Deputy Assistant Adjutant-General

DAB Daily Audience Barometer *(BBC, q.v.)*

DAC Development Assistance Committee *(of the OECD, q.v.)*; Deutsche *(West German)* Aero Club; *(Caribbean)* Democratic Action Congress

DAD Deputy Assistant Director

DADMS Deputy Assistant Director of Medical Services

DADOS Deputy Assistant Director of Ordnance Services

DAES Diploma in Advanced Educational Studies

DAF Department of Agriculture and Fisheries

DAFS Department of Agriculture and Fisheries, Scotland

DAG Deputy Adjutant General; *(West Germany)* Deutsche Angestellen Gewerkschaft *(Salaried Employees Union)*

DAJAG Deputy Assistant Judge Advocate General

DAMHB Directorate of Ancient Monuments and Historic Buildings *(DOE, q.v.)*

D and D Drunk and Disorderly

DAQMG Deputy Adjutant Quartermaster General

DAR Daughters of the American Revolution

DARE Zanu *(q.v.)* Executive

DAS Development Advisory Service *(World Bank)*; Disablement Advice Service; Dramatic Authors' Society

DASE Diploma in Advanced Studies in Education

DATA Draughtsmen's and Allied Technicians Association

DATAR *(France)* Délégation à l'Aménagement du Territoire et à l'Action Régionale *(Delegation concerned with land and regional operations)*

DAvMed Diploma in Aviation Medicine

DAWN Drugs, Alcohol, Women, Nationality

DB Domesday Book; Day Book *(accountancy); (West Germany)* Deutsche Bundesbahn *(Federal Railway); (West Germany)* Deutsche Bundesrepublik *(Federal Republic)*

dB Decibel

dBA Absolute Decibels

DBC Deaf Broadcasting Campaign

DBE Dame Commander of the Order of the British Empire

DBO Diploma of the British Orthoptic Council; District Building Officer *(NHS, q.v.)*

DBS Direct Broadcast by Satellite

DC Design Council; Deputy Commissioner; Direct Current *(electricity)*; Detective Constable; District Council; Divisional Court; 600 *(Roman numeral); (Italy)* Partito Democrazia Cristiana *(Christian Democratic Party)*; District of Columbia *(USA)*

dc *(music)* da capo *(repeat from the beginning)*

DCAS Deputy Chief of Air Staff

DCB Dame Commander of the Order of the Bath

DCC Diploma of Chelsea College; 700 *(Roman numeral); (USA, New York)* Dramatic Critics' Circle

DCCC 800 *(Roman numeral)*; Domestic Coal Consumers' Council

DCE Domestic Credit Expansion

DCG Diploma in Careers Guidance; Deputy Chaplain-General

DCGS Deputy Chief of the General Staff

DCH Diploma in Child Health

DChD Doctor of Dental Surgery

DCJ *(USA)* District Court Judge

DCL Doctor of Civil Laws

DCLF Diploma in Contact Lens Fitting

DCLP Diploma in Contact Lens Practice of the British Optical Association

DCM Distinguished Conduct Medal; Don't-Come-Monday *(had-enough-of-you-on-Saturday)*

DCMG Dame Commander of the Order of St. Michael & St. George

DCNI Department of the Chief of Naval Intelligence

DCNS Deputy Chief of Naval Staff

DCO Dominions, Colonies and Overseas

DCR,MU Diploma of the College of Radiographers in Medical Ultra Sound

DCR,NM Diploma of the College of Radiographers in Nuclear Medicine

DCR(R) Diploma of the College of Radiographers

DCR(T) Diploma of the College of Radiographers

DCS Deputy Chief of Staff; Deputy Clerk of Session

DCSO Deputy Chief Scientific Officer

DCSP Scottish Diploma in Contact Lens Practice

DCVO Dame Commander of the Royal Victorian Order

DD Doctor of Divinity; Diploma in Dermatology; Drunk and Disorderly

d . . . . d damned

DDA Dangerous Drugs Act; Disabled Drivers' Association; German Employers' Association

DDAG Disabled Drivers' Action Group

DDG Deputy Director General

DDHBirm Diploma in Dental Health, University of Birmingham

DDI Divisional Detective Inspector

DDL Deputy Director of Labour

DDME Deputy Director of Mechanical Engineering

DDMI Deputy Director of Military Intelligence

DDMS Deputy Director of Medical Services

DDMT Deputy Director of Military Training

DDNI Deputy Director of Naval Intelligence

DDO District Dental Officer *(NHS, q.v.)*; Diploma in Dental Orthopaedics

DDOrthRCPS Glas Diploma in Dental Orthopaedics of the Royal College of Physicians and Surgeons, Glasgow

DDPR Deputy Director of Public Relations

DDPS Deputy Director of Personal Services

DDR *(East Germany)* Deutsche Demokratische Republik *(German Democratic Republic)*; East German International Motor Vehicle Registration Letters

DDRA Deputy Director Royal Artillery

DDRB Doctors' and Dentists' Review Body

DDS Director of Dental Services; Doctor of Dental Surgery

DDSc Doctor of Dental Science

DDST Deputy Director of Supplies and Transport

DDT Dapsone Dichlordiphenyl-trichlorethane *(insecticide)*

DDWE & M Deputy Director of Works, Electrical and Mechanical

DE Department of Environment/Employment/Education *(see also DOE)*; District Engineer; *(Eire)* Dail Eireann *(House of Representatives)*

DEA *(USA)* Drug Enforcement Agency

DEB Dental Estimates Board *(NHS, q.v.)*

Dec December

dec *(music)* decrescendo *(decrease volume)*; decimetre
Decd Deceased
deg C degrees Centigrade
deg F degrees Fahrenheit
Del Delaware *(USA State)*
delineavit *(Latin)* He/she drew it
DEMYC, EDS & UEJDC Three European Conservative and Democratic Student Organisations
Den Denmark
D en D *(France)* Docteur en Droit *(Doctor of Laws)*
DEng Doctor of Engineering
D en L *(France)* Docteur en Leyes *(Doctor of Law)*
D en M *(France)* Docteur en Médécine *(Doctor of Medicine)*
DEP Department of Employment and Productivity
Dep Deputy
Dep/dep Departure/departure
Dept Department
DER Development Engineering Review *(Naval RADAR, q.v.)*
Derbys Derbyshire
DEREC Definitive Election Results Evaluation Computer
DERV Diesel Engine Road Vehicle
DES Department of Education and Science
DESI Division of Economic and Social Information *(UN, q.v.)*
D ès L *(France)* Docteur ès Lettres *(Doctor of Literature)*
DesRCA Designer of the RCA, *q.v.*
Det Detective
Det Con Detective Constable
Det Insp Detective Inspector
Det Sgt Detective Sergeant
DETA Mozambique Airline
DF Dean of the Faculty; Direction Finder; Development Forum *(UN, q.v., newspaper)*; *(Latin)* Defensor Fidei *(Defender of the Faith)*
DFC Distinguished Flying Cross
DFI Directorate of Food Investigation
DFLP Democratic Front for the Liberation of Palestine
DFM Distinguished Flying Medal; Diploma in Forensic Medicine
DFO District Finance Officer *(NHS, q.v.)*
DFR Deutscher Frauenring *(West German NCW, q.v.)*
DFT Development Foundation of Turkey
DFYB Don't-Forget-Your-Bucket
DG Director General; Dragoon Guards; *(Latin)* Dei Gratia *(by the Grace of God)*; *(Latin)* Deo Gratias *(thanks to God)*
DGAA Distressed Gentlefolks' Aid Association
DGAMS Director General Army Medical Service

DGB *(West Germany)* Deutsche Gewerkschaftsbund *(German Trade Union Federation)*
DGE *(France)* Le Délégué Général à l'Energie *(Deputy General of the Department of Energy)*
DGH District General Hospital
DGI Director General of Information
DGLF Dark Green Leaf Vegetable
DGMS Director General of Medical Services
DGMT Director General of Military Training
DGMW Director General of Military Works
DGP Director General of Personnel
DGSE *(France)* Counter-Espionage Service
DHA District Health Authority *(NHS, q.v.)*
DHA(T) District Health Authority (Teaching), *(NHS, q.v.)*
DHE Diploma in Horticulture Edinburgh
DHL Doctor of Hebrew Literature
DHM Dirham *(Monetary unit of Morocco)*
DHMSA Diploma in the History of Medicine, Society of Apothecaries
DHQ Director of Headquarters; District Headquarters
DHSS Department of Health & Social Security
DI Detective Inspector; Divisional Inspector; District Inspector
DIA *(USA)* Defense Intelligence Agency
diag diagonal
DIAL Disablement Information and Advisory Service, Derby
diam diameter
DIC Diploma of Membership of the Imperial College of Science and Technology
dic dictionary
DIG Disablement Income Group; Deputy Inspector-General; Pressure Group *(acting on behalf of the metal detector industry)*
DIH Diploma in Industrial Health
dim *(music)* diminuendo *(gradually decrease volume)*
DIN *(Honduras)* Secret Police
DINA *(Chile)* Secret Police
D in D *(Italy)* Dottore in Diritto *(Doctor of Law)*
DIng *(Latin)* Doctor Ingeniariae *(Doctor of Engineering)*; *(Italy)* Dottore Ingeniere *(Doctor of Engineering)*; *(France)* Docteur en génie civil *(Doctor of Engineering)*
Dioc Diocesan; Diocese
Dip Diploma
DipAd Diploma in Art and Design
DipAE Diploma in Adult Education
DipArch Diploma in Architecture
DipBact Diploma in Bacteriology

DipCAM Diploma in Communication Advertising and Marketing Education Foundation

DipCD Diploma in Community Development; Diploma in Civic Design

DipClinPath Diploma in Clinical Pathology

DipCOT Diploma of the College of Occupational Therapists

DipDB Diploma in Education

DipED Diploma in Education

DipEdAdmin Diploma in Educational Administration

DipEdStud Diploma in Educational Studies

DipEduc Diploma in Education

DipEF Diploma in Executive Finance

DipEMA Diploma in Executive Finance for Non-Accountants

DipEngLit Diploma in English Literature

DipFD Diploma in Funeral Directing

DipHE Diploma of Higher Education

DipH-WU Diploma of Heriot-Watt University

DipIB(Scot) Diploma of the Institute of Bankers in Scotland

DipIPA Diploma in International Phonetic Alphabet; Diploma in Public Administration

DipLE Diploma in Land Economy

Dipl Ing *(France)* Diplôme d'Ingénieur *(Engineer's Diploma)*

DipLP Diploma in Legal Practice

DipM Diploma in Marketing

DipMusEd Diploma in Musical Education

DipOS Diploma in Operational Salesmanship

DipPA Diploma of Practitioners in Advertising *(now DipCAM, q.v.)*

DipPharmMed Diploma in Pharmaceutical Medicine

DipPhot Diploma in Photography

DipPsych Diploma in Psychology

DipRAM Diploma of the Royal Academy of Music

DipRCM Diploma of the Royal College of Music

DipRMS Diploma of the Royal Microscopical Society

DipSc Diploma in Science

DipTE Diploma in Transportation Engineering

DipTech Diploma of Technology

DipTech(Eng) Diploma of Technology (Engineering)

DipTM Diploma in Training Management

DipTP Diploma in Town Planning

DipVEN Diploma in Venereology

DipWCF Diploma of the Worshipful Company of Farriers

DIS Diploma in Industrial Studies

Dis/dis Discount/discount

DISK *(Turkey)* Devrimci Isçi Sendikalari Konfederasyonu *(Turkish Trade Union Revolutionist Confederation)*

DISM *(USA project)* Delayed Action Space Missile

DIW *(West Germany)* Deutsches Wirtschafts Institut *(Institute for Economic Research)*

DIY Do-It-Yourself

DJ Disc Jockey; *(USA)* Diploma in Journalism

DJA Disc Jockey Association

DJAG Deputy Judge Advocate General

DJF Disc Jockey Federation

DJP *(Korea)* Democratic Justice Party

DJur Doctor of Jurisprudence

DK Denmark International Motor Vehicle Registration Letters; Krone *(Monetary unit of Denmark)*

DKN *(Denmark)* Danske Kvinders Nationalraad *(NCW, q.v.)*

DKP *(West Germany)* Communist Party

DLAS Defence of Literature and Art Society

DLC(Eng) Diploma of Loughborough College

DLC(Sci) Diploma of Loughborough College

DLES Doctor of Letters in Economic Studies

DLF Disabled Living Foundation

DLH *(West Germany)* Deutsche Lufthansa *(airline)*

DLitt Doctor of Letters

DLO Diploma in Laryngology and Otology; Dead Letter Office *(now RLO, q.v.)*

DLOs Direct Labour Organisations

DLP *(Australia and Barbados)* Democratic Labour Party

DLT Development Land Tax

DM Doctor of Medicine; Director of Music; District Manager; Deutsche Mark *(Monetary unit of West Germany)*

DMA Diploma in Municipal Administration

DMC District Manpower Committee; District Medical Committee *(NHS, q.v.)*; *(Israel)* Democratic Movement for Change

DME Doctor in Mechanical Engineering

DMedRehab Diploma in Medical Rehabilitation

DMet Doctor of Metallurgy

Dm Deutschmark *(Monetary Unit of West Germany)*

DMHS Director of Medical Health Service

DMI *(South Africa)* Department of Military Intelligence; Director of Military Intelligence

DMJ(Clin) Diploma in Medical Jurisprudence (Clinical)

DMJ(Path) Diploma in Medical Jurisprudence (Pathological)

DMK *(Indian Provincial)* Dravidan Welfare Association

DML Doctor of Modern Languages

DMO District Medical Officer

DMP Diploma in Medical Psychology

DMR Diploma in Medical Radiology

DMRD Diploma in Medical Radio-Diagnosis

DMRE Diploma in Medical Radiology and Electrology

DMRT Diploma in Medical Radio Therapy

DMS Director of Medical Services; Diploma in Management Studies

DMT District Management Team *(NHS, q.v.)*; Director of Military Training

DMus Doctor of Music

DMusCantuar The Archbishop of Canterbury's Doctorate in Music

DMV Doctor of Veterinary Medicine; Deserted Medieval Village

DN Diploma in Nutrition

d . . n damn

DNA Disposal Notification Area *(Community · Land Act)*; Deoxyribonucleic Acid *(in genetic cells, see also RNA)*

DNAD Director of Naval Aircraft Division

DNB Dictionary of National Biography

DNE Director of Naval Equipment

DNES Director of Naval Education Service

DNI Director of Naval Intelligence

DNO District Nursing Officer *(NHS, q.v.)*

Dnr Dinar *(Monetary unit of Yugoslavia)*

DNS Department of National Security

DO Diploma in Ophthalmology; Diploma in Osteopathy; District Office; Drawing Office; Divisional Officer *(RN, q.v.)*; Direction Officer *(RN, q.v.)*

do ditto *(the same)*

DOBETA Domestic Oil Burning Equipment Testing Association

DObst RCOG Diploma Royal College of Obstetricians & Gynaecologists

DOC District Officer Commanding; *(Italy)* Denominazione de Origine Controllata *(Government Wine Quality Label)*

Doc/doc Document/document; Doctor *(informal)*

DocEng Doctor of Engineering

DOE Department of the Environment

DoE Department of Education; Department of Energy

DoI Department of Industry

dol *(music)* dolce *(sweet)*; *(music)* doloroso *(mournfully, sadly)*

DOM Dominican Republic; Dirty-Old-Man; Dominican International Motor Vehicle Registration Letters

DomRep Dominican Republic

DOMS Diploma in Ophthalmic Medicine and Surgery

DomSc Domestic Science

DONS *(South Africa)* Department of National Security *(formerly BOSS, q.v.)*

DOpt Diploma in Ophthalmic Optics

DORA Defence of the Realm Act

DOrth Diploma in Orthoptics of the British Optical Association

DOrth RCSEng Diploma in Orthodontics, Royal College of Surgeons of England

DOS Director of Ordnance Services; Disc Operating System; Diploma in Orthopaedic Surgery

DOT Diploma in Occupational Therapy; *(USA)* Department of Occupational Titles

DoT Department of Overseas Trade; Department of Transport

DP Democratic Party; Data Processing; Diploma in Psychiatry; District Pharmacist *(NHS, q.v.)*; Displaced Person

DPA Discharged Prisoners' Aid; Deutsche Press Agentur *(West German Press Agency)*; Diploma in Public Administration

DPAS Discharged Prisoners' Aid Society

DpBact Diploma in Bacteriology

DPCP Department of Prices and Consumer Protection

DPD Diploma in Public Dentistry

DPH Diploma in Public Health

DPHRCSEng Diploma in Public Health Royal College of Surgeons of England

DPhil Doctor of Philosophy

DPhO District Pharmaceutical Officer *(NHS, q.v.)*

DPI Diploma of the Plastics Institute; Department of Public Information *(UNO, q.v.)*

DPM Diploma in Psychological Medicine

DPO District Personnel Officer *(NHS, q.v.)*

DPP Director of Public Prosecutions

DPR Director of Public Relations

DPS Director of Postal Services; Diploma in Pastoral Studies and Applied Technology; Diploma in Professional Studies; *(USA)* Department of Political Science

DPW Department of Public Works

DQMG Deputy Quartermaster General

DQR Directory Enquiry Record *(telephone number supplied if caller knows name and address)*

DR Diploma in Radiology; Dead Reckoning *(navigation)*

Dr Doctor; Director; Debtor; Drachma *(Monetary unit of Greece)*

Dr(RCA) Doctor of the Royal College of Art

DRDRCSEd Diploma in Restorative Dentistry, Royal College of Surgeons, Edinburgh

DRE Director of Religious Education; Diploma in Remedial Electrolysis

DRF Dutch Reformed Church; Dutch Research Foundation

DrIng (West Germany) Doctor of Engineering

DRO Disablement Resettlement Office

DRSAM Diploma of the Royal Scottish Academy of Music and Drama

DS Detective Sergeant

ds (music) dal segno (repeat from previous sign)

DSandT Director of Supplies and Transport

DSC Doctor of Surgical Chiropody; Distinguished Service Cross

DSc Doctor of Science

DScA (France) Docteur en Sciences Agricoles (Doctor of Agricultural Sciences)

DScAgri Doctor of Science in Agriculture

DScEcon Doctor in the Faculty of Economics and Social Studies

DSc(Econ) Doctor of Science Economics (or "in Economics")

DSc(Eng) Doctor of Science (Engineering)

DSc (Social Sciences) Doctor of Science in the Social Sciences

DSc(Tech) Doctor of Technical Science

DSD Director Staff Duties

DSIR Department of Scientific & Industrial Research (now SSRC, q.v.)

DSM Distinguished Service Medal

DSO (Companion of the) Distinguished Service Order; Defence Sales Organisation

DSOC Deputy Signal Office in Chief

DSoc Diploma of Sociology

DSocSc Doctor of Social Science

DSS Director of Social Services (Local Authority)

DSSc (USA) Doctor of Social Science

DST Daylight Saving Time; Director of Supplies Transport; (France) Division de la Sécurité Territoriale (Secret Service)

DSTA Diploma Member of the Swimming Teachers' Association

DStJ Dame (of Grace/of Justice) of the Order of St. John of Jerusalem

DSU Disabilities Study Unit

DSW (USA) Department of Social Welfare

DSWA Diplomatic Service Wives' Association

DT Diphtheria and Tetanus (immunisation)

DTA Differential Thermal Analysis; (Namibia) Democratic Turnhalle Alliance

DTCD Department of Technical Co-Operation for Development (UNO, q.v.); Diploma in Tuberculosis and Chest Diseases

DTCH Diploma in Tropical Child Health

DTech Doctor of Technology

DTH Diploma in Tropical Hygiene

DTheol Doctor of Theology

DTI Department of Trade and Industry

DTM&H Diploma in Tropical Medicine and Hygiene

DTNM Date – Time – Next Meeting

DTP Diphtheria, Tetanus and Pertussis (immunisation)

DTs Delirium Tremens

DTVM Diploma in Tropical Veterinary Medicine

DU (Honorary) Doctor of the University of Essex

DUA Department of Urban Archaeology

DUB Department of Utter/Utmost Boredom

DUniv Doctor of the University

DUP (Ulster) Democratic Unionist Party; (France) Docteur de l'Université de Paris (Doctor of Paris University)

dup duplicate

DUS Diploma of the University of Southampton

DV (Latin) Deo Volente (God be willing!)

DVA Diploma in Veterinary Anaesthesia

DVetMed Doctor of Veterinary Medicine

DVH Diploma in Veterinary Hygiene

DVI Dust Veil Index (from volcanic eruption)

DVLC Driver and Vehicle Licensing Centre

DVM Doctor of Veterinary Medicine

DVM&S Doctor of Veterinary Medicine and Surgery

DVR Diploma of Veterinary Radiology

DVS Director of Veterinary Services

DVSc Doctor of Veterinary Science

DWCA Doctors for a Woman's Choice on Abortion

DWO District Works Officer (NHS, q.v.)

dwt pennyweight

DY Benin International Motor Vehicle Registration Letters

Dy Dysprosium

DYN (Argentina) News Agency

DYS (USA/Massachusetts) Department of Youth Service

DZ Doctor of Zoology; Dropping Zone (RAF, q.v.); Algerian International Motor Vehicle Registration Letters

DZF (West Germany) Deutsche Zentrale für Fremdenverkehr (Tourist Office)

E

E East; Spanish International Motor Vehicle Registration Letter

ea each

EAA Electrical Appliance Association; East African Airways; European Athletic Association; Edinburgh Architectural Association

EAAA European Association of Advertising Agencies

EAAP European Association for Animal Production *(FAO, q.v., see also FEZ)*

EAC Engineering Advisory Council; Education Advisory Council

EAGGF European Agricultural Guidance & Guarantee Fund

EAK Kenyan International Motor Vehicle Registration Letters

EAM-78 Argentine World Cup Organising Body, 1978

EAN European Article Numbering

E & OE/e & oe Errors and Omissions Excepted

EAPM European Association for Personnel Management

EAPS European Association of Professional Secretaries

EAS Educational Advisory Service

EAT Employment Appeal Tribunal; Equal Appeals Tribunal *(EOC, q.v.)*; Economic and Technical Committees on "packaging" *(see also IOP, PIRA and INCPEN)*; European Appeal Tribunal; Tanzanian International Motor Vehicle Registration Letters

EAU Ugandan International Motor Vehicle Registration Letters

EAW Electrical Association for Women

EAWL East African Women's League

EBAE European Bureau of Adult Education

EBC European Brewery Convention *(FAO, q.v.)*; *(USA)* Educational Broadcasting Corporation

EBF European Baptist Federation

EBS European Broadcasting Systems

EBU European Broadcasting Union; European Boxing Union

EC European Community; European Committees *(see also under CE, EG, EP and EK)*; Episcopal Church; Ecuador International Motor Vehicle Registration Letters; Emergency Commission; Executive Council

ECA European Confederation of Agriculture; Educational Centres Association; Economic Co-operation Administration; Economic Commission for Africa *(see also CEA)*; Electrical Contractors' Association

ECAC European Commission for Civil Aviation

ECAFE Economic Commission for Asia and the Far East *(now ESCAP, q.v.)*

ECBA European Communities Biologists' Association

ECBO European Conference of British Bus and Coach Operators

Eccl Ecclesiastic§Ecclesiastical

ECCS Emergency Core Cooling System

ECE Economic Commission for Europe, *(UN, q.v., see also CEE)*; Export Council for Europe

ECF European Cultural Foundation *(EEC, q.v.)*

ECG Electrocardiograph

ECGD Export Credits Guarantee Department

ECHO Equipment for Charity Hospitals Overseas

ECICW/EC-ICW European Centre of the International Council of Women *(see also CECIF)*

ECJ European Court of Justice

ECLA Economic Commission for Latin America *(UN, q.v., see also CEPAL)*

ECM European Common Market *(see also EEC)*; Electric Coding Machine; Electric Cipher Machine *(Coding)*

ECME Economic Commission for the Middle East

ECN Energy Centre of the Netherlands

ECNR European Council for Nuclear Research

ECO Ecology Party

ECOSA European Coach Service Operators' Association

ECOSOC Economic and Social Committee *(European Community)*

ECOWAS Economic Community of West African States *(Mauritania, Senegal, Guinea, Mali, Niger, Liberia, Ivory Coast, Upper Volta, Ghana, Togo and the Republic of Benin)*

ECP English Collective of Prostitutes; European *(Organisation)* for Cancer Prevention *(Studies)*

ECPS Environment and Consumer Protection Service *(European Community)*

ECR European Court *(Law)* Reports

ECS European Communications Systems

ECSC European Coal & Steel Community

ECT Electro-Convulsive Therapy

ECU European Currency Unit; English Church Union

Ecua Ecuador

ECWA Economic Commission for Western Asia

ECWS European Centre for Work and Society *(EEC, q.v.)*

ED Education Department; Existence Doubtful *see also PD (on old maps and*

charts); Efficiency Decoration; *(USA)* Doctor of Engineering

Ed Editor

EDA Electrical Development Association

EDC Economic Development Council; European Defence Committee; European Defence Council; Expected Date of Confinement

EDCS Economic Development Co-operative Society *(World Bank for Poor Countries)*

EDF *(France)* Electricité de France *(Electricity Board)*; European Development Fund

EDH Efficient Deck Hand

EDIK *(Greece)* Enosis Dimocratikou Kentrou *(Unions of the Democratic Centre)*

Edin Edinburgh

EDM Early Day Motion *(Parliament)*

EDP Electronic Data Processing *(Computer Terminology)*; Emergency Defence Plan *(see also NATO)*

EDS, DEMYC & UEJDC Three European Conservative and Democratic Student Organisations

EDU European Democratic Union *(anti-Marxist)*

EE Electrical Engineer; Employment Exchange

E-E Envoy Extraordinary

E-E and MP Envoy Extraordinary and Minister Plenipotentiary

EEB European Environmental Bureau

EEC European Economic Community *(Common Market)*; Eurocontrol Experimental Centre

EEF Engineering Employers' Federation

EEG Electroencephalograph *(instrument for measuring brain activity)*

EEIBA Electrical and Electronic Institutes Benevolent Association

EEPTU Electrical, Electronic, Plumbing & Telecommunications Union *(also known as EETPU)*

EEOC *(USA)* Equal Employment Opportunities Commission

EERT European Educational Research Trust

EETPU See EEPTU

EETS Early English Text Society

EF Expeditionary Force

EFE Spanish News Agency

EFL English as a Foreign Language; External Financing Limit *(Government)*

EFP Electron Field Production *(Television)*

EFTA European Free Trade Association

EFTPoS Electronic Funds Transfer at Point of Sale

EFU European Football Union

EFVA Educational Foundation for Visual Aids

EG *(Netherlands)* Europese Gemeenschappen *(European Community)*

eg *(Latin)* exempli gratia *(for example)*

EGA Elizabeth Garrett Anderson *(Hospital)*

EGE *(Greece)* Enosis Gynekon Ellados *(Women's Union)*

EGM Extraordinary General Meeting

EGO Eccentric Geophysical Observatory *(see also OGO and POGO)*

EGP *(Guatemala and Nicaragua)* Ejército Guerrillero de los Pores *(Guerrilla Army of the Poor)*

EGSA Educational Guidance Service for Adults

EHF Extremely High Frequency

EHO Environmental Health Officer

EHOA Environmental Health Officers' Association

EHRR European Human Rights Reports

EHT Extra High Tension

EHV Extra High Voltage

EIA Environmental Impact Analysis

EIB European Investment Bank

EIEIO Engineering Industries Export Intelligence Officer

E-in-C Engineer in Chief

EIR Eire *(Southern Ireland)*

EIS Educational Institute of Scotland

EIU Economist Intelligence Unit

EK *(Denmark)* De Europoeiske Kelleskaber *(European Community)*

EKKE *(Greece)* Epanastatiko Komma Ellados *(Young People's Organisation)*

EL AL Israeli Airline

ELB Environment Liaison Board

elcb earth leakage current breaker *(electricity)*

ELDO European Launching Development Organisation

ELEC European League for Economic Co-operation

ELF Eritrea Liberation Front; Extremely Low Frequency

ELN *(Colombia)* Ejército Liberación Naciónal *(National Liberation Army)*

ELP *(Portugal)* Ejército para Libertaçao de Portugal *(Liberation Army)*

ELT English Language Teacher *(British Council)*

ELTSA End-Loans-To-South-Africa

ELWA Edinburgh and Lothian Women's Aid

ELWAR East London Workers Against Racialism

EM Edward Medal; European Movement; Electrical Mechanic

em electromagnetic

EMA European Monetary Agreement; Educational Maintenance Allowances; Engineers' and Managers' Association

EMAP East Midlands Allied Press

EMAS Employment Medical Advisory Service

EMB Egg Marketing Board

EMEU East Midlands Educational Union

emf electro motive force

EMI Electrical and Musical Industries; Electromagnetic Interference

EMIC Emergency Maternity and Infant Care

EMIDEC Computer at Ministry of Pensions & National Insurance

EMMS Edinburgh Medical Missionary Society

EMP European Member of Parliament *(see also MEP)*; Electro-magnetic pulse

EMR Electronic Magnetic Resonance

EMRIAE East Midlands Regional Institute of Adult Education

EMS European Monetary System; Emergency Medical Service

EMT *(Spain, Madrid)* Municipal Bus Co.

EMU European Monetary Union *(EEC, q.v.)*

emu electromagnetic unit

EN · Enrolled Nurse

ENA English Newspaper Association; Ethiopian News Agency; *(France)* Ecole Nationale d'Administration *(National School of Management)*

ENABAS *(Nicaragua)* Empresa Nicaragüensa Abastecimienta *(State Grain Marketing Company)*

ENAC *(France)* Ecole Nationale de l'Aviation Civile *(National School of Civil Aviation)*

ENAP *(Chile)* Empresa Nacional de Petroleo *(National Petroleum Authority)*

Enc/enc Enclosed/enclosed; Enclosure/enclosure

END European Nuclear Disarmament

ENDAS *(Italy)* Ente Nationale della Assis Fente Sociale *(Social Workers' Association)*

ENE East North-East

ENEA European Nuclear Energy Agency

ENG Engineer; England/English; Electronic Newsgathering; Enrolled Nurse, General

ENG(M) Enrolled Nurse, General *(Mental Nursing)*

ENG(MS) Enrolled Nurse, General *(Mental Sub-normal Nursing)*

Engr Engineer

ENIT *(Italy)* Ente Nazionale Industrie Turistiche *(State Tourist Office)*

ENO English National Opera

ENON English National Opera North

ENOSIS *(Cyprus)* Union with Greece *(see also EOKA)*

ENP English National Party

ENSA Entertainments National Service Association *(now CSE, q.v.)*

ENT Ear, Nose & Throat

EO Education Officer; Executive Officer; Engineering Officer *(RN, q.v.)*

EOB *(USA)* Executive Officers' Building

EOC Equal Opportunities Commission

EOD Explosive Ordnance Disposal *(Royal Engineers)*

EOKA *(Cyprus)* Ethnika Organosis Kypriakou Agonas *(National Organisation of Struggle to Unite with Greece, see also ENOSIS)*

EONR European Organisation for Nuclear Research

EORTC European Organisation for Research in the Treatment of Cancer

EOTP European Organisation for Trade Promotion

EP European Parliament *(also Europees Parlement, Europa-Parlamentet, Europäisches Parlement, see also EC and PE)*; European Patent; *(Peru)* Aerolineas Peruanas *(Airline)*; Electro-Plate *(see also EPNS)*; Employment Protection

EPA Equal Pay Act; *(USA)* Environmental Protection Agency; Emergency Powers (Defence) Act *(successor of DORA, q.v.)*; European Productivity Agency *(of OEEC, q.v., see also FAO)*

EPC Economic and Planning Council; European Political Community

EPD Excess Profits Duty

EPEA Electrical Power Engineers' Association

EPG European Programme Group *(of NATO, q.v.)*

EPI Employers' Protection Insurance

Epil Epilogue

Epiph Epiphany

EPL *(Colombia)* Ejército Popular de Liberacion *(Populist Liberation Army)*

EPLF Eritrea People's Liberation Front

EPNDB Effective Perceived Noise Decibel

EPNS Electro-Plated Nickel Silver *(see also EP)*

EPOC Equal Pay and Opportunities Campaign; Equal Pay and Opportunities Commission; Economic Policy and Organisation Committee

EPOS Electronic Point Of Sale

EPP European People's Party *(EEC, q.v.)*

EPPO European and Mediterranean Plant Protection Organisation *(FAO, q.v.)*

EPRP Ethiopia People's Revolutionary Party

EPT Excess Profits Tax

EPTA Expanded Programme of Technical Assistance *(UNO, q.v.)*

EPU European Payments Union

EQUITY Union of actors and actresses

equiv equivalent

EQ(S) European Questions *(Cabinet Steering Committee)*

ER *(Latin)* Elizabetha Regina *(Queen Elizabeth)*

Er Erbium

ERA Electrical Research Association; *(USA)* Equal Rights Amendments

ERB Engineers' Registration Board

ERC Electronics Research Council

ERD Emergency Reserve Decoration

ERDA *(USA)* Energy Research and Development Administration

ERDF European Regional Development Fund

ERG Ecology Research Group

erg unit of energy

ergo *(Latin)* therefore

ERICCA Equal Rights in Clubs Campaign for Action

ERM Enfants Refugiés du Monde *(Refugee Children of the World)*

ERNIC Earnings Related National Insurance Contribution

ERNIE Electronic Random Number Indicator Equipment

ERO Emergency Relief Organisation

EROM Erasable ROM, *q.v. (Computer Terminology)*

ERP European Recovery Programme; *(El Salvador)* Ejército Revolucionario del Pueblo *(People's Revolutionary Party)*

ERS Electoral Reform Society; Electoral Reform Secretariat

ERT *(Greece)* National Radio and Television

ERTS Earth Resources Technology Satellite

ERW Enhanced Radiation Weapon *(neutron bomb)*

ES El Salvadorean International Motor Vehicle Registration Letters

Es Einsteinium

ESA Employment Services Agency; European Space Agency; Engineers and Scientists of America; Entomological Society of America; *(Spain)* Basque Separatist Organisation

ESB English Speaking Board

Esc Escudo *(Monetary unit of Portugal)*

ESCAP Economic and Social Commission for Asia and the Pacific *(UN, q.v.)*

ESCO Educational, Scientific and Cultural Organisation *(UN, q.v.)*

ESDP European Social Development Programme *(UN, q.v.)*

ESDWGP Economic & Social Welfare Department Working Group on Population Questions *(unit of the International Council of Women)*

ESE East South-East

ESH Human Resources, Institutions and Agrarian Reform Division *(unit of the International Council of Women)*

ESHH Home Economics & Social Programme Service *(unit of the International Council of Women)*

ESL English as a Second Language

ESLA European Space Laboratory

ESLO European Satellite Launching Organisation

ESN Educationally Sub-Normal

ESP Extra-Sensory Perception

espress *(music)* espressivo *(with expression)*

Esq Esquire

ESRO European Space Research Organisation

ESSP Employers' Statutory Sick Pay

EST *(USA)* Eastern Standard§Summer Time; *(USA)* Earliest Start Time; Ehrhart Sensitivity Training *(USA Club)*

Est Established

ESTEC European Space Technology Centre *(set up by ESRO, q.v.)*

ESTI European Space Technology Institute

E-SU English-Speaking Union

ET Entertainments Tax; Extra-Terrestrial; Ephemera's Time; Egyptian International Motor Vehicle Registration Letters; Emerging Technology

et al *(Latin)* et alibi *(and elsewhere)*; *(Latin)* et aliter *(and otherwise)*

et seq *(Latin)* et sequentia *(and the following)*

ETA *(Spain)* Euzkadi Ta Askatasun *(Marxist Guerrilla Organisation)*; Expected Time of Arrival

ETA-M *(Spain)* Euzkadi Ta Askatasun-Militar *(Military wing of ETA, q.v.)*

ETA-PM *(Spain)* Euzkadi Ta Askatasun-Politico Militar *(Political military wing of ETA, q.v.)*

ETAP Expanded Programme of Technology Assistance *(part of FAO, q.v.)*

ETB English Tourist Board

ETC Environmental Test Centre

etc *(Latin)* et cetera *(and so on)*; *(France)* en tout cas *(at all events)*

ETD Expected Time of Departure

ETS Employment Transfer Scheme

ETSU Energy Technology Support Unit

ETU Electrical Trades Union

ETUC European Trade Union Congress; European Trade Union Confederation

ETUI European Trade Union Institute

ETV Educational Television

EU Evangelical Union

Eu Europium

EUA European Units of Account

EUDISED European Documentation and Information Service for Education

EURATOM European Atomic Energy Commission

EUROCO-OP European Consumer Co-Operatives' Association *(EEC, q.v.)*

EUW European Union of Women

ev electron volt

evg evening

EVP Electronic Voice Phenomena

EWA Electrical Association for Women

EWO Educational Welfare Officer;

Engineering Works Officer

EWONA Education Welfare Officers' National Association

EWR Early Warning Radar

EWRS European Weed Research Society

EWS Early Warning System

EWTU Except-What-Turns-Up

ex div ex dividend *(without dividend)*

ex lib *(Latin)* ex libris *(from the library)*

Ex Off/ex off *(Latin)* Ex Officio/ex

officio *(by virtue of one's office)*

EXCO *(Zimbabwe)* Transitional Executive Council

EXIT Voluntary euthanasia group

Exor Executor

EYF European Youth Foundation

EZE *(West Germany)* Evangelische Zentralstelle für Entwicklungshilfe *(Evangelical Central Bureau for Development Help)*

F

F Fahrenheit; Female; Fellow; Fluorine; French International Motor Vehicle Registration Letter

f following; folio; franc *(see Fr/fr) (music)* Forte *(loud)*

FA Football Association; Family Allowance *(was also known as FAM)*; Field Artillery; Faculty of Actuaries

FAA Fellow of the Australian Academy of Science; Film Artistes Association; *(USA)* Federal Aviation Administration

FAAA Fellow of the American Academy of Arts and Sciences

FAAI Fellow of the Institute of Administrative Accounting and Data Processing

FAAS Fellow of the American Association for the Advancement of Science

FAB Families-Against-the-Bomb; Family Advice Bureau; Feminists Against Benyon *(pro-abortion group)*

Fac Faculty

FAcA Fellow of the Acupuncture Association

FACC Food and Agricultural Consultative Council/Committee; Food Additives and Contaminants Council; Fellow of the Australian College of Cardiology

FACCP Fellow of the American College of Chest Physicians

FACD Fellow of the American College of Dentistry

FACE Fellow of the Australian College of Education; Field Artillery Computing Equipment

FACO Fellow of the Association of Dispensing Chemists

FACOG Fellow of the American College of Obstetrics and Gynaecologists

FACP Fellow of the American College of Physicians

FACR Fellow of the American College of Radiology

FACS Fellow of the American College of Surgeons

FACT Federation Against Copyright Theft

FACTS Football Association Coaching-Tactics Skills

FADO Fellow of the Association of Dispensing Opticians

FADO(Hons) Fellow of the Association of Dispensing Opticians with Honours Diploma

FADO(Hons)CL Fellow of the Association of Dispensing Opticians with honour diploma and Diploma in Contact Lens Fitting

FAFS Farm and Food Society

FAGO Fellowship in Australia in Obstetrics and Gynaecology

FAGS Fellow of the American Geographical Society

FAHA Fellow of the Australian Academy of the Humanities

FAHE Fellow of the Association of Home Economists

FAI Fédération Aeronautique Internationale *(International Aeronautic Federation)*; Football Association of Ireland

FAIA Fellow of the Association of International Accountants; Fellow of the American Institute of Architects

FAIAA Fellow of the American Institute of Aeronautics and Astronautics

FAIAS Fellow of the Australian Institute of Agricultural Science

FAIB Fellow of the Association of Insurance Brokers

FAIC Fellow of the American Institute of Chemists

FAIE Fellow of the British Association of Industrial Editors

FAIM Fellow of the Australian Institute of Management

FAIP Fellow of the Australian Institute of Physics

FAIR Family Action Information and Rescue

FAK *(South Africa)* Federasie van

Afrikaanse Kulturvenenings *(part of the secret Boer-Broederbond Organisation)*

FALN *(Puerto Rico)* Fuerzas Armadas de Liberacion Nacional *(Armed National Liberation Force)*

FALPA *(Angola)* People's Armed Forces

FAM Family Allowance *(see also FA)*

Fam Family Division *(Law Reports)*

FamD Family Division *(of the High Court of Justice)*

FAMS Fellow of the Ancient Monuments Society; Fellow of the Association of Medical Secretaries, Practice Administrators and Receptionists

FAmSCE Fellow of the American Society of Civil Engineers

FAN Feminist Arts News

FANE *(France)* Fédération d'Action Nationaliste Européenne *(European Federation of Nationalist Action, i.e. fascist, outlawed 1980, see also FEN and FNE)*

FANY First Aid Nursing Yeomanry

FAO Food and Agriculture Organisation *(UN, q.v.)*; Fleet Accountant Officer; For the Attention Of

FAP First Aid Post; *(Portugal)* Força Aera Portuguesa *(Air Force)*

FAPA Fellow of the American Psychiatric Association

FAPC *(Congo)* Popular Armed Forces

FAPHA Fellow of the American Public Health Association

FARC *(Colombia)* Fuerzas Armadas Revolucionaria de Colombia *(Revolutionary Armed Forces)*

FARE Federation of Alcoholic Residential Establishments

FARI Foreign Affairs Research Institute

FARN *(El Salvador)* Fuerzas Armadas de la Resistancia Nacional *(Armed National Resistance Forces, terrorist group)*

FAS Fetal Alcohol Syndrome; Faculty of Architects and Surveyors; Federation of American Scientists; Fellow of the Antiquarian Society; Faculty of Astrological Studies; Film Availability Services *(Department of the BFI, q.v.)*; *(France)* Association Française pour l'Avancement de Science *(Association for the Advancement of Science)*

FASA Fellow of Australian Society of Accountants

FASCE Fellow of the American Society of Civil Engineers

FASE Fellow of the Antiquarian Society, Edinburgh

FASI Fellow of the Ambulance Service Institute

FASIC Association for All Speech-Impaired Children

FASP *(France)* Fédération Autonome des Syndicats de Police *(Autonomous Federation of Police Syndicates)*

FASSA Fellow of the Academy of the Social Sciences in Australia

FAWA Federation of Asian Women's Associations

FAWCE Farm Animal Welfare Co-ordinating Executive

f/b full board

FBA Fellow of the British Academy; Fellow of the British *(Theatrical)* Arts Association; Federation of British Artists

FBAA Fellow of the British Association of Accountants and Auditors

FBBO Fellow of the British Ballet Organisation

FBCO Fellow of the British College of Ophthalmic Opticians; Fellow of the British College of Optometrists

FBCS Fellow of the British Computer Society

FBEI Fellow of the Institution of Body Engineers

FBHA Fellow of the British Hypnotherapy Association

FBHI Fellow of the British Horological Institute

FBHS Fellow of the British Horse Society

FBI Federation of British Industry *(now merged with CBI, q.v.)*; *(USA)* Federal Bureau of Investigation

FBIA Fellow of the Bankers' Institute of Australasia

FBID Fellow of the British Institute of Interior Design

FBIE Fellow of the British Institute of Embalmers

FBIM Fellow of the British Institute of Management

FBIS Fellow of the British Interplanetary Society; *(USA)* Foreign Broadcast Information Service

FBIST Fellow of the British Institute of Surgical Technologists

FBKS Fellow of the British Kinematograph Sound and Television Society

FBOA Fellow of the British Optical Association

FBOA-HD Higher Diploma of the FBOA, *q.v.*

FBOU Fellow of the British Ornithologists' Union

FBPsS Fellow of the British Psychological Society

FBPW Federation of Business & Professional Women

FBR Fast Breeder Reactor *(plutonium-fuelled reactor)*

FBS Fellow of the Building Societies Institute

FBSC Fellow of the British Society of Commerce

FBSE Fellow of the Botanical Society Edinburgh

FBSI Fellow of the Boot and Shoe Institution

FBT Fellow of the Association of Beauty Teachers

FBU Federation of Broadcasting Unions; Fire Brigades' Union

FC Football/Fencing Club *(usually preceded by initial of Borough or County)*

FCA Fellow of the Institute of Chartered Accountants; Fuel Cost Adjustment; Federation of Canadian Artists; *(USA)* Farm Credit Administration

FCAI Fellow of the New Zealand Institute of Cost Accountants

FCAM Fellow of the Communication Advertising and Marketing Education Foundation

fcap See fcp

FCASI Fellow of the Canadian Aeronautics and Space Institute

FCBSI Fellow of the Chartered Building Societies Institute

FCC *(USA)* Federal Communications Commission

FCCA Fellow of the Association of Certified Accountants

FCCEd Fellow of the College of Craft Education

FCCC Fellow of the Commonwealth Chambers of Commerce

FCCS Fellow of the Corporation of Certified Secretaries *(now FCS, q.v.)*

FCEA Fellow of the Association of Cost and Executive Accountants

FCEC Federation of Civil Engineering Contractors

FCES Flight Control Electronics System

FCFC Free Church Federal Council

FCFI Fellow of the Clothing and Footwear Institute

FCGI Fellow of City & Guilds of London Institute

FChemSoc Fellow of the Chemical Society

FChS Fellow of the Society of Chiropodists

FCI Fellow of the Institute of Commerce

FCIA Fellow of the Corporation of Insurance Agents

FCIArb Fellow of the Chartered Institute of Arbitrators

FCIB Fellow of the Corporation of Insurance Brokers

FCIBS Fellow of the Chartered Institution of Building Societies *(formerly FIHVE)*

FCIC Fellow of the Chemical Institute of Canada

FCII Fellow of the Chartered Insurance Institute

FCILA Fellow of the Chartered Institute of Loss Adjusters

FCIOB Fellow of the Chartered Institute of Building

FCIS Fellow of the Institute of Chartered Secretaries and Administrators

FCIT Fellow of the Chartered Institute of Transport

FCL Farriers Company of London

FCLA *(Angola)* National Front for the Liberation of Angola

FCM Faculty of Community Medicine

FCMA Fellow of the Institute of Cost and Management Accountants

FCO Foreign and Commonwealth Office

FCOG(SA) Fellow of the South African College of Obstetrics and Gynaecology

FCP Fellow of the College of Preceptors

FCP(SoAf) Fellow of the College of Physicians (South Africa)

fcp foolscap

FCPath Fellow of the College of Pathologists

FCPO Fleet Chief Petty Officer

FCPSO(SoAf) Fellow of the College of Physicians and Surgeons and Obstetricians (South Africa)

FCRA Fellow of the College of Radiologists of Australia

FCS Fellow of the Chemical Society; Fellow of the Corporation of Secretaries; Federation of Conservative Students

FCS(SoAf) Fellow of the College of Surgeons (South Africa)

FCSI Fellow of the Construction Surveyors' Institute

FCSP Fellow of the Chartered Society of Physiotherapy

FCST Fellow of the College of Speech Therapists

FCTB Fellow of the College of Teachers of the Blind

FCWA Fellow of the Institute of Cost and Works Accountants *(amalgamated with FCMA, q.v.)*

FD Family Division *(of the High Court)*; *(Latin)* Fidei Defensor *(Defender of the Faith)*

fd forward

FDA First Division Association *(of Civil Servants, also CSFDA, q.v.)*; *(USA)* Food and Drug Administration

FDB Family Discussion Bureau *(now IMS, q.v.)*

FDDip Funeral Directors' Diploma

FDF *(Belgium)* Democratic Organisation of French-speaking Belgians

FDO Flight Deck Officer *(RN, q.v.)*; Faculty of Dispensing Opticians

FDP *(West Germany)* Freie Demokratische Partei *(Free Democratic Party)*

FDS Fellow in Dental Surgery

FDSRCS Fellow in Dental Surgery, Royal College of Surgeons

FDSRCPS Glas Fellow in Dental Surgery of the Royal College of Physicians and Surgeons of Glasgow

FDSRCS Ed Fellow in Dental Surgery of the Royal College of Surgeons in Edinburgh

FDSRCSEng Fellow in Dental Surgery of the Royal College of Surgeons in England

Fe *(Latin)* Ferrum *(Iron)*

FEAF Far East Air Force

FEATS Festival of European Anglophone Theatrical Societies

Feb February

FEC *(USA)* Federal Election Commission

FECI Fellow of the Institute of Employment Consultants

FED/Fed *(USA)* Federal Reserve Bank

FEG Feminist Education Group

FEI Fédération d'Equitation Internationale *(International Equestrian Federation, see also IEF)*

FEIS Fellow of the Educational Institute of Scotland

FEK The Theatre of the Eccentric Actor

FELCO Federation of English Language Course Organisers

Fem/fem Female/female

FEN *(France)* Fédération d'Education Nationale *(Federation of National Education, neo-nazi group. See also FANE and FNE)*

FEOGA Fond Européen d'Orientation et de Garantie Agriculture *(European Agricultural Guidance and Guarantee Fund, see also EAGGF)*

FERA *(India)* Foreign Exchange Regulation Act

FES Fellow of the Entomological Society; Fellow of the Ethnological Society; Family Expenditure Survey

FEU Further Education Unit *(replaced Further Education Curriculum Review and Department Unit); (Spain)* Federación de Estudiantes Universitarios *(Federation of University Students)*

FEVER Friends of the Education Voucher Experiment in Representative Regions

FEZ Fédération Européenne de Zootechnic *(European Association for Animal Production, FAO, q.v., see also EAAP)*

FF Falklands Factor *(1982);* Field Force

ff following; *(music)* fortissimo *(very loud)*

FFA Fellow of the Faculty of Actuaries *(in Scotland);* Female Financial Advisers

FFARACS Fellow of the Faculty of Anaesthetists, Royal Australian College of Surgeons

FFARCS Eng Fellow of the Faculty of Anaesthetists, Royal College of Surgeons in England

FFARCSI Fellow of the Faculty of Anaesthetists, Royal College of Surgeons Ireland

FFAS Fellow of the Faculty of Architects and Surveyors

FFB Fellow of the Faculty of Building

FFCM Fellow of the Faculty of Community Medicine

FFCS Fellow of the Faculty of Secretaries and Administrators

FFDO Fellow of the Faculty of Dispensing Opticians

FFDRCSIrel Fellow of the Faculty of Dentistry, Royal College of Surgeons in Ireland

FFF Free French Forces *(Second World War)*

FFHom Fellow of the Faculty of Homeopathy

FFI Finance For Industry; *(France)* Forces Françaises de l'Intérieur *(Forces of the Interior);* Free From Infection

FFOM Fellow of the Faculty of Occupational Medicine

FFPS Fauna and Flora Preservation Society

FFR Fellow of the Faculty of Radiologists *(now FRCR, q.v.)*

FFRRCSIrel Fellow of the Faculty of Radiologists Royal College of Surgeons Ireland

FFS Fellow of the Faculty of Architects and Surveyors

FFTCom Fellow of the Faculty of Teachers in Commerce

ffz *(music)* molto sforzando *(strongly accentuated)*

FG Federal Government

FGA Fellow of the Gemmological Association

FGCL Fellow of the Guild of Cleaners and Launderers

FGI Fellow of the Greek Institute; Fellow of the Institute of Certificated Grocers

FGO Fleet Gunnery Officer

FGM-CFDT *(France)* Fédération Générale de la Métallurgie – Confédération Française Démocratique du Travail *(Metal Workers Union)*

FGPT Fellow of the Guild of Professional Toastmasters

FGR Federal German Republic; Fibre Glass Reinforced

FGS Fellow of the Geological Society

FGSM Fellow of the Guildhall School of Music and Drama

FGTO French Government Tourist Office

FHA Fellow of the Institute of Health Service Administrators; Finance Houses' Association

FHANG Federation of Heathrow Anti-Noise Groups *(see also HACAN)*

FHAS Fellow of the Highland & Agricultural Society *(of Scotland)*

FHB Family-Hold-Back *(on food, if un-expected visitors arrive, see also FKO)*

FHCIMA Fellow of the Hotel Catering and Institutional Management Association

FHG Fellow of the Institute of Heraldic and Genealogical Studies

FHI Fellow of the Horological Institute

FHL Food Hygiene Laboratory

FHR *(USA)* Federal House of Representatives

FHS Forces Help Society

FHTTA Fellow of the Highway and Traffic Technicians' Association

FH-WC Fellow of Heriot-Watt University, Edinburgh

FI Falkland Islands

FIA Fellow of the Institute of Actuaries; Fédération Internationale de l'Automobile *(International Automobile Federation, includes 50 nations)*; Freedom In Advertising

FIAA Fellow of the Incorporated Association of Architects and Surveyors *(Architects)*; Fellow of the Institute of Administrative Accounting and Data Processing

FIAA & S Fellow of the Incorporated Association of Architects & Surveyors

FIAAS Fellow of the Institute of Australian Agricultural Science

FIAF Fédération Internationale des Archives du Film *(International Federation of Film Archives)*

FIAgrE Fellow of the Institution of Agricultural Engineers

FIAI Fellow of the Institute of Industrial and Commercial Accountants

FIAL Fellow of the International Institute of Arts and Letters

FIAM Fellow of the International Academy of Management

FIAPF Fédération Internationale des Associations de Producteurs de Films *(International Federation of Film Producers Associations)*

FIArb Fellow of the Institute of Arbitrators

FIAS Fellow of the Incorporated Association of Architects and Surveyors *(Surveyors)*

FIAT Fellow of the Institute of Animal Technicians; Fellow of the Institute of Asphalt Technology

FIAWS Fellow of the International Academy of Wood Sciences

FIB Fellow of the Institute of Bankers; Fellow of the Institute of Building

FIB(Scot) Fellow of the Institute of Bankers in Scotland

FIBA Fellow of the Institution of Business Agents; Federation of International Basketball Associations

FIBCO Fellow of the Institution of Building Control Officers

FIBD Fellow of the Institute of British Decorators *(and Interior Decorators)*

FIBEF Fédération Internationale des Bureaux d'Extraits de Presse *(International Federation of Press-Cutting Bureaux)*

FIBF Fellow of the Institute of British Foundrymen

FIBICC Fellow of the Incorporated British Institute of Certified Carpenters

FIBiol Fellow of the Institute of Biology

FIBP Fellow of the Institute of British Photographers

FIBS Financial Incentive Bonus Scheme *(Work Study)*

FIB(Scot) Fellow of the Institute of Bankers in Scotland

FICA Fellow of the Commonwealth Institute of Accountancy

FICAI Fellow of the Institute of Chartered Accountants in Ireland

FICD Fellow of the Institute of Civil Defence

FICE Fellow of the Institution of Civil Engineers; Fédération Internationale des Communautés d'Enfants *(International Federation of Children's Committees)*

FICeram Fellow of the Institute of Ceramics

FIChemE Fellow of the Institution of Chemical Engineers

FIChor Fellow of the Benesh Institute of Choreology

FICI Fellow of the Institute of Chemistry of Ireland; Fellow of the International Colonial Institute

FICM Fellow of the Institute of Credit Management

FICO Fellow of the Institute of Careers Officers

FICorrT Fellow of the Institution of Corrosion Science and Technology

FICP Fédération Internationale des Clubs de Publicité *(a permanent Secretariat of the UN, q.v.)*

FICS Fellow of the Institute of Chartered Shipbrokers; Fellow of the International College of Surgeons

FICW Fellow of the Institute of Clerks of Works of Great Britain Incorporated

FID Fédération Internationale de la Documentation *(International Documentation Federation)*

Fid Def *(Latin)* Fidei Defensor *(Defender of the Faith, see also FD)*

FIDA International Women's Legal Organisation; *(Malay)* Federal Industrial Development Authority

FIDE Fédération de l'Industrie Dentaire en Europe *(Federation of the European Dental Industry)*; Fédération Internationale des Echecs *(World Chess Federation)*

FIDO Fog Intensive Dispersal Operation; Film Industry Defence Organisation

FIDs Falkland Islands Dependencies

FIDTA Fellow of the International Dance Teachers' Association

FIE Fédération Internationale de l'Escrime *(International Fencing Federation)*

FIED Fellow of the Institution of Engineering Designers

FIEE Fellow of the Institution of Electrical Engineers

FIEEE Fellow of the Institution of Electrical and Electronics Technician Engineers

FIEF Fédération Internationale pour l'Economie Familiale *(International Federation of Home Economics, FAO, q.v., see also IFHE)*

FIEJ Fédération Internationale des Editeurs de Journaux et Publications *(International Federation of Editors of Newspapers and Publications)*

FIEM Fellow of the Institute of Executives and Managers

FIERE Fellow of the Institution of Electronic and Radio Engineers

FIEx Fellow of the Institute of Export

FIExE Fellow of the Institute of Executive Engineers and Officers

FIExpE Fellow of the Institute of Explosives Engineers

FIFA Fédération Internationale des Football Associations *(International Federation of Football Associations)*

FIFireE Fellow of the Institution of Fire Engineers

FIFM Fellow of the Institute of Fisheries Management

FIFO First-In-First-Out

FIFor Fellow of the Institute of Forestry

FIFST Fellow of the Institute of Food Science and Technology

FIG Fraud Investigators Guide

FIGasE Fellow of the Institution of Gas Engineers

FIGD Fellow of the Institute of Grocery Distribution

FIGeol Fellow of the Geological Society

FIGO International Federation of Gynaecology and Obstetrics

FIH Fellow of the Institute of Hygiene; Fellow of the Institute of Housing

FIHE Fellow of the Institute of Health Education; Fellow of the Institution of Highway Engineers

FIHM Fellow of the Institute of Housing Managers

FIHospE Fellow of the Institute of Hospital Engineering

FIIM Fellow of the Institution of Industrial Managers

FIInfSc Fellow of the Institute of Information Scientists

FIInst Fellow of the Imperial Institute

FIIP Fellow of the Institute of Incorporated Photographers

FIISE Fellow of the International Institute of Social Economics

FIISec Fellow of the Institute of Industrial Security

FIL Fellow of the Institute of Linguists; Fédération Internationale de Laiterie *(International Dairy Federation, FAO, q.v., see also IDF)*

FILCLC Fédération Internationale de Femmes de Carrières Libérales et Commerciales *(International Federation of Career Women)*

FILGA Fellow of the Institute of Local Government Administration

FILLM Fédération Internationale des Langues et Littératures Modernes *(International Federation of Modern Language and Literature)*

FIllumES Fellow of the Illuminating Engineering Society

FIM Fellow of the Institution of Metallurgists

FIMA Fellow of the Institute of Mathematics and its Applications

FIManf Fellow of the Institute of Manufacturing

FIMarE Fellow of the Institute of Marine Engineers

FIMBI Fellow of the Institute of Medical and Biological Illustration

FIMC Fellow of the Institute of Management Consultants

FIMechE Fellow of the Institution of Mechanical Engineers

FIMF Fellow of the Institute of Metal Finishing

FIMGTechE Fellow of the Institution of Mechanical and General Technician Engineers

FIMH Fellow of the Institute of Military History; Fellow of the Institute of Materials Handling

FIMI Fellow of the Institute of the Motor Industry

FIMinE Fellow of the Institution of Mining Engineers

FIMIT Fellow of the Institute of Musical Instrument Technology

FIMLS Fellow of the Institute of Medical Laboratory Sciences

FIMLT Fellow of the Institute of Medical Laboratory Technology

FIMM Fellow of the Institution of Mining and Metallurgy; Fellow of the Institute of Male Masseurs

FIMS Fellow of the Institute of Mathematical Statistics

FIMTA Fellow of the Institute of Municipal Treasurers & Accountants

FIMunE Fellow of the Institution of Municipal Engineers

FIN *(Guatemala)* Frente de Integracion

Nacional *(Front for National Integration)*

Fin Finland

FInstAM Fellow of the Institute of Administrative Management

FInstBB Fellow of the Institute of British Bakers

FInstBCA Fellow of the Institute of Burial and Cremation Administrators

FInstBRM Fellow of the Institute of Baths and Recreation Management

FInstCH Fellow of the Institute of Chiropodists

FInstCM Fellow of the Institute of Commercial Management

FInstD Fellow of the Institute of Directors

FInstE Fellow of the Institute of Energy

FInstF Fellow of the Institute of Fuel

FInstFF Fellow of the Institute of Freight Forwarders

FInstLEx Fellow of the Institute of Legal Executives

FInstM Fellow of the Institute of Marketing; Fellow of the Institute of Meat

FInstMC Fellow of the Institute of Measurement and Control

FInstMSM Fellow of the Institute of Marketing and Sales Management

FInstNDT Fellow of the British Institute of Non-Destructive Testing

FInstP Fellow of the Institute of Physics

FInstPet Fellow of the Institute of Petroleum

FInstPI Fellow of the Institute of Patentees and Inventors

FInstPkg Fellow of the Institute of Packaging

FInstPRA Fellow of the Institute of Park and Recreation Administration

FInstPS Fellow of the Institute of Purchasing and Supply

FInstR Fellow of the Institute of Refrigeration

FInstRM Fellow of the Institute of Recreation Management

FInstSM Fellow of the Institute of Sales Management

FInstSWM Fellow of the Institute of Solid Wastes Management

FInstSWM(Hon) Honorary Fellowship of the Institute of Solid Wastes Management

FInstTA Fellow of the Institute of Traffic Administration

FInstWPC Fellow of the Institute of Water Pollution Control

FINucE Fellow of the Institution of Nuclear Engineers

FIO Fellow of the Institute of Ophthalmology

FIOA Fellow of the Institute of Acoustics

FIOD Fellow of the Institute of Directors

FIOP Fellow of the Institute of Plumbing; Fellow of the Institute of Printing

FIPA Fellow of the Institute of Practitioners in Advertising

FIPC Fellow of the Institute of Production Control

FIPHE Fellow of the Institution of Public Health Engineers

FIPlantE Fellow of the Institution of Plant Engineers

FIPM Fellow of the Institute of Personnel Management

FIPR Fellow of the Institute of Public Relations

FIPRE Fellow of the Incorporated Practitioners in Radio and Electronics

FIProdE Fellow of the Institution of Production Engineers

FIQ Fellow of the Institute of Quarrying

FIQA Fellow of the Institute of Quality Assurance

FIQPS Fellow of the Institute of Qualified Private Secretaries

FIQS Fellow of the Institute of Quantity Surveyors

FIR Fédération Internationale des Résistants *(International Federation of Resistance Movements)*

FIRA Furniture Industry Research Association

FIRE *(USA)* Fellow of the Institute of Radio Engineers

FIREE(Aust) *(Australia)* Fellow of the Institution of Radio and Electronic Engineers

FIRSE Fellow of the Institute of Railway Signal Engineers

FIS Family Income Supplement; Fellow of the Institute of Statisticians; Fédération Internationale du Commerce des Semences *(International Federation of the Seed Trade, FAO, q.v.)*; Fédération Internationale de Ski *(International Ski Federation)*

FISA Fellow of the Incorporated Secretaries' Association

FISE Fellow of the Institute of Sanitary Engineers

FISICAL Freedom in Sport International Committee and Lobby

FISM Fellow of the Institute of Supervisory Management

FISOB Fellow of the Incorporated Society of Organ Builders

FIST Fellow of the Institute of Science Technology

FISTC Fellow of the Institute of Scientific and Technical Communicators

FISTD Fellow of the Imperial Society of Teachers in Dancing

FISTM Fellow of the Institute of Sales

Technology and Management

FIStructE Fellow of the Institution of Structural Engineers

FISW Fellow of the Institute of Social Welfare

FITD Fellow of the Institute of Training and Development

FITE Fellow of the Institution of Electrical and Electronics Technician Engineers

FITO Fellow of the Institute of Training Officers of the IISE, *q.v.*

FITPASC Fédération Internationale des Travailleurs des Plantations d'Agriculture et des Secteurs Connexes *(Federation of Plantation Agricultural and Allied Workers, see also IFPAAW, FAO, q.v.)*

FITSA Fellow of the Institute of Trading Standards Administration

FIWES Fellow of the Institution of Water Engineers and Scientists

FIWHTE Fellow of the Institution of Works and Highway Technician Engineers

FIWM Fellow of the Institution of Works Managers

FIWO Fellow of the Institute of Welfare Officers

FIWSc Fellow of the Institute of Wood Science

FIWSOM Fellow of the Institute of Practitioners in Work Study, Organisation and Methods

FJCEE Fédération des Jeunes Chefs d'Entreprise *(Federation of Young European Businessmen)*

FJI Fellow of the Institute of Journalists; Fiji International Motor Vehicle Registration Letters

FKC Fellow of King's College *(London)*

FKO Family-Keep-Off *(food, if unexpected visitors arrive, see also FHB)*

FL Football League; Lichtenstein International Motor Vehicle Registration Letters

FL/fl Florin *(Monetary unit of the Netherlands)*

FLA Fellow of the Library Association

Fla Florida *(USA State)*

FLAC Lord Flower's Liquidation Action Committee *(scheme to amalgamate hospitals)*

FLAG Food Law Action Group; Feminist Legislation Action Group

Flak Flugzeugabwehrkanone *(anti-aircraft gun/gunfire/shell-fire)*

FLB *(USA)* Federal Land Bank

FLCM Fellow of the London College of Music

FLCSP(Phys) Fellow of the London and Counties Society of Physiologists

FLEC *(Angola)* Black Guerrilla Movement

FLHS Fellow of the London Historical Society

FLI Fellow of the Landscape Institute

FLIC Foreign Languages for Industry and Commerce

FLM *(Italy)* Metal Workers' Union

FLNC *(Congo)* Front pour la Libération Nationale du Congo *(National Liberation Front)*; *(Corsica)* Front pour la Libération Nationale de Corse *(National Liberation Front)*

Flor Florida *(USA State)*

FLOSY Front for the Liberation of Occupied South Yemen

fl oz fluid ounce

FLP *(El Salvador)* Fuerzas de Liberación Popular *(Popular Liberation Forces)*

FLQ *(Canada)* Fédération pour la Libération de Québec *(Federation for the Liberation of Quebec)*

FLS Fellow of the Linnean Society

Flt Flight

FM Field Marshal; Frequency Modulation

Fm Fermium

FMA Fellow of the Museums Association

FMANZ Fellow of the Medical Association of New Zealand

FMB Federation of Master Builders; *(USA)* Federal Maritime Board

FMC Fatstock Market Corporation; *(Cuba)* Frente de Mujeres Cubanas *(Women's Movement)*

FMD Foot and Mouth Disease *(Veterinary)*

FMF Food Manufacturers' Federation

FMI Financial Management Initiative

FMPA Fellow of the Master Photographers' Association

FMR Fellow of the Association of Health Care Information and Medical Records Officers *(NHS, q.v.)*

FMS Fellow of the Metals Society; Fellow of the Institute of Management Services

FMSA *(USA)* Fellow of the Mineralogical Society

FMTA-CMT Fédération Mondiale de Travailleurs Agricoles *(World Federation of Agricultural Workers, see also WFAW-CMT)*

FNAEA Fellow of the National Association of Estate Agents

FNCR *(Costa Rica)* Ferrocarril del Norte de Costa Rica *(Northern Railway)*

FNCRT Fellow of the National College of Rubber Technology

FNE *(France)* Faisceaux Nationalists Européens *(European National Fascists, see also FEN and FANE)*

FNF Fault Not Found; Families Need Fathers

FNFL *(Luxembourg)* Fédération Nationale des Femmes Luxembourgeoises

(NCW, q.v.)

FNI Fellow of the Nautical Institute; Fellow of the National Institute of Sciences in India

FNIH Fellow of the National Institute of Hardware

FNIMH Fellow of the National Institute of Medical Herbalists

FNLA *(Zaire)* Military Organisation; *(Kenya)* National Movement; *(Spain and Angola)* Frente Nacional de Alianza Libre *(National Liberation Front)*

FNSEA *(France)* Fédération Nationale des Syndicats d'Exploitants Agricoles *(National Federation of Agricultural Syndicates)*

FNU Fonds des Nations Unies *(United Nations Emergency Fund, same as UNREF, q.v.)*

FNUI Fellow of the National University of Ireland

FNV *(Netherlands)* Federatie Nederlandse Vakvereniginge *(Federation of Trade Unions)*

FNZIA Fellow of the New Zealand Institute of Architects

FNZIAS Fellow of the New Zealand Institute of Agricultural Science

FNZIC Fellow of the New Zealand Institute of Chemistry

FNZIE Fellow of the New Zealand Institution of Engineers

FO Foreign Office; Field Officer; Flying Officer

fob free on board

FOC Free Of Charge; Father of the Chapel *(Printing Unions)*

FOCEP *(Peru)* Frente Obrero, Campesino i Estudiantil de Peru *(Workers, Peasants and Students Popular Front)*

FOCUS Film Conservation & Utilisation Society

FOE Friends of the Earth

FOG Frequency of Gobbledegook *(of language)*

FOHC Friends of Highgate Cemetery

FOIC Flag Officer In Charge

fol folio

FOMS Fellow of the Organisation and Methods Society

FOPRA Federation of Private Residents' Associations

FOREST Freedom Organisation for the Right to Enjoy Smoking Tobacco

FORTRAN Formula Translation *(Computer Terminology)*

FOSDIC *(USA)* Film Optical Sensing Device for Computer Input *(Census Bureau)*

FOSCOR *(South Africa)* Phosphate Development Corporation

FP Former Pupils; Federal Parliament

fp *(music)* forte piano *(loudly, then softly)*; freezing point

FPA Family Planning Association; Film Producers' Association; Fire Protection Association; Foreign Press Association

FPB Fast Patrol Boat

FPC Family Practitioner *(Medical)* Committee

FPEA Fellow of the Physical Education Association

FPhS Fellow of the Philosophical Society of England

FPLP Front Populaire pour la Libération de la Palestine *(Popular Front for the Liberation of Palestine)*

FPMI Fellow of the Pensions Management Institute

FPO Field Post Office; *(Austria)* Freie Partei Oesterreich *(Liberal Party)*; Fire Prevention Officer

FPP Foster Parents Plan

FPRI Fellow of the Plastics and Rubber Institute

FPRS Federation of Professional Railway Staff

FPS Fellow of the Pharmaceutical Society; Federation of Personnel Services; *(Spain)* Federaçion de Partidos Socialistas *(break-away Socialist Party, now defunct)*; Fauna Preservation Society

FPU Family Policy Unit

FR Faroe Islands International Motor Vehicle Registration Letters; Federal Republic

Fr French; Friar; Francium

Fr/fr franc *(Monetary unit of France, Switzerland, Belgium, Luxembourg and a number of other countries)*

FRACDS Fellow of the Royal Australian College of Dental Surgeons

FRACI Fellow of the Royal Australian Chemical Institute

FRACP Fellow of the Royal Australasian College of Physicians

FRACS Fellow of the Royal Australasian College of Surgeons

FRAD Fellow of the Royal Academy of Dancing

FRAeS Fellow of the Royal Aeronautical Society

FRAgS Fellow of the Royal Agricultural Societies

FRAHS Fellow of the Royal Australian Historical Society

FRAI Fellow of the Royal Anthropological Institute

FRAIA Fellow of the Royal Australian Institute of Architects

FRAIB Fellow of the Royal Australian Institute of Building

FRAIC Fellow of the Royal Architectural Institute of Canada

FRAM Fellow of the Royal Academy of Music

FRAME Fund for the Replacement of Animals in Medical Experiments

FRANZCP Fellow of the Royal Australian and New Zealand College of Psychiatrists

FRAP *(Spain)* Frente Revolucionario Anti-Fascista y Patriotico *(Anti-fascist Revolutionary Patriotic Front); (Chile)* Frente de Acción Popular *(Popular Action Front)*

FRAPI Fellow of the Royal Australian Planning Institute

FRAS Fellow of the Royal Astronomical Society; Fellow of the Royal Asiatic Society

FRASB Fellow of the Royal Asiatic Society of Bengal

FRASE Fellow of the Royal Agricultural Society of England

FRBS Fellow of the Royal Society of British Sculptors; Fellow of the Royal Botanic Society

FRCA Fellow of the Royal College of Art

FRCGP Fellow of the Royal College of General Practitioners

FRCM Fellow of the Royal College of Music

FRCN Fellow of the Royal College of Nursing

FRCO Fellow of the Royal College of Organists

FRCO(CHM) Fellow of the Royal College of Organists (Choir Training Diploma)

FRCOG Fellow of the Royal College of Obstetricians and Gynaecologists

FRCP Fellow of the Royal College of Physicians of London

FRCP&S(Canada) Fellow of the Royal College of Physicians and Surgeons of Canada

FRCP(C) Fellow of the Royal College of Physicians (Canada)

FRCPath Fellow of the Royal College of Pathologists

FRCPEdin Fellow of the Royal College of Physicians of Edinburgh

FRCPI Fellow of the Royal College of Physicians of Ireland

FRCPRCPSGlas Fellow of the Royal College of Physicians and Surgeons of Glasgow

FRCPSGlasg Fellow of the Royal College of Physicians and Surgeons of Glasgow

FRCPsych Fellow of the Royal College of Psychiatrists

FRCR Fellow of the Royal College of Radiologists

FRCS Fellow of the Royal College of Surgeons

FRCSEdin Fellow of the Royal College of Surgeons of Edinburgh

FRCSEng Fellow of the Royal College of Surgeons of England

FRCSGlas Fellow of the Royal College of Surgeons of Glasgow

FRCS(Irel) Fellow of the Royal College of Surgeons of Ireland

FRCSoc Fellow of the Royal Commonwealth Society

FRCUS *(Denmark)* Fellow of the Royal College of University Surgeons

FRCVS Fellow of the Royal College of Veterinary Surgeons

FREconS Fellow of the Royal Economics Society

FRED Fast Reactor Experiment Dounreay *(nuclear power experiment)*

FREE Forum on the Rights of Elderly People to Education; A charitable organisation for the curing of drug and alcohol addiction

FREGG Free Range Egg

FREI *(Australia)* Fellow of the Real Estate Institute

FRES Fellow of the Royal Entomological Society

FRFP Fédération Européenne et Internationale des Responsables des Femmes Patronnes *(European and International Federation of Professional and Business Women)*

FRG Family Rights Group; Federal Republic of Germany

FRGS Fellow of the Royal Geographical Society

FRHistS Fellow of the Royal Historical Society

FRHS Fellow of the Royal Horticultural Society

Fri Friday

FRIAS Fellow of the Royal Incorporation of Architects of Scotland

FRIBA Fellow of the Royal Institute of British Architects

FRICS Fellow of the Royal Institution of Chartered Surveyors

FRIDA Fund for Research and Investment for the Development of Africa

FRIH Fellow of the Royal Institute of Horticulture of New Zealand

FRIIA Fellow of the Royal Institute of International Affairs

FRIN Fellow of the Royal Institute of Navigation

FRINA Fellow of the Royal Institution of Naval Architects

FRIPHH Fellow of the Royal Institute of Public Health and Hygiene

FRMCM Fellow of the Royal Manchester College of Music

FRMetS Fellow of the Royal Meteorological Society

FRMS Fellow of the Royal Microscopical Society

FRNCM Fellow of the Royal Northern College of Music

FRNS Fellow of the Royal Numismatic Society

FRNs Floating Rate Notes

FRNSA Fellow of the Royal Navy School of Architecture

FRPS Fellow of the Royal Photographic Society

FRPSL Fellow of the Royal Philatelic Society of London

FRS Fellow of the Royal Society

FRSA Fellow of the Royal Society of Arts

FRSAI Fellow of the Royal Society of Antiquaries, Ireland

FRSAMD Fellow of the Royal Scottish Academy of Music and Drama

FRSC Fellow of the Royal Society of Chemistry; Fellow of the Royal Society of Canada

FRSCM Fellow of the Royal School of Church Music

FRSE Fellow of the Royal Society of Edinburgh

FRSGS Fellow of the Royal Scottish Geographical Society

FRSH Fellow of the Royal Society of Health

FRSI Fellow of the Royal Sanitary Institute

FRSL Fellow of the Royal Society of Literature

FRSM/FRSocMed Fellow of the Royal Society of Medicine

FRSNZ Fellow of the Royal Society, New Zealand

FRSS Fellow of the Royal Statistical Society

FRSSA Fellow of the Royal Scottish Society of Arts

FRSSAf Fellow of the Royal Society of South Africa

FRST Fellow of the Royal Society of Teachers

FRSTM & H Fellow of the Royal Society of Tropical Medicine and Hygiene

FRTPI Fellow of the Royal Town Planning Institute

FRU Free Representative/Representation Unit

FRVA Fellow of the Rating and Valuation Association

FRVC Fellow of the Royal Veterinary College

FRZS Fellow of the Royal Zoological Society

FRZS(Scot) Fellow of the Royal Zoological Society (Scotland)

FS Fabian Society; Film Society *(usually preceded by initial of Borough or County)*

FSA Fellow of the Society of Antiquaries of London

FSA(Scot) Fellow of the Society of Antiquaries (Scotland)

FSAE Fellow of the National Society of Art Education

FSAM Fellow of the Society of Art Masters

FSAO Fellow of the Scottish Association of Opticians

FSASM Fellow of the South Australian School of Mines

FSAW Federation of South African Women

FSBTh Fellow of the Society of Health and Beauty Therapists

FSC Fellow of the Society of Chiropodists; Friends Service Council; Field Studies Council; *(USA)* Federal Supreme Court

FSCA Fellow of the Society of Company and Commercial Accountants

FSCT Fellow of the Society of Commercial Teachers; Fellow of the Society of Cardiological Technicians; Floyd Satellite Communications Terminal

FSDC Fellow of the Society of Dyers and Colourists

FSE Fellow of the Society of Engineers

FSERT Fellow of the Society of Electronic and Radio Technicians

FSF *(Pakistan and Baluchistan)* Federal Security Force

FSG Fellow of the Society of Genealogists

FSGT Fellow of the Society of Glass Technology

FSIA Fellow of the Society of Investment Analysts

FSIAD Fellow of the Society of Industrial Artists and Designers

FSL First Sea Lord

FSLAET Fellow of the Society of Licensed Aircraft Engineers and Technologists

FSLN *(Nicaragua)* Frente Sandinista Liberacion Nacional *(Sandinista National Liberation Front)*

FSMC Fellow of the Worshipful Company of Spectacle Makers

FSMC(Hons) FSMC, *q.v.* (Honours)

FSP *(Portugal)* Frente Socialista Popular *(Popular Socialist Front)*; *(Pakistan)* Federal Security

FSRG Fellow of the Society of Remedial Gymnasts

FSS Fellow of the Finnish Sauna Society

FSSF Fellow of the Society of Shoe Fitters

FST Financial Secretary to the Treasury

FSTA Fellow of the Swimming Teachers' Association

FSTD Fellow of the Society of Typographic Designers

FSU Family Service Units

FSVA Fellow of the Incorporated Society of Valuers and Auctioneers

ft foot/feet

FTA Freight Transport Association

FTAT Furniture Timber and Allied Trades' Union

FTB First Time *(House)* Buyer; Fast

Torpedo Boat *(RN, q.v.)*

FTC Full Technological Certificate *(of City and Guilds of London Institute)*; *(USA)* Federal Trade Commission

FTCD Fellow of Trinity College Dublin

FTCL Fellow of the Trinity College of Music, London

FTI Fellow of the Textile Institute

FTII Fellow of the Institute of Taxation

FTRO Fellow of the Toastmasters for Royal Occasions

FTS Fellow of the Australian Academy of Technological Sciences; Flying Training School

FTSC Fellow in the Technology of Surface Coatings

FTT Full-Time Tutorial

FTUA *(USSR)* Free Trade Union Association *(dissident group of the Soviet Working People)*

FU Farmers' Union *(see also NFU)*

FUFTB Full-Up-Fit-To-Bust

FUME Foam Upholstery Must End *(RoSPA, q.v.)*

FUMIST Fellow of the University of Manchester Institute of Science and Technology

FUMO *(Mozambique)* United Democratic Front

FUNAI *(Brazil)* Fundacão pra os Asuntos Indios *(Indian Affairs Foundation)*

Fur/fur Furlong/furlong

FUW Farmers' Union of Wales

FUZZ Slang for police officer

FVA *(Argentina)* Fatherland Volunteers Association

FWA Family Welfare Association; Factories and Workshops Act; Fellow of the World Academy of Arts & Sciences; Football Writers' Association

FWAG Farming and Wildlife Advisory Group

FWCF Fellow of the Worshipful Company of Farriers

Fwd/fwd Forward/forward

FWeldI Fellow of the Welding Institute

FWF Forum World Features *(News Agency)*

FWH Flexible Working Hours

FWI Federation of Women's Institutes; Federation of West Indies *(also WIF, q.v.)*

FWSOM Fellow of the Institute of Practitioners in Work Study, Organisation and Method

FWZ Federation of Women Zionists

fz *(music)* sforzando *(emphasis on chord or note)*

FZS Fellow of the Zoological Society

G

GA Geographical Association; Geologists' Association; Gamblers Anonymous

Ga Georgia *(USA State)*; Gallium

GAB General Agreements to Borrow *(from IMF, q.v., Fund)*

GAC General Advisory Council

GAI *(USA)* Guaranteed Annual Income

GAL *(West Germany)* Grün-Alternativen *(Green Alternatives' List – combination of "Greens" and other peace groups)*

GALS Girls-Alone-in-London-Service

GAMS *(France)* Groupe de Femmes pour l'Abolition des Mutilations Sexuelles *(Group against female circumcision)*

G and EI Gilbert and Ellice Islands

GAO *(USA)* The General Accounting Office

GAP *(Nicaragua and San Salvador)* Ejército Guerrillero de los Pobres *(Guerrilla Army of the Poor)*

GAPAN Guild of Air Pilots and Air Navigators

GAPS Girls and Physical Sciences

GASP Group Against Smoking Pollution/Group Against Smoking in Public

GATCO Guild of Air Traffic Control Officers

GATT General Agreement on Tariffs and Trade

GB Great Britain; Great Britain and Northern Ireland International Motor Vehicle Registration Letters

GBA Alderney International Motor Vehicle Registration Letters

GBE Knight or Dame Grand Cross of the Order of the British Empire

GBG Guernsey International Motor Vehicle Registration Letters

GBGSA Association of Governing Bodies of Girls' Public Schools

GBH Grievous Bodily Harm

GBJ Jersey International Motor Vehicle Registration Letters

GBM Isle of Man International Motor Vehicle Registration Letters

GBS George Bernard Shaw

GBSM Graduate of the Birmingham School of Music

GBW Good Bears of the World

GBZ Gibraltar International Motor Vehicle Registration Letters

GC George Cross *(civilian VC, q.v.)*; Grand Cross of the Order of Chivalry; Golf Club *(usually preceded by name of*

club); General Council *(NHS, q.v.)*

GCA Ground Control Approach *(aviation);* Guatemala International Motor Vehicle Registration Letters

GCB Knight or Dame Grand Cross of the Order of the Bath

GCBS General Council of British Shipping

GCE General Certificate of Education

gcf greatest common factor *(mathematics)*

GCH Knight Grand Cross of Hanover

GCHQ Government Communications Headquarters

GCIE Knight Grand Commander of the Indian Empire

GCLH *(France)* Grand-Croix du Légion d'Honneur *(Grand Cross of the Legion of Honour)*

gcm greatest common multiple *(mathematics)*

GCMG Knight or Dame Grand Cross of the Order of St. Michael and St. George

GCP Gift Coupon Programme *(UNESCO, q.v., became Co-Action, q.v.)*

GCR Ground Control Radar

GCSE General Certificate of Secondary Education

GCSG Knight Grand Cross of the Order of St. Gregory the Great

GCSI Knight Grand Commander of the Order of the Star of India

GCStJ Bailiff or Dame Grand Cross of the Order of St. John of Jerusalem

GCT Giro Credit Transfer

GCVO Knight or Dame Grand Cross of the Royal Victorian Order

Gd Gladolinium

GDBA Guide Dogs for the Blind Association

GDC General Dental Council

Gdns Gardens

GDP/gdp Gross Domestic Product/gross domestic product

GDR German Democratic Republic *(East Germany)*

GDUP *(Portugal)* Grupos Democráticos de Unideade Popular *(Union of Popular Democratic Groups)*

GE General Election

GEI General and Engineering Industries

GEMBAT see GMBATU

GEMS Global Environmental Monitoring System *(UNO, q.v.)*

Gen/Genl General

Gent Gentleman

GENTA *(Zimbabwe)* Government Import Agency for Oil

Geo Georgia *(USA State)*

GEOD Geodesy *(science of measuring the earth)*

Geog Geography

Geol Geology

Geom Geometry

Ger German/Germany

GES Government Economic Service

GESTAPO Geheime Staats Polizei *(Hitler's Political Police)*

GEW West German Teachers' Union

GFR German Federal Republic *(West Germany)*

GFS Girls' Friendly Society

GFTU General Federation of Trade Unions

GG Grenadier Guards; Georgian Group; Governor General; Girl Guides

GGA Girl Guides' Association

GGF Glass and Glazing Federation

GGL Guild of Guide Lecturers

GH Ghanaian International Motor Vehicle Registration Letters

GHI Good Housekeeping Institute

GHQ General Headquarters

GHS General Household Survey

GI Government Issue; Gunnery Instructor *(RN, q.v.);* *(USA)* General Issue *(Enlisted Army Private)*

GIA Groupement des Indèpendants Africains *(Independent-Africans Group);* *(France)* Group for Information and Shelter *(of Mental Patients)*

Gib Gibraltar

GICS Government Industrial Civil Service

GIGN *(France)* Groupe d'Intervention de la Gendarmerie Nationale *(elite national police intervention group)*

GIMechE Graduate of the Institution of Mechanical Engineers

GIMI Graduate of the Institute of the Motor Industry

GInstM Graduate of the Institute of Marketing

GIST Girls Into Science and Technology

GJC Grand Junction Canal

GKN Guest Keen Nettlefolds

GL Grand Lodge *(masonic)*

GLA *(South Africa)* General Law Amendment Bill

GLAA Greater London Arts Association

GLAD Greater London Association for the Disabled

GLAP Gay Legal Advice Project

Glas Glasgow

GLB Girls' Life Brigade

GLC Greater London Council

GLCM Graduate Diploma of the London College of Music

Gld/gld Guilder *(Monetary unit of the Netherlands)*

GLH *(West Germany)* Grüne Liste Hessen *(ecology political party, Hesse)*

Glos Gloucestershire

GLS General Lighting Service *(Electric Light Bulb)*

GLU *(West Germany)* Grüne Liste Umweltschütz *(World Ecology Political*

Party)

GLW *(West Germany)* Grüne Liste West-falen *(ecology political party, West-phalia)*

GLYC Greater London Young Conservatives

GM General Manager; George Medal; Grand Master; Guided Missile; International Society for Research on Peat/Turf *(FAO, q.v., see also IGM)*

GMAG Genetic Manipulation Advisory Group

GMASI Graduate Member of the Ambulance Service Institute

GMBATU General and Municipal Boilermakers and Allied Trades Union *(amalgamation of GMWU, q.v., and ASBSBSW, q.v., in 1982)*

GmbH *(West Germany)* Gesellschaft mit beschränkter Haftung *(Limited Company)*

GMC General Medical Council; Guild of Memorial Craftsmen; General Management Committee

GME General Ministerial Examination

GMF Glass Manufacturers' Federation

GMHQ Guardsmen's HQ, *q.v.*

GMT Greenwich Mean Time

GMusRNCM(Hons) Graduate of the Royal Northern College of Music

GMWU General and Municipal Workers' *(merged 1982 with ASBSBSW, q.v. to become GEMBAT, q.v.)*

GMWU/GMU See GEMBAT

GNC General Nursing Council

GNP Gross National Product

GNSM Graduate of the Northern School of Music *(now Royal Northern School of Music)*

GO General Officer; *(France)* Grand Officer *(Grand Officier of the Legion of Honour)*

GOC General Optical Council; General Officer Commanding

GOC-in-C General Officer Commanding-in-Chief

GOE General Ordination Examination

GOES Geostatic Orbiting Environmental Satellite

GOM Grand Old Man

GOP *(USA)* Grand Old Party *(Republican Party)*

GOPWO *(Uganda)* Grossly Over-Promoted Warrant Officers

GOQ Genuine Occupational Qualification

Goth Gothic

Gov Governor

Gov. Gen. Governor General

Govt Government

GP General Practitioner *(medical)*; Grand Prix *(first prize)*; *(Latin)* Gloria Patri *(Glory to the Father)*; *(music)* General Pause

GPC General Purposes Committee

GPDST Girls' Public Day School Trust

GPh Graduate in Pharmacy

GPM Grand Past Master *(freemason)*

GPMFJ Ghana People's Movement for Freedom and Justice

GPMG General Purpose Machine Gun

GPO General Post Office

GPP *(Nicaragua)* Guerra Popular Prolongada *(Prolonged Popular War)*

GPS Generalised Preference Scheme

GPT Guild of Professional Toast-masters

GPU *(USSR)* Gasudarstvenol Politicheskol Ypravlenie *(Special Police, same as OGPU, q.v.)*

GQG *(France)* Grand Quartier Général *(General HQ, q.v.)*

GR General Reserve; Greek International Motor Vehicle Registration Letters; *(Latin)* Georgius Rex *(King George)*

Gr Greek; Greece

GRA Greyhound Racing Association

GRACE Graphic Arts Composing Equipment

Grad Graduate

GradBHI Graduate of the British Horological Institute

GradICeram Graduate of the Institute of Ceramics

GradIISec Graduate of the Institute of Industrial Security

GradIMA Graduate of the Institute of Mathematics and its Applications

GradIManf Graduate Member of the Institute of Manufacturing

GradIMF Graduate of the Institute of Metal Finishing

GradIMS Graduate of the Institute of Management Specialists

GradInstBE Graduate of the Institute of British Engineers

GradInstNDT Graduate of the British Institute of Non-Destructive Testing

GradInstPS Graduate of the Institute of Purchasing and Supply

GradIOP Graduate of the Institute of Printing

GradIPM Graduate of the Institute of Personnel Management

GradIPRE Graduate, Incorporated Practitioners in Radio and Electronics

GradISM Graduate of the Institute of Supervisory Management

GradIStructE Graduate of the Institute of Structural Engineers

GradNIH Graduate of the National Institute of Hardware

GradPRI Graduate of the Plastics and Rubber Institute

GradRIC Graduate Member of the Royal Institute of Chemistry

GradSLAET Graduate of the Society of Licensed Aircraft Engineers and Technologists

GradSTA Graduate Member of the Swimming Teachers' Association

Graduate ITE Graduate of the Institution of Electrical and Electronics Technician Engineers

GradWeldI Graduate of the Welding Institute

GRAPO *(Spain)* 1st October Anti-Fascist Revolutionary Group

GRAS *(USA)* Generally Regarded As Safe *(list of food additives)*

GRC Government Research Corporation; Glass Reinforced Cement

GRE Grant-Related Expenditure

GRIM Glass Reflected Index Measurement

GRIT Graduated Reciprocated Initiatives in Tension Reduction

GRNCM Graduate of the Royal Northern College of Music

GRO General Register Office

GRP Glass Reinforced Plastic

Grp. Capt. Group Captain *(RAF, q.v.)*

GRSC Graduate of the Royal Society of Chemistry

GRSM Graduate of the Royal Schools of Music

GRU *(USSR)* Glavnoye Razvedivatelnoye Ypravlenie *(Chief Military Intelligence Directorate)*

GS General Secretary; General Staff; General Service; Geographical Survey; Geological Survey; Grammar School

GSA *(USA)* General Services Administration

GSD German Shepherd Dog

GSEE *(Greece)* Geniki Sinemospontia Ergaton Ellados *(General Confederation of Unions)*

GSG-g *(West Germany)* Grenzschutzgruppe *(para-military frontier force)*

GSIEN French Research Group

GSM General Service Medal

GSMD Guildhall School of Music & Drama

GSO Giro Standing Order; General Staff Officer

GSP Generalised System of Preferences

GSS Government Statistical Service

GSU *(Kenya)* General Service Unit

Gt. Brit. Great Britain

GTC Government Training Centre; General Teaching Council

GTCL Graduate Diploma of Trinity College of Music London

GTO *(USSR)* Gotov K Trudu i Oberone *(ready for work and defence)*

GTS General Thinking Skills

Guar Guaranteed

Guat Guatemala

GUD *(France)* Groupe pour Union et Défence *(Extreme right-wing student union)*

GUFFAW Government-Undertaking-For-Finding-Another-Way *(Parliamentary slang)*

Guil Guilder *(florin, Monetary unit of the Netherlands)*

Guin Guinea

GUM *(USSR)* Gosudarstvenni Universalni Magazin *(State Universal General Store)*

GUY Guyana International Motor Vehicle Registration Letters

GV *(France)* Grande Vitesse *(express transport)*

GWB General Welfare for the Blind

GWCMD Graduate Diploma of the Welsh College of Music and Drama

Gym Gymnasium/Gymnastics

H

H Hydrant; Hydrogen; Hungarian International Motor Vehicle Registration Letter

h henry *(unit of inductance)*

h & c hot and cold *(water)*

H-A Hautes-Alpes *(Department of France)*

HA Highways Act; Heavy Artillery; Horse Artillery; Hostile Aircraft; Historical Association

HA and M Hymns Ancient and Modern

HAA Heavy Anti-Aircraft

HAC High Alumina Cement; Honourable Artillery Company

HACAN Heathrow Association for the Control of Aircraft Noise *(see also FHANG)*

HACTU Human Action Counselling and Training Unit

HAG Housing Action Group *(usually preceded by initial of Town, County or Borough)*

HANG Highland Anti-Nuclear Group

Hants Hampshire

HAPA Handicapped Adventure Playground Association

HARM High-speed Anti-Radar Missile *(USA)*

HARCVS Honorary Associate of the Royal College of Veterinary Surgeons

HARP Heating and Rent Payment *(Birmingham City Council Scheme for Pensioners)*

HART Halt All Racist Tours

Harv Harvard

HAS Hospital Advisory Service

HASS Home Accident Surveillance System

HASU - 2 High Flying Reconnaissance Aircraft

h/b half-board

HBG Historic Buildings Group

HBM Her/His Britannic Majesty

HC House of Commons; Headmasters' Conference; Health Certificate; Heralds' College; High Church; Higher Certificate *(Education)*; Holy Communion

hc hot and cold *(water)*; *(Latin)* honoris causa *(for the sake of the honour)*

HCB House of Commons Bill

HCF Honorary Chaplain to the Forces

hcf highest common factor *(mathematics)*

HChD Higher Chiropodial Theory Diploma of the Institute of Chiropodists

HCIMA Hotel Catering and Institutional Management Association

HCPT Historic Churches Preservation Trust; Health Care Planning Team *(NHS, q.v.)*

HCR High Commission for Refugees *(UN, q.v.)*

HCS Home Civil Service

HCSA Hospital Consultants & Specialists Association

HCSG Hyper-Active Children's Support Group

HCVO Heating and Ventilating Contractors' Organisation

HD Haemodialysis *(artificial kidney machine treatment)*

HDA *(Australia)* Hawkesbury Diploma in Agriculture

HDC Home Defence Circular

HDCR (R) Higher Award in Radio Diagnosis, College of Radiographers

HDCR (T) Higher Award in Radio Therapy, College of Radiographers

HDD Higher Dental Diploma

HDF Home Defence Force

HDL High Density Lipoproteins

HDTV High Definition Television

HE His/Her Excellency; His Eminence; Health Education

He Helium

HEA Health Education Authority

Heb Hebrew

HEBA Home Extension Building Association

HEC Home Extension Consultancy; Health Education Council

HEH His/Her Exalted Highness

HELT Hedonism Limitation Talks

Herts Hertfordshire

HEW *(USA)* Department of Health, Education & Welfare

HF Home Fleet; Home Forces; High Frequency

Hf Hafnium

HFARA Honorary Foreign Associate of the Royal Academy

HFPA Hollywood Foreign Press Association

HFRA Honorary Foreign Member of the Royal Academy

HG His/Her Grace; Home Guard *(Local Defence Volunteers, 2nd World War)*; Horse Guards

Hg *(Latin)* Hydrargyrum *(Mercury)*

HGH Human Growth Hormone

HGV Heavy Goods Vehicle

HH His/Her Highness; His Holiness; His/Her Honour

hh hands high *(horse measurement)*

HHD *(USA)* Doctor of Humanities

HIDB Highlands and Islands Development Board

HiFi High Fidelity *(radio recording)*

HIH His/Her Imperial Highness

HIM His/Her Imperial Majesty

HIVOS *(Netherlands)* Humanistisch Instituut voor Ontwikkelingssamenwerking *(Humanist Institute for co-operation with Developing Countries)*

HJS *(Latin)* Hic Jacet Sepultus *(here lies buried)*

HJSC Hospital Junior Staff Committee *(of BMA, q.v.)*

HK House of Keys *(Manx Parliament)*; Columbia Civil Air Line; Hong Kong International Motor Vehicle Registration Letters

HKJ Hong Kong trade advisory group; Jordanian International Motor Vehicle Registration Letters

HL House of Lords

HLA *(West Germany)* Stop-Foreign-Immigration Party

HLCC Home Laundering Consultative Council; Home Laundering Care Code

HLI Highland Light Infantry

HLM *(France)* Habitation à Loyer Modérée *(Subsidised Housing Unit)*

HM Her/His Majesty; Headmaster; Headmistress; Harbour Master *(RN, q.v.)*

HMAS Her/His Majesty's Australian Ship

HMC Her/His Majesty's Customs; Headmasters' Conference; Hospital Management Committee; Historical Manuscripts Commission

HMCS Her/His Majesty's Canadian Ship

HMG Her/His Majesty's Government

HMHS Her/His Majesty's Hospital Ship

HMI Her/His Majesty's Inspector

HMNZS Her/His Majesty's New Zealand Ship

HMOCS Her/His Majesty's Overseas Civil Service

HMS Her/His Majesty's Service/Ship

HMS/M Her/His Majesty's Submarine

(RN, q.v.)

HMSO Her/His Majesty's Stationery Office

HNC Higher National Certificate *(Technical Education)*

HNCIP Housewives' Non-Contributory Invalidity Pension

HND Higher National Diploma

HNP *(South Africa)* Herstigte Nationale Party *(Right-wing Nationalist Party)*

HNWI *(USA)* High Network Individual *(creditworthiness)*

HO Home Office; Head Office; House Officer

Ho Holmium

HOBRA Heart-of-Bromley Residents' Association

H of C House of Commons

H of L House of Lords

HOLLAND Hope-Our-Love-Lives-And-Never-Dies!

HOLS Help Organise Local Schemes *(for children's school holidays)*

Hon Honourable; Honorary; Honour

Hon Sec Honorary Secretary

HonARAM Honorary Associate of the Royal Academy of Music

HonARCM Honorary Associate Royal College of Music

HonASTA Honorary Associate of the Swimming Teachers' Association

Hond Honduras

HonDrRCA Honorary Doctorate of the Royal College of Art

HonFBID Honorary Fellow of the British Institute of Interior Design

HonFEIS Honorary Fellow of the Educational Institute of Scotland

HonFHCIMA Honorary Fellow of the Hotel, Catering and Institutional Management Association

HonFIGasE Honorary Fellow of the Institution of Gas Engineers

HonFIIM Honorary Fellow of the Institution of Industrial Managers

HonFIIP Honorary Fellow of the Institute of Incorporated Photographers

HonFIMarE Honorary Fellow of the Institute of Marine Engineers

HonFIMechE Honorary Fellow of the Institution of Mechanical Engineers

HonFIMM Honorary Fellow of the Institution of Mining and Metallurgy

HonFInstMC Honorary Fellow of the Institute of Measurement and Control

HonFInstNDT Honorary Fellow of the Institute of Non-Destructive Testing

HonFIOP Honorary Fellow of the Institute of Printing

HonFIQA Honorary Fellow of the Institute of Quality Assurance

HonFIRSE Honorary Fellow of the Institution of Railway Signal Engineers

HonFITD Honorary Fellow of the Institute of Training and Development

HonFIWHTE Honorary Fellow of the Institution of Works and Highways Technician Engineers

HonFPRI Honorary Life Member of the Plastics and Rubber Institute

HonFRAM Honorary Fellow of the Royal Academy of Music

HonFRPS Honorary Fellow of the Royal Photographic Society

HonFSE Honorary Fellow of the Society of Engineers

HonFSGT Honorary Fellow of the Society of Glass Technology

HonFSLAET Honorary Fellow of the Society of Licensed Aircraft Engineers and Technologists

HonWeldI Honorary Fellow of the Welding Institute

HonGSM Honorary Member of the Guildhall School of Music and Drama

HonIPRE Honorary Member, Incorporated Practitioners in Radio and Electronics

HonMInstE Honorary Member of the Institute of Energy

HonMInstNDT Honorary Member of the British Institute of Non-Destructive Testing

HonMRIN Honorary Member of the Royal Institute of Navigation

HonMWES Honorary Member of the Women's Engineering Society

HonRAM Honorary Member of the Royal Academy of Music

HonRCM Honorary Member of the Royal College of Music

HonRNCM Honorary Member of the Royal Northern College of Music

HonRSCM Honorary Member of the Royal School of Church Music

Hons Honours

Hon Sec Honorary Secretary

HOPE Horticultural Organisation for Purposeful Employment

Hort Horticulture/Horticultural

Hosp Hospital

HOWL Hands Off Wildlife

HP House Physician; Horse Power; Hire Purchase; Half Pay; Panama Airline

HPPA Horses' and Ponies' Protection Association

HQ Headquarters

HR Highland Regiment; *(USA)* House of Representatives

hr hour

HRA Horse Rangers Association; Habitable Rooms per Acre

HRC Holy Roman Church; High Rupturing Capacity *(electric fuses)*

HRCA Honorary Royal Cambrian Acadamician

HRH His/Her Royal Highness

HRHA Honorary Member of the Royal Hibernian Academy

HRI Honorary Member of the Royal

Institute of Painters in Water Colours
HRIP *(Latin)* Hic requiescat in pace *(here rests in peace, usually RIP, q.v.)*
HROI Honorary Member of the Royal Institute of Oil Painters
HRSA Honorary Member of the Royal Scottish Academy
HRSW Honorary Member of the Royal Scottish Water Colour Society
HRT Hormone Replacement Therapy
HS House Surgeon; Home Service *(BBC, q.v.)*; Hansard Society; High School; *(Latin)* Hic Sepultus *(here lies buried)*
HSA Hospital Saving Association
HSACP Hospital Saving Association Crown Plan
HSC Hospital Safety Commission; Health and Safety Commission; Higher School Certificate
HSE Health & Safety Executive
HSF Hospital Saturday Fund
HSH His/Her Serene Highness
HSS *(Latin)* Historical Societatis Socius *(Fellow of the Historical Society)*
HST High Speed Train
HT High Tension
Ht/Rhin Haut-Rhine *(Department of France)*
Hte/Gar Haute-Garonne *(Department of France)*
Hte/L Haute-Loire *(Department of France)*
Hte/M Haute-Marne *(Department of France)*
Hte/Sao Haute-Saône *(Department of France)*

Hte/Sav Haute-Savoie *(Department of France)*
Htes/Alpes Hautes-Alpes *(Department of France)*
Htes-Pr (or H-P) Hautes-Pyrénées *(Department of France)*
Htes/Pyr Hautes-Pyrénées *(Department of France)*
HTGR High Temperature Gas-Cooled Reactor
HTL Hearing Threshold Level
HTM Half-Term Movement *(Organisation for co-ordinating half-term school holidays)*
HTV Harlech Television
HUD *(USA)* Housing and Urban Development
HULA Home for Unwanted and Lost Animals
Hum Humanity; Humanities *(Classics)*
Hung Hungary
Hunts Huntingdonshire
HUP Hydrogen Uranyl Phosphate *(source of energy)*
HV High Velocity; High Voltage; Health Visitor *(now RHV, q.v.)*
HVA Health Visitors' Association
HVCert Health Visitors' Certificate
HW High Water
HWLB High Water, London Bridge
HWM High Water Mark
HWR Heavywater Reactor
Hwy Highway
HYMA Hebrew Young Men's Association

I

I Island; Isle; Iodine; Idaho *(USA State)*; 1 *(Roman Numeral)*
IA Institute of Actuaries; Institute of Agriculture; Indian Army
Ia Iowa *(USA State)*
IAA International Association of Art *(UNESCO, q.v.)*
IAAA Irish Amateur Athletic Association; Irish Association of Advertising Agencies
IAAE International Association of Agricultural Economists *(FAO, q.v.)*
IAAF International Amateur Athletic Federation
IAAS Incorporated Association of Architects and Surveyors
IAB Industrial Advisory Board
IABA International Amateur Boxing Association
IAC Institute of Amateur Cinema-

tographers; International Athletes Club
IACS Insurance Agency for Civil Servants
IACW Inter-American Commission of Women
IAE Institution of Automobile Engineers
IAEA International Atomic Energy Agency *(UN, q.v.)*
IAES Institute of Aeronautical Sciences
IAF International Aeronautical Federation; Indian Air Force; Indian Auxiliary Force; International Abolitionist Federation
IAgrE Institution of Agricultural Engineers
IAHM Incorporated Association of Headmasters
IAIAS Inter-American Institute of Agricultural Sciences

IAL Irish Academy of Letters

IALA International Association of Lighthouse Authorities

IALS Institute of Advanced Legal Studies

IAM Institute of Administrative Management; Institute of Advanced Motorists; Institute of Aviation Medicine

IAMA Incorporated Advertising Managers' Association

IAMCR International Association for Mass Communication Research

IAMFE International Association on Mechanisation of Field Experiments *(FAO, q.v.)*

IAMLEP Medical Programme of the World Health Organisation

IAMTACT Institute of Advanced Machine Tool and Control Technology

I and V Immunisation and Vaccination *(NHS, q.v.)*

IAPA International Airline Passengers' Association

IAPS Incorporated Association of Preparatory Schools

IArb Institute of Arbitrators

IARC International Agency for Research on Cancer

IAS Institute of Accounting Staff; Institute of Aeronautical Sciences; *(USA)* Institute of Advanced Studies; *(Chicago)* Institute of Applied Science; *(USA)* Institute of Aerospace Sciences

IASC International Accounting and Standards Committee

IASM *(Italy)* Instituto per l'Assistenzo alla Sviluppo del Mezzogiorno *(Institute for Assistance in the Development of the South)*

IASS International Association for Scandinavian Studies

IAT International Atomic Time

IATA International Air Transport Association

IATM International Association of Tour Managers

IATSE *(USA and Canada)* International Alliance of Theatrical Stage Employees and Moving Picture Machine Operators

IATUL International Association of Technical University Libraries

IAU International Association of Universities; International Astronomical Union

IAW International Alliance of Women

IB Information Bureau; Intelligence Branch; International Bank; Institute of Bankers; Institute of Building; International Baccalauréat *(International Bachelor's Degree)*

ib/ibid *(Latin)* ibidem *(in the same place)*

IBA Independent Broadcasting Authority; International Bar Association; Israel Broadcasting Authority

I-BA Indo-British Association

IBB Invest in Britain Bureau

IBBY International Board on Books for Young People

IBCE Indo-British Cultural Exchange

IBE Institution of British Engineers

IBELs Interest-Bearing Eligible Liabilities *(sterling)*

IBG Institute of British Geographers

IBI *(Japan)* International Broadcasting Institute

IBiol Institute of Biology

IBM Intercontinental Ballistic Missile *(usually ICBM, q.v.)*; International Business Machines

IBNS Inter-Borough Nomination Scheme

IBP Institute of British Photographers; International Biological Programme *(UNESCO, q.v.)*

IBPGR International Board for Plant Genetic Resources *(FAO, q.v.)*

IBRD International Bank for Reconstruction and Development *(UN, q.v.)*

IBS Incentive Bonus Scheme *(Work Study)*

IBSTP International Bureau for the Suppression of Traffic in Persons

IBT International Broadcasting Trust

IC Intelligence Corps

i/c in charge

ICA Institute of Chartered Accountants; Institute of Company Accountants; Institute of Contemporary Arts; International Co-operative Alliance; Ignition Control Additive; Invalid Car Allowance; Invalid Care Allowance; Institute of Amateur Cinematographers; International Coffee Agreement

ICAA Invalid Children's Aid Association

ICAC *(Hong Kong)* International Commission Against Corruption

ICAE International Council for Adult Education

ICAI International Commission for Agriculture and Food Industries *(FAO, q.v., see also CIIA)*

ICAL Institute of Chartered Accountants in Ireland

ICAMAS International Centre for Advanced Mediterranean Agronomic Studies *(FAO, q.v., see also CIHEAM)*

ICAN International Commission for Air Navigation

ICAO International Civil Aviation Organisation *(UN, q.v.)*

ICAOPA International Council of Aircraft Owners' and Pilots' Associations

ICAP International Code of Advertising Practice

ICAR International Cannabis Alliance

Reform; *(Romania)* Instituli de Cercetari Agronomice al Romîniei *(Agricultural Research Institute)*

ICARDA International Centre for Agricultural Research in Dry Areas

ICAS Institute of Chartered Accountants, Scotland

ICASC International Contraception, Abortion and Sterilisation Campaign

ICBM Inter-Continental Ballistic Missile

ICBP International Council for Bird Preservation

ICC International Chamber of Commerce; International Christian Committee; International Association for Cereal Chemistry *(FAO, q.v.)*; International Cricket Conference

ICCA International Cocoa Agreement

ICCB *(Switzerland)* International Catholic Child Bureau

ICCC International Council of Christian Churches

ICCH International Commodities Clearing House

ICCO International Cocoa Organisation; *(Netherlands)* Interkerkelijke Coordinatie Commissie Ontwikkelingshulp *(Protestant Inter-Church Economic Coordination Committee for Development aid)*

ICD Institute of Civil Defence

ICE Institution of Civil Engineers; Internal Combustion Engine; Institution of Chemical Engineers; Inner City Enterprises *(Conservative Party Proposal)*

ICEM Inter-governmental Committee for European Migration *(UN, q.v.)*

ICES International Council for the Exploration of the Sea

ICF Industrial Christian Fellowship

ICFC International Centre of Films for Children; Industrial and Commercial Finance Corporation

ICFCYP International Centre of Films for Children and Young Persons *(see also CIFEJ)*

ICFTU International Confederation of Free Trade Unions

IChemE Institution of Chemical Engineers

ICHEO Inter-University Council for Higher Education Overseas

ICI Imperial Chemical Industries

ICID International Commission on Irrigation and Drainage *(FAO, q.v.)*

ICIFI International Council of Infant Food Industry

ICJ International Court of Justice; International Commission of Jurists; International Court of Justice Law Reports

ICJW International Council of Jewish Women

ICL International Computers Ltd.

ICLH Imperial College London Hospital *(Joint Operation)*

ICM International Confederation of Midwives; Institute of Commercial Management

ICMA Institute of Cost and Management Accountants

ICN International Council of Nurses

ICO International Coffee Organisation; Institute of Careers Officers

ICOM Industrial Common Ownership Movement; International Council of Museums; International College of Oriental Medicine

ICOMOS International Council of Monuments and Sites

ICPA International Commission for the Prevention of Alcoholism

ICPO International Criminal Police Organisation *(see also INTERPOL)*

ICR International Christian Relief; Industrial Cases Law Reports

ICRA International Catholic Charitable Rural Association *(FAO, q.v.)*

ICRC International Committee of the Red Cross

ICRF Imperial Cancer Research Fund

ICRISAT International Crops Research Institute for the Semi-Arid Tropics

ICRP International Commission on Radiological Protection

ICRPMA International Committee for Recording the Productivity of Milk Animals *(FAO, q.v., see also CICPLB)*

ICS Institute of Chartered Secretaries and Administrators; Institute of Chartered Shipbrokers; International Correspondence Schools; International Chamber of Shipping; Indian Civil Service

ICSA Spanish equivalent of the Public Opinion Poll

ICSC International Civil Service Commission

ICSDW International Council of Social Democratic Women

ICSL Inns of Court School of Law

ICSS International Committee for the Sociology of Sport

ICST Imperial College of Science and Technology

ICSU International Council of Scientific Unions *(FAO, q.v., see also CIUS and COGENE)*

ICSW International Council on Social Welfare *(FAO, q.v.)*

ICT International Computers and Tabulators

ICTA *(Trinidad)* Imperial College of Tropical Agriculture

ICTU Irish Congress of Trade Unions

ICU Intensive Care Unit

ICVA International Council for Voluntary Agencies

ICW International Council of Women

(see also CIF)

ICWG International Co-operative Women's Guilds

ID Information Department; Intelligence Department

Id Idaho *(USA State)*

id *(Latin)* idem *(the same)*

IDA International Development Association *(UN, q.v.)*; Irish Development Agency; *(Eire)* Industrial Development Authority

Ida Idaho *(USA State)*

IDB Industrial Development Board

IDD International Direct Dialling *(telephone)*

IDEA Institute of Directors European Association

IDF International Dairy Federation *(FAO, q.v., see also FIL)*; International Dental Federation; Israel Defence Force

IDHE Institute of Domestic and Heating Engineers

IDL International Date Line

IDP International Driving Permit

IDS Income Data Service; Industrial Data Services; Institute of Development Studies; Institute of Dental Surgery; International Dendrology Society

IDT Industrial Design Technology

IDTA International Dance Teachers' Association

IDU International Democratic Union, *see also UDI (International Marxist Group)*

ie *(Latin)* id est *(that is)*

IEA Institute of Economic Affairs

IEE Institution of Electrical Engineers

IEETE Institution of Electrical and Electronics Technician Engineers

IEF International Equestrian Federation *(see also FEI)*

IERE Institution of Electronic & Radio Engineers

IES Illuminating Engineering Society; Institution of Engineers and Shipbuilders in Scotland; Indian Educational Service

I et L Indre-et-Loire *(Department of France)*

I et V Ille-et-Vilaine *(Department of France)*

IF Intermediate Frequency

IFA Irish Football Association; International Federation of Actors

IFAD International Fund for Agricultural Development *(UNO, q.v.)*

IFALPA International Federation of Airline Pilots' Association

IFAP International Federation of Agricultural Producers

IFATCA International Federation of Air Traffic Controllers' Association

IFAW International Fund for Animal Welfare

IFBPW International Federation of Business & Professional Women

IFC International Finance Corporation *(UN, q.v.)*

IFCL International Faculty of Comparative Law

IFCTU International Federation of Christian Trade Unions

IFF Identifies Friend or Foe *(RAF, q.v., instrument)*

IFFLP International Federation for Family Life Promotion

IFHE International Federation of Home Economics *(FAO, q.v. see also FIEF)*

IFIP International Federation for Information Processing

IFireE Institution of Fire Engineers

IFL International Friendship League

IFLA International Federation of Library Associations

IFMA Independent Film Makers' Association

IFOP *(France)* Institut Français d'Opinion Publique *(Institute of Public Opinion)*

IFPAAW International Federation of Plantation, Agricultural and Allied Workers *(FAO, q.v., see also FITPASC)*

IFR Instrument Flight Rules *(aviation)*

IFRB International Frequency Registration Board

IFS Irish Free State

IFSW International Federation of Social Workers

IFUW International Federation of University Women

IFWEA International Federation of Workers Educational Associations

IFWL International Federation of Women Lawyers

IG Instructor in Gunnery; Imperial Gallon

IGasE Institution of Gas Engineers

IGM International Society for Research on Peat/Turf *(FAO, q.v., see also GM)*; *(West Germany)* Internationale Gesellschaft für Moorforschung *(International Society for Research on Moors)*; *(Italy)* Instituto Geografico Militare *(Military Geographic Institute)*

IGN *(Guatemala)* Instituto Geografico Nacional *(National Geographic Institute)*

IGO Inter-Governmental Organisation

IGU International Geographical Union; International Gas Union

IGY International Geophysical Year *(1957–58, actually lasted 18 months . . . 1/7/57 to 1/12/58 to enable 57 countries to participate in the meteorological survey)*

IHA Institute of Hospital Administrators; International Hotels Association; Issuing Houses Association

IHE Institution of Highway Engineers; Institute of Higher Education

IHS *(Latin)* Jesus Hominum Salvator *(Jesus, Saviour of Mankind)*

IHSA Institute of Health Service Administrators

IHVE Institution of Heating and Ventilating Engineers

II 2 *(Roman numeral)*

IIAL International Institute of Arts and Letters

IIASA International Institute for Applied Systems Analysis

IIED International Institute for the Environment and Development

IIF Institut International du Froid *(International Institute of Refrigeration, see also IIR)*

III 3 *(Roman numeral)*

IIOE International Indian Ocean Expedition *(1963)*

IIP Institute of Incorporated Photographers

IIR International Institute of Refrigeration *(see also IIF)*

IIS Irish Institute of Secretaries; International Institute of Sociology

IISE International Institute of Social Economics

IISS International Institute for Strategic Studies

IIW International Institute of Welding

IJI Illegal Jewish Immigrant *(designation applied by Great Britain in 1945–48 during the occupation of Palestine)*

IKV *(Netherlands)* Interkerkelijk Vredesberaad *(Inter-church Peace Council)*

IL Institute of Linguists; Israeli International Motor Vehicle Registration Letters

ILA Institute of Landscape Architects; International Law Association

ILAA International Legal Aid Association

ILEA Inner London Education Authority

ILJW International League of Jewish Women

Ill Illinois *(USA State)*

ILMI Index Linked Mortgage and Investment

ILO International Labour Organisation *(FAO, q.v., see also BIT)*; International Labour Office

ILocoE Institute of Locomotive Engineers

ILP Independent Labour Party

ILPA Index-Linked Pensions Association

ILPH International League for the Protection of Horses

ILR Independent Local Radio; International Law Reports; International Labour Review

ILS Instrument Landing System *(aviation)*

ILTF International Lawn Tennis Federation

ILTO Industrial Liaison Technical Officers

IM Institution of Metallurgists

IMA International Music Association; Irish Medical Association

IMarE Institute of Marine Engineers

IMBUSA International Meeting of the Bishops of the Union of South Africa

IMC Institute of Management Consultants

IMCO Intergovernmental Maritime Consultative Organisation *(UN, q.v., now IMO, q.v.)*

IME Institution of Mechanical Engineers; Institution of Municipal Engineers

IMEA Incorporated Municipal Electrical Association

IMechE Institution of Mechanical Engineers

IMF International Monetary Fund; International Metalworkers' Federation

IMG International Marxist Group

IMH Institute of Materials Handling

IMI Institute of the Motor Industry; Imperial Metals Industry

IMinE Institution of Mining Engineers

IMLS Institute of Medical Laboratory Sciences

IMLT Institute of Medical Laboratory Technology

IMM Institution of Mining & Metallurgy

IMO International Maritime Organisation *(UN, q.v., formerly IMCO, q.v.)*

Imp Imperial

IMPA International Maritime Pilots Association

IMR Institute for Market Research

IMS Institute of Marital Studies *(see also FDB)*; Indian Medical Service; International Military Service; Institute of Management Services

IMU International Mathematical Union; *(Sweden)* Institutet för Marknadsundersökningar *(Institute for Market Research)*

IMunE Institution of Municipal Engineers

IN Indian Navy; Netherlands Indies; Instructor

In Indium

INC *(Latin)* In Nomine Christi *(in the name of Christ)*

Inc Incorporated *(USA equivalent of Limited)*

incog *(Latin)* incognito *(under disguised name)*

Incorp Incorporated, see Inc.

INCPEN Industry Committee for Packaging and the Environment *(see also IOP, PIRA & EAT)*

IND *(Latin)* In nomine Dei *(in God's name)*; Indian International Motor Vehicle Registration Letters

Ind Indiana *(USA State)*; Independent

INDEC Independent Nuclear Disarmament Election Committee

INDECS Interactive Design of Control

Systems

Ind-et-L Indre-et-Loire *(Department of France)*

Indo-Eur Indo-European

Ind-Rep Independent Republican

IndT *(USA)* Indian Territory

INF Intermediate-Range Nuclear Forces; Iran National Front

Inf Information; Infant; Infantry

INFANT Test-tube *(baby)* charity

infra dig *(Latin)* infra dignitatem *(beneath dignity)*

Ing *(France)* Ingénieur *(engineer)*; *(Italy)* Ingegnere *(engineer)*

INGO International Non-Governmental Organisation

INJ *(Latin)* In Nomine Jesu *(in the name of Jesus)*

INLA Irish National Liberation Army

INMOS Microelectronics Company *(of the NEB, q.v.)*

INPOL *(West Germany)* Centralised Police Computer

INRA *(France)* Institut National de Récherche Agronomique *(National Institute for Agronomical Research)*

INRDP *(France)* L'Institut National de Recherche et Documentation Pédagogiques *(Research Institute for Teachers, see also CRDP)*

INRI *(Latin)* Jesus Nazarenus Rex Judaeorum *(Jesus of Nazareth, King of the Jews)*

INS International News Service; *(USA)* Information Naturalisation Service

INSEAD Institut Européen d'Administration des Affaires *(European Institute of Business Administration, see also MBA)*

INSEE *(France)* L'Institut National de Statistiques et d'Etudes Economiques *(National Institute of Statistics and Economic Studies)*

Insp Inspector

INST *(Latin)* In Nomine Sanctae Trinitatus *(In the name of the Holy Trinity)*

Inst Institute; Institution; Current month

Inst. de France Institut de France *(Association of five French Academies)*

InstMM Institution of Mining and Metallurgy

INSTRAW Institute for Training and Research for the Advancement of Women

INTELSAT International Telecommunications Satellite Organisation

INTERPOL International Police *(see also ICPO)*

IntLR International Law Reports

INucE Institution of Nuclear Engineers

IO Intelligence Officer

Io Ionium

IOB Institute of Bankers

IOBS Institute of Bankers in Scotland

IOC International Olympic Committee *(Olympic Games)*

IOCU International Organisation of Consumer Unions

IOD Institute of Directors

IODE Imperial Order of the Daughters of the Empire

IOF Institute of Fuel; Independent Order of Foresters

I of M Isle of Man

IOGT International Order of Good Templars

IOJ International Organ of Journalists

IoJ Institute of Journalists *(members are MJI, q.v.)*

IOM Indian Order of Merit; Isle of Man

IOOC International Olive Oil Council, *(FAO, q.v., see also COI)*

IOOF Independent Order of Oddfellows

IOP Institute of Painters in Oil Colours; Institute of Petroleum; Institute of Packaging *(see also PIRA, INCPEN and EAT)*

IOR Institute of Religious *(Works)*; *(Italy)* Institute per Opera di Religione *(Vatican Bank)*

IoT Institute of Transport

IOU I owe you

IoW Isle of Wight

IPA Institute of Practitioners in Advertising; International Phonetic Alphabet; International Playground Association; International Police Association; Industrial Participation Association

IPBM Inter-Planetary Ballistic Missile

IPC *(USA)* Indo-China Peace Campaign

IPCL *(France)* Institut du Pétrole, des Carburants et Lubrifiants *(Fuel Research Institute)*

IPCS Institution of Professional Civil Servants

IPD Institute for Professional Development; Intrapenile Device *(contraceptive)*

IPE Institution of Plant Engineers; *(Spain)* Unión de Patriotas Españoles *(Union of Patriots)*

IPEX Instant Purchase Excursion Fares *(airlines)*

IPFA Member of the Chartered Institute of Public Finance and Accountancy

IPHE Institution of Public Health Engineers

IPI International Press Institute; Institute of Professional Investigators

IPlantE Institution of Plant Engineers

IPM Institute of Personnel Management

IPPA Independent Programme Producers' Association *(TV, q.v.)*; International Planned Parenthood Association

IPPF International Planned Parenthood Federation

IPPNW International Physicians for Prevention of Nuclear War

IPPS Institute of Physics and the Physical Society

IPR Institute of Public Relations

IPRA International Public Relations Association

IProdE Institute of Production Engineers

IPS International Primate-ological Society; Institute for Palestinian Studies

IPSE International Political and Social Economy *(Forum)*

IPTC International Press Telecommunications Council

IPTIC International Pulse Trade and Industry Confederation *(FAO, q.v., see also CICILS)*

IPU Inter-Parliamentary Union *(not specifically British)*; International Postal Union

IQ Intelligence Quotient

IQED *(Usually QED, q.v.)*

IQPS Institute of Qualified Private Secretaries

IQS Institute of Quantity Surveyors

IR Infra-Red; Industrial Relations; Inland Revenue; Irish Law Reports; Inside Right *(football)*; Iranian International Motor Vehicle Registration Letters; Iran Airline

Ir Ireland; Irish; Iridium

IRA Irish Republican Army; *(USA)* Individual Retirement *(Bank)* Account

IRAD Institute for Research on Animal Diseases

IRAS Infra-Red Astronomical Satellite

IRBM Intermediate Range Ballistic Missile

IRC International Red Cross

IRCA International Record Critics Award

IRCS International Research Communication System

Ire Ireland

IREE (Aust) *(Australia)* Institution of Radio & Electronics Engineers

IRF International Road Federation

IRIS Industrial Research Information Services

IRL Republic of Ireland International Motor Vehicle Registration Letters

IRN Independent Radio News

IRNA Iranian News Agency

IRO International Refugee Organisation; Industrial Relations Officer; Inland Revenue Office

IRP *(Iran)* Islamic Republican Party; Iranian Revolutionary Party

IRQ Iraq International Motor Vehicle Registration Letters

IRR Institute of Race Relations

IRRI International Rice Research Institute

IRRR Industrial Relations Review Report

IRS *(USA)* Inland Revenue Service

IRSF Inland Revenue Staff Federation

IRSO Institute of Road Safety Officers

IRSP Irish Republican Socialist Party

IRTE Institute of Road Transport Engineers

IRTU Industrial Research Training Unit

IRU Immediate Response Unit *(Police)*; International Raiffeisen Union *(FAO, q.v.)*

IS International Socialist; International Society *(of Sculptors, Painters and Engravers)*; Institute of Statisticians; Iceland International Motor Vehicle Registration Letters

Is Island(s)

ISA Incorporated Society of Authors; International Seabed Authority

ISBA Incorporated Society of British Advertisers

ISBN International Standard Book Number

ISC Institute for the Study of Conflict; Imperial Service College; Incest Survivors' Campaign; International Sericultural Commission, *FAO, q.v., see also CSI)*

ISCA International Steering Committee for Consumer Affairs

ISCh Incorporated Society of Chiropodists

ISDD Institute for the Study of Drug Dependence

ISES International Solar Energy Society

ISFA International Scientific Film Association

ISG Inland Shipping Group

ISI International Statistical Institute

ISIRAN *(Iran)* Information Systems Computer Agency

ISIS Independent Schools Information Services; Oxford University News Sheet *(named after the river)*; International Shipping Information Services

ISKON International Society for Krishna Consciousness *(religious sect)*

ISL Internally-Silvered Lamp *(electricity bulb)*

ISM Imperial Service Medal; Institute of Sales Management; Incorporated Society of Musicians

ISMA Incorporated Sales Managers' Association

ISMRC Inter-Services Metallurgical Research Council

ISO Imperial Service Order; International Standardisation Organisation *(FAO, q.v.)*

ISP Institute of Sales Promotion

ISPA International Society for the Protection of Animals; *(Switzerland)* Institut Suisse de Prophylaxie de l'Alcoolisme *(Institute for the Prevention of Alcoholism)*

ISPCC Irish Society for the Prevention of Cruelty to Children

ISPH International Society for the Protection of Horses

ISPP International Society for Prenatal Psychology

ISS International Social Services

ISSA Information Service of South Africa

ISSHG Incest Survivors' Self-Help Group

ISSS International Society of Soil Science *(FAO, q.v., see also AISS)*

IST Institute of Science and Technology

ISTA Independent Secretarial Training Association

ISTC Iron & Steel Trades Confederation

ISTD Imperial Society of Teachers of Dancing

IStructE Institution of Structural Engineers

ISU Immigration Service Union

ISVA Incorporated Society of Valuers and Auctioneers

IT Information Technology; Institute of Technology; Income Tax; Infantry Training; International Times *(British underground newspaper)*; Intermediate Treatment *(of child offenders)*; *(USA)* Indian Territory; Sex-appeal

It Italy

ITA Independent Television Authority *(now IBA, q.v.)*; Initial Teaching Alphabet; International Tea Agreement; International Tin Agreement

ITAG Invalid Tricycle Action Group

Ital Italian

ITAP Information Technology Advisory Panel

ITB Industrial Training Board; Industry Training Board; Irish Tourist Board; Insurance Technical Bureau

ITC International Trade Centre; *(USA)* International Trade Commission

ITCA Independent Television Companies Association

ITDG Intermediate Technology Development Group

ITE Institution of Electrical and Electronics Technician Engineers

ITEM Independent Treasury Economic Model *(group of economists)*

ITF International Transport Federation

ITMA Institute of Trade Mark Agents

ITN Independent Television News

ITO International Trade Organisation

ITP Independent Television Publishers

ITR Industrial Tribunal Reports

ITSA Institute of Trading Standards Association

ITTA Independent Taxation with Transferable Allowance

ITU International Telecommunications Union *(UN, q.v.)*

ITV Independent Television

ITY Information Technology Year *(1982)*

IUA International Union of Architects

IUB International Union of Biochemistry

IUBS International Union of Biological Sciences *(FAO, q.v.)*

IUC Inter-University Council *(for Higher Education Overseas)*

IUCE International Union of Cinematograph Exhibitors

IUCN International Union for the Conservation of Nature and Natural Resources *(see also CITES)*

IUCW International Union for Child Welfare

IUD Inter-Uterine Device *(contraceptive)*

IUEF International University Exchange Fund

IUFO International Union of Family Organisations

IUFRO International Union of Forestry Organisations

IUP Association of Independent Unionist Peers

IUPAC International Union of Pure and Applied Chemistry

IUPAP International Union of Pure and Applied Physics

IUPS International Union of Physiological Sciences

IUTEP International Urban Technology Exchange Programme

IV 4 *(Roman numeral)*

IVS International Voluntary Service

IW Isle of Wight

IWA Inland Waterways Association; Indian Workers' Association

IWandD Inland Waterways and Docks

IWC International Whaling Commission; International Wheat Council

IWES Institution of Water Engineers

IWGC Imperial War Graves Commission

IWM Institution of Works' Managers

IWN International Women's News

IWO International Vine and Wine Office *(FAO, q.v., see also OIV)*

IWS Industrial Welfare Society

IWSOM Institute of Practitioners in Work Study, Organisation and Methods

IWSP Institute of Work Study Practitioners

IWW Industrial Workers of the World

IWY International Women's Year *(1975)*

IX 9 *(Roman numeral)*

IY Imperial Yeomanry *(1900-1914)*

IYC International Year of the Child *(1980)*

IYDP International Year of Disabled People *(1981)*

J

J Judge; Justice; Japanese International Motor Vehicle Registration Letter

JA Judge Advocate; Jamaican International Motor Vehicle Registration Letters

JACOPIS Joint Advisory Committee on Pets in Society

JACS Jewish Association of Cultural Societies

JAG Judge Advocate General

JAIL Justice Against Identification Laws

JAL Japan Airline

JAMA Japanese Automobile Manufacturers' Association

Jan January

JANE Journalists Against Nuclear Extermination

Jap Japan/Japanese

JASP Joint Approach to Social Policy *(UN, q.v.)*

JAT *(Yugoslavia)* Jugoslovenski Aero-Transport *(Airline)*

JB John Bull *(typifying an Englishman)*; Junior Boys *(School Department)*

JBG Jewish Board of Guardians

JC Jesus Christ; Justices' Clerk *(Scottish Legal Appointment)*; Jockey Club; Joint Committee; Judiciary Cases *(Scotland)*

JCB Bachelor of Canon Law; These initials are also widely used to describe a big mechanical digger

JCC Joint Consultative Committee *(NHS, q.v.)*; Joint Co-Ordinating Committee

JCD *(Latin)* Juris Canonici Doctor *(Doctor of Canon Law)*

JCL *(Latin)* Juris Canonici Licentiatus *(Licentiate of Canon Law)*

JCO Joint Consultative Organisation

JCP Job Creation Programme

JCR Junior Common Room

JCS Journal of the Chemical Society; Joint Chiefs of Staff; Justices' Clerks' Society

Jct Junction

JCTUA *(Sri Lanka)* Joint Committee for Trade Union Action

JCWI Joint Council for the Welfare of Immigrants

JD Doctor of Jurisprudence

JDipMA Joint Diploma in Management Accounting Services

JET Joint European Torus *(European Community Nuclear Energy Programme)*

JG Junior Girls *(School Department)*; Junior Grade

JHS *(Latin)* Jesus Hominum Salvator *(Jesus, Saviour of Man)*

JI Institute of Journalists

JIA Jewish Israeli Appeal

JIB Joint Industry Board

JIC Joint Intelligence Committee; Joint Industrial Council

JICRAR Joint Industry Committee for Radio Audience Research

JICTAR *(IBA, q.v.)* Joint Industry Committee for Television Advertising Research

JInstE Junior Institution of Engineers

JJ Justices *(Law)*

JLB Jewish Lads' Brigade

JLP Jamaican Labour Party

Jly July

JMB Joint Matriculation Board

JNC Joint Negotiating Committee/Council

JNF Jewish National Fund

Jnr Junior

JOC *(France)* Jeunes Ouvriers Chrétiens *(Young Christian Workers)*

JOCF *(France)* Jeunes Ouvrières Chrétiennes Féminines *(Young Christian Women Workers)*

JP Justice of the Peace; Jet Propulsion

JPA Joint Palestine Appeal *(of Great Britain and Ireland)*

JPB Joint Production Board

JPS Joint Parliamentary Secretary

JPW Japanese Women's Party

Jr Junior

JRC Job Responsibility Council

JSB Joint Stock Bank

JSCC Joint Staff Consultative Committee

JSD *(Bangladesh)* Jatiya Samaytanbrook Dal *(National Socialist Party)*; *(Latin)* Jurum Sciential Doctor *(Doctor of Juristic Science)*

JSSC Joint Shop Stewards Committee

Jt/jt Joint/joint

Jt/Ac Joint Account

JTC Junior Training Corps

JUD *(Latin)* Juris Utruisque Doctor *(Doctor of Canon and Civil Laws)*

Jun June; Junior

Junc Junction

JW Jehovah's Witness

JWC Joint Women's Council *(Isle of Man)*

K

K Kampuchea Airline; *(Latin)* Kalium *(Potassium)*; Kilohm

k See Kr

KADU Kenya African Democratic Union

KAHS Kenya Agricultural & Horticultural Society

KAL Korea Airline

k and b kitchen & bathroom

KANNUP Karachi Nuclear Power Plant

Kans Kansas *(USA State)*

KANU Kenya African National Union

KAR King's African Rifles

KB King's Bench *(Division of the High Court)*; King's Bench *(Law Reports)*; Knight of the Bath *(before 1815, now KCB, q.v.)*

KBE Knight Commander of the Order of the British Empire

KBTG Keep Britain Tidy Group

KBW *(West Germany)* Kommunistischer Bund Westdeutschlands *(Communist Federation)*

KC King's College, London; King's Counsel; Kennel Club *(usually preceded by name of the Club)*

kc/s kilocycle(s) per second

KCB Knight Commander of the Order of the Bath

KCC Commander of the Order of the Crown *(Belgian & Congo Free State)*; Kenya Co-operative Creameries

KCH King's College Hospital; Knight Commander of Hanover

KCHS Knight Commander of the Order of the Holy Sepulchre

KCIA Korean Central Intelligence Agency

KCIE Knight Commander of the Order of the Indian Empire

KCL King's College London

KCMG Knight Commander of the Order of St. Michael & St. George

KCNA Korean Official News Agency

KCSI Knight Commander of the Star of India

KCVO Knight Commander of the Royal Victorian Order

KD/Kd Kuwait Dinar *(Monetary unit of Kuwait)*

KDG King's Dragoon Guards

KDPI *(Iraq)* Kurdish Democratic Party

KFA Kenya Farmers' Association

KG Knight of the Order of the Garter

KGB *(USSR)* Komitet Gossudarstvennoi Bezopastnosti *(Committee of State Security – secret police)*

KH Knight of Hanover

KHC Honorary Chaplain to the King

KHDS Honorary Dental Surgeon to the King

KHNS Honorary Nursing Sister to the King

KHP Honorary Physician to the King

KHS Honorary Surgeon to the King; Knight of the Holy Sepulchre

KHz Kilohertz

Kilo Kilogram

KKE *(Greece)* Kommunistiko Komma Ellados *(Communist Party)*

KKK *(USA)* Ku-Klux-Klan *(secret association)*

KLM *(Netherlands)* Koninklijke Luchtvaart Maatschappij *(Royal Dutch Airline)*

KM Knight of Malta

km kilometre

KNCW Korean National Council of Women

KNP Korea National Party

KO Knock Out; Kick-off

KOMSOMOL *(USSR)* Kommunistichestei Soyuz Mologozhei *(Communist Youth League)*

KOR *(Poland)* Komitet Obrony Robotnikow *(Committee for the Defence of Workers ... banned organisation)*; The Koran; Korea; Type of Russian submarine

KOROC Keep-Out-of-Reach-Of-Children

KORR King's Own Royal Regiment

KOSB King's Own Scottish Borderers

KOYLI King's Own Yorkshire Light Infantry

KP Knight of the Order of St. Patrick

KPM King's Police Medal

KPN *(Poland)* Komitet Polski Niezaleznej *(Committee for Independent Poland ... banned organisation, hostile to USSR)*

KPNLF Khmer People's National Liberation Front; Kampuchea Catholic Pax Faction

KPU Kenya Political Party

Kr Krone *(Monetary unit of Denmark, Norway and Sweden)*; Krypton

KRC Knight of the Red Cross

KRR King's Royal Rifles

KRRC King's Royal Rifle Corps

KRS Kinematograph Reters' Society *(Now SFD, q.v.)*

KS King's Scholar

KSG Knight of St. Gregory

KSLI King's Shropshire Light Infantry

KStJ Knight of the Order of St. John of the Hospital of Jerusalem

KT Knight of the Order of the Thistle; Knight Templar

Kt Knight

KTA *(West Germany)* Kertechnischer Ausschuss *(Nuclear Technical Commission)*; Netherlands Cable Television Network

KTU Kidney Transplant Unit *(NHS, q.v.)*
kV/kv kilovolt
kW/kw kilowatt
kWh/kwh kilowatt hours
KWOC Key Word Out Of Context
KWT Kuwaiti International Motor Vehicle Registration Letters

KY Kentucky *(USA State)*; *(Israel)* Kol Yisroel *(Israeli Broadcasting Service)*
KY/Ky Kyat *(Monetary unit of Burma)*
KYP *(Greece)* Kendriki Iperisia Pliroforion *(Central Intelligence Organisation)*
Kz Konzentrationslager *(Concentration Camp - Nazi)*

L

L Learner driver; Liberal *(political)*; Licentiate; Lake; Lira *(Monetary unit of Italy)*; *(Latin)* Libra *(pound)*; 50 *(Roman numeral)*; Luxembourg International Motor Vehicle Registration Letter
l litre; left
LA Law Agent; Legislative Assembly; Library Association; Los Angeles; Local Association; Licensing Act; Literate in Arts; Liverpool Academy
La Louisiana *(USA State)*; Lanthanum
LAA Library Association of Australia
LAAI Licentiate of the Institute of Administrative Accounting and Data Processing
LAANC Local Authorities Aircraft Noise Council
LAB London Association for the Blind
Lab Labour *(political)*
LAC Leading Aircraftsman; London Athletic Club; London Advisory Committee *(broadcasting)*; Licentiate of Apothecaries
LACE London Association for Continuing Education; London Association for Community Education
LACES London Airport Cargo Scheme
LACW Leading Aircraftswoman *(in WRAF, q.v.)*
LADA *(Argentina)* Líneas Aéreas Domésticas *(domestic airline)*
LAFTA Latin American Free Trade Association
LAG Legal Action Group
LAGER Liberal *(Party)* Action Group for Electoral Reform
LAH (Dublin) Licentiate of the Apothecaries' Hall (Dublin)
LAI *(Italy)* Linie Aera Italia *(airline)*
LAIR Animal Welfare Organisation
LAMDA London Academy of Music and Dramatic Art
LAMPS London Area Mobile Physiotherapy Service
LAMRTPI Legal Associate Member of the Royal Town Planning Institute
Lancs Lancashire
LAO Licentiate in Obstetrics; Laos

International Motor Vehicle Registration Letters
LAP Labour Action for Peace
LAPADA London and Provincial Antique Dealers' Association
LAR Libyan Arab Republic; Libyan International Motor Vehicle Registration Letters
LARC Labour Abortion Rights Campaign
LArts Licentiate in Arts
LAS Lord Advocate of Scotland; Land Agents' Society; League of Arab States
LASDA Liberal and Social Democrat Alliance/Social Democrat and Liberal Alliance
LASER Light Amplification by Stimulated Emission of Radiation *(light beams, see also MASER)*
LASH Lighter Aboard Ship
LASI Licentiate of the Ambulance Service Institute
Lat Latitude; Latin
LATA London Amenity & Transport Association
LAW Light Anti-tank Weapon
LB Liberian International Motor Vehicle Registration Letters
lb pound *(weight)*
LBA London Boroughs Association; Local Broadcasting Authority *(recommended by the Annan Committee)*
LBC London Broadcasting Company
LBEI Licentiate of the Institution of Body Engineers
LBID Licentiate of the British Institute of Interior Design
LBIST Licentiate of the British Institute of Surgical Technologists
LBS London Business School
LBSC Licentiate of the British Society of Commerce
LBW Low Birth Weight
lbw leg before wicket *(cricket)*
LC Lord Chancellor; *(USA)* Library of Congress
LCC London County Council *(now GLC, q.v.)*; London Chamber of Com-

merce; Labour Co-ordinating Committee

LCCI London Chamber of Commerce and Industry

LCD Lord Chancellor's Department; London College of Divinity; Liquid Crystal Display *(mathematics)*

lcd lowest common denominator

LCEA Licentiate of the Association of Cost and Executive Accountants

LCh Licentiate in Surgery; Licentiate in Chiropody

LCIOB Licentiate of the Chartered Institute of Building

LCJ Lord Chief Justice

LCL Licentiate of Canon Law

LCM London College of Music

lcm lowest common multiple

LCMSC London Common Market Safeguards Committee

LCO Landing Control Officer *(aviation)*

LCol Lieutenant Colonel

LCP Licentiate of the College of Preceptors

LCPC London Co-operative Political Centre

L/Cpl Lance-Corporal

LCR Landing Craft, Rubber; Logarithmic Correlators Radiometer

LCSI Licentiate of the Construction Surveyors' Institute

LCSS London Council of Social Services

LCST Licentiate of the College of Speech Therapists

LCWIO Liaison Committee of Women's International Organisations

LCY *(Yugoslavia)* League of Communists

LD Lethal Dose

Ld Lord

LDB *(Yemen)* Local Development Board

LDC London Diocesan Council

LDCs Least Developed Countries *(UN, q.v.)*

LDDC London Docks Development Corporation

LD50 Median Lethal Dose

Ldg Leading

LDiv Licentiate in Divinity

LDL Low Density Lipoproteins

LDP *(Japan)* Liberal Democratic Party

LDS Licentiate in Dental Surgery

LDSRCPSGlas Licentiate in Dental Surgery of the Royal College of Physicians and Surgeons, Glasgow

LDSRCSEd Licentiate in Dental Surgery of the Royal College of Surgeons of Edinburgh

LDSRCSEng Licentiate in Dental Surgery of the Royal College of Surgeons in England

LDSRCSIrel Licentiate in Dental Surgery of the Royal College of Surgeons of Ireland

LDT Land Development Tax

LDV Local Defence Volunteers (2nd

World War, *subsequently the HG, q.v.)*

LEA Local Education Authority

LEAA *(USA)* Law Enforcement Assistance Administration

LEAP Life Education for the Autistic Person

LEB London Electricity Board

LECC London Electricity Consultative Council

LECHRA Department of the Environment's Housing Subsidy Computer

Lect Lecture; Lecturer

LED Light Emitting Diode

LEG Liberal Ecology Group

leg *(music)* legato *(bind notes smoothly)*

Leics Leicestershire

LEM Lunar Excursion Module

Lem Lempira *(Monetary unit of Honduras)*

len *(music)* lento *(slow, but not so slow as previously)*

LENTA National Enterprise Agency

LEPRA Leprosy Relief Association

L ès L *(France)* Licencié ès Lettres *(Licentiate in Letters)*

L ès Sc *(France)* Licencié ès Sciences *(Licentiate in Science)*

LEV Lunar Excursion Vehicle; Leyland Experimental Vehicle

LF Low Frequency; Lancashire Fusiliers

LFA Less Favoured Area *(EEC, q.v.)*

LFB London Fire Brigade

LFCS Licentiate of the Faculty of Secretaries

LFS Licentiate of the Faculty of Architects and Surveyors; Labour Force Survey

LFSC Librarians For Social Change

LGB Local Government Board

L-Gen Lieutenant-General

LGORU Local Government Operational Research Unit

LGSM Licentiate of the Guildhall School of Music and Drama

LGU Ladies Golf Union

LH Legion of Honour; Left Hand; Leading Hand *(RN, q.v.)*

LHA Licentiate of the Institute of Health Service Administrators; Local Health Authority

LHAG London Health Advisory Group

LHCIMA Licentiate of the Hotel, Catering and Institutional Management Association

LHD *(Latin)* Literarum Humaniorum Doctor *(Doctor of Literature)*

lhd left hand drive

LHE Licentiate in Ecclesiastical History

LHG Licentiate of the Institute of Heraldic and Genealogical Studies

LHMC London Hospital Medical College

LHS Left Hand Side

LI Light Infantry; *(USA)* Long Island; 51 *(Roman numeral)*

Li Lithium

Lib Liberal *(political)*

LIBD Licentiate of the Incorporated Institute of British Decorators and Interior Decorators

LIBOR London Interbank Offered Rate *(lending rate between banks)*

LIC London Industrial Centre

LicAc Licentiate of Acupuncture

LicBAA Licentiate of the British Association of Accountants and Auditors

LICC League for the Introduction of Canine Controls

LICeram Licentiate of the Institute of Ceramics

LicMed Licentiate in Medicine

LICW Licentiate of the Institute of Clerks of Works

Lieut Lieutenant

LIFE Anti-abortion group

LIFFE London International Financial Futures Exchange

LIFO Last In First Out

LIFT London International Festival Theatre

LIHM Licentiate of the Institute of Housing Managers

LIKUD *(Israel)* Right-wing Political Party

LIMA Licentiate of the Institute of Mathematics and its Applications

LIMF Licentiate of the Institute of Metal Finishing

Lincs Lincolnshire

LInstBB Licentiate of the Institute of British Bakers

LInstBCA Licentiate of the Institute of Burial and Cremation Administration

LInstPRA Licentiate of the Institute of Park and Recreation Administration

LIR Licentiate of the Institute of Population Registration

LISTD Licentiate of the Imperial Society of Teachers of Dancing

LIT Local Income Tax *(proposal as substitute for rates)*

LitD/LittD *(Latin)* Literarum/Litterarum Doctor *(Doctor of Literature/Doctor of Letters)*

Lit Hum *(Latin)* Literae Humaniores *(Classics)*

LIX 59 *(Roman numeral)*

LJ Lord Justice

LJJ Lords Justices

LJW League of Jewish Women

LLA Lesotho Liberation Army; Lady Literate in Arts *(Scottish University Degree)*

LLAM Licentiate of the London Academy of Music and Dramatic Art

LLB Bachelor of Laws

LLCM Licentiate of the London College of Music

LLCM(TD) Licentiate of the London College of Music (Teachers' Diploma)

LLD *(Latin)* Legum Doctor *(Doctor of Laws)*

LLI Licence in Laws

LLM Master of Laws

LLMRCPIrel}
LLMRCSIrel} Conjoint Diplomas of Licentiate and Licentiate in Midwifery, the Royal College of Physicians and of Surgeons of Ireland

LM Licentiate in Midwifery; *(music)* Long Metre

LMC Local Medical Committee *(NHS, q.v.)*

LMCC Licentiate of the Medical Council of Canada

LME London Metal Exchange

LMR London Midland Region

LMRSH Licentiate Member of the Royal Society of Health

LMRTPI Legal Member of the Royal Town Planning Institute

LMS London Missionary Society; London Midland and Scottish *(Railway)*

LMSSALond Licentiate in Medicine, Surgery and Midwifery of the Society of Apothecaries of London

LMusLCM Licentiate in Music of the London College of Music

LMusTCL Licentiate in Music, Trinity College of Music, London

LNAT Liberal National

LNCRT Licentiate of the National College of Rubber Technology

LNCW Lesotho NCW, *q.v.*

LNFWO Liberian National Federation of Women's Organisations

LNHS London Natural History Society

LO Liaison Officer; *(Sweden and Denmark)* Landsorganisationen *(Trade Unions Confederation)*

LOA Leave of Absence

LOAs Local Overseas Allowances *(BAOR, q.v.)*

LOB Location of Offices Bureau

LOCB London Orchestral Concerts Board

L of C Lines of Communication

log logarithm

long longitude

LONTA Intermediate Technology Voluntary Development Agency *(UN, q.v.)*

loq *(Latin)* loquitur *(he/she speaks)*

LORAN Long Range Navigational Aids

LOX Liquid Oxygen

LP Labour Party *(political)*; Lord Provost; Long-Playing Record

LPA Loyalist Prisoners' Association *(Northern Ireland Political Prisoners)*

LPC Lord President of the Council; Less Prosperous Country *(EEC, q.v.)*

LPG Liquid Petroleum Gas

LPM Leading Patrolman *(RN, q.v.)*

LPO London Philharmonic Orchestra

L'pool Liverpool

LPRI Licentiate of the Plastics and Rubber Institute

LPS Lord Privy Seal

LPU Low Pay Unit

LPYS Labour Party Young Socialists

LR Lloyds Register; Leading Rate/Rating *(RN, q.v.)*; Leading Regulator *(RN, q.v.)*

Lr Lawrencium

lr lira *(Monetary unit of Italy)*

LRAD Licentiate of the Royal Academy of Dancing

LRAM Licentiate of the Royal Academy of Music

LRBM Long Range Ballistic Missile

LRC Labour Representation Committee

LRCC London Rape Crisis Centre

LRCM Licentiate of the Royal College of Music

LRCP Licentiate of the Royal College of Physicians

LRCPEdin Licentiate of the Royal College of Physicians, Edinburgh

LRCPI Licentiate of the Royal College of Physicians, Ireland

LRCP/MRCS Eng Licentiate of the Royal College of Physicians/Member of the Royal College of Surgeons, England

LRCPSGlasg Licentiate of the Royal College of Physicians and Surgeons of Glasgow

LRCS Licentiate of the Royal College of Surgeons; League of Red Cross Societies *(including Crescent, Lion and Sun)*

LRCSEdin Licentiate of the Royal College of Surgeons Edinburgh

LRCSI Licentiate of the Royal College of Surgeons, Ireland

LRCVS Licentiate of the Royal College of Veterinary Surgeons

LRD Labour Research Department

LRIBA Licentiate of the Royal Institute of British Architects

LRPS Licentiate of the Royal Photographic Society

LRS Lloyds Register of Shipping

LRSC Licentiate of the Royal Society of Chemistry

LRSM Licentiate of the Royal Schools of Music

LS Law Society; Leading Seaman; Loud Speaker *(sound amplifier)*; Lesotho International Motor Vehicle Registration Letters

ls left side

LSA Licentiate of the Society of Apothecaries

LSC London Salvage Corps *(Fire)*

LSc Licence in Science

LSc(Econ) Licence in Science (Economics)

LSCP(Assoc) Associate of the London and Counties Society of Physiologists

LSD Lysergic Acid Diethylmide *(hallucination drug)*; Labour Saving Devices; Lightermen, Stevedores, Dockers; Pounds, Shillings, Pence *(obsolete)*

LSE London School of Economics; London Stock Exchange

LSHTM London School of Hygiene & Tropical Medicine

LSIA Licentiate of the Society of Industrial Artists and Designers

LSNSW Linnean Society of New South Wales

LSO London Symphony Orchestra

LSPGA London School of Printing & Graphic Arts

LSSP *(Sri Lanka)* Leftist Sama Samaj Party

LT Licentiate in Teaching; London Transport

Lt Lieutenant

LTA Lawn Tennis Association; London Teachers' Association

LTB London Transport Board *(now LTE, q.v.)*

LTC Lawn Tennis Club; Loving Tender Care

LTCL Licentiate of Trinity College of Music London

LtCol Lieutenant Colonel

LtComdr Lieutenant Commander

Ltd Limited

LTE London Transport Executive

LtGen Lieutenant General

LTH London Teaching Hospitals *(NHS, q.v.)*

LTh Licentiate in Theology

LTI Licentiate of the Textile Institute

Lt.Inf Light Infantry

LtRN Lieutenant Royal Navy

LTSC Licentiate in the Technology of Surface Coatings

LU Liberal Unionst *(political)*

Lu Lutetium

LUA Liverpool Underwriters' Association *(marine insurance)*

LUAR *(Portugal)* Liga Unida de Accão Revolucionária *(League of Unity for Revolutionary Action)*

LUOTC London University Officers' Training Corps

Lux Luxemburg

LUYC London Union of Youth Clubs

LV 55 *(Roman numeral)*; Luncheon Voucher; Licensed Victualler

LVNDL Licensed Victuallers' National Defence League

LW Low Water; Long Wave

LWCMD Licentiate of the Welsh College of Music and Drama

LWF Lutheran World Federation

LWR Light Water Reactor

LWT London Weekend Television

LX 60 *(Roman numeral)*

LXV 65 *(Roman numeral)*

M

M   *(Followed by a number)* Motorway; Member; 1000 *(Roman numeral)*; Malta International Motor Vehicle Registration Letter; Monsieur *(Mr.)*; Megohm

M̄   One million *(Roman numeral)*

m   male; metre; million; married; *(music)* mezzo *(half)*

M1   Money Supply Monitoring *(notes and coins in circulation, including sight deposits)*

M3   As M1 above, but including private and public deposits and foreign currency deposits

MA   Master of Arts; Magistrates' Association; Military Academy; Maternity Alliance; Maternity Allowance; Morocco International Motor Vehicle Registration Letters; Medical Attendant

mA   milliampere

MA(Architectural Studies)   Master of Arts (Architectural Studies)

MA(Econ)   Master of Arts in Economic and Social Studies

MA(ECS)   Master of Arts (European Community Studies)

MA(Ed)   Master of Arts in Education

MA(LD)   Master of Arts (Landscape Design)

MA(Mus)   Master of Arts (Music)

MA(RCA)   Master of Arts (Royal College of Art)

MA(Theol)   Master of Arts in Theology

MA(UrbDes)   Master of Arts in Urban Design

MAA   Master-At-Arms *(Navy)*; Motor Agents Association; Microlight Aircrafts Association; Manufacturers' Agents Association

MAAM   Movement Against A Monarchy

MAAS   Member of the American Academy of Arts and Sciences

MAB   Metropolitan Asylums Board; Man and the Biosphere *(UNESCO, q.v. Programme)*

MAC   Medical Advisory Committee *(NHS, q.v.)*; Martial Arts Commission; *(Wales)* Mudiad Amddiffyn Cymru *(Movement for the Defence of Wales)*; Multipoint Analogue Component *(satellite television transmission)*

MACA   Mental After Care Association

MAcA   Member of the Acupuncture Association

MAcc   Master of Accountancy

MACE   Member of the Association of Conference Executives; Member of the Australian College of Education

MACS   Member of the American Chemical Society

MAD   Mutually Assured Destruction *(nuclear armament countries)*; Management and Administration Department *(of the Court of Protection)*; *(West Germany)* Militärischer Abschirm Dienst *(Military Counter-Intelligence)*

MADD   *(USA)* Mothers Against Drunk Drivers

MAEE   Marine Aircraft Experimental Establishment

MAFF   Minister of Agriculture, Fisheries & Food; Member of Food Additives and Contaminants Committee

MAG   Migrants' Action Group

Mag   Magazine; Magneto

MAgr   Master of Agriculture

MAgrSc   Master of Agricultural Science

MAHE   Member of the Association of Home Economists

MAI   *(Latin)* Magister in Arte Ingeniaria *(Master of Engineering)*

MAIAA   Member of the American Institute of Aeronautics and Astronautics

MAIAC   *(Spain)* Movement for the Autonomy and Independence of the Canary Archipelago

MAICE   Member of the American Institute of Consulting Engineers

MAIChE   Member of the American Institute of Chemical Engineers

MAIE   Member of the British Association of Industrial Editors

Maj   Major

Maj Gen   Major General

MAL   Malaysian International Motor Vehicle Registration Letters

MAM   Medical Association of Malta

MAMA   Meet-A-Mum-Association

MAMS   Member of the Association of Medical Secretaries, Practice Administrators and Receptionists

MAMSPAR   Member of the Association of Medical Secretaries, Practice Administrators and Receptionists

Man   Manitoba *(Canada)*

MAO   Master of Obstetrics

MAOT   Member of the Association of Occupational Therapists

MAP   Medical Aid Post; Ministry of

Aircraft Production; Microprocessor Application Project; Moroccan News Agency

MAppSci Master of Applied Science

Mar March

marc *(music)* marcato *(with emphasis)*

MArch Master of Architecture

Marq Marquis; Marquess

MARS *(USA/California)* Manned Astronautical Research Station

MAS Malaysian Airline System

MASAE Member of the American Society of Agricultural Engineering

MASAW Manx Association of Scientists Artists and Writers

Masc Masculine

MASCE Member of the American Society of Civil Engineers

MASEE Member of the Association of Supervising and Executive Engineers

MASER Microwave Amplification by Stimulated Emission of Radiation *(see also LASER)*

MASH/M★A★S★H Military Advanced Service Hospital; Mobile Army Surgical Hospital

MASME Member of the American Society of Mechanical Engineers

Mass Massachusetts *(USA State)*

MATCH Mothers Apart From Their Children

Math Mathematics; Mathematical

Mats Matinees

MATSA Management Administrative Technical and Supervisory Association

Max Maximum

MB Bachelor of Medicine; Medical Board

mb millibar

MBA Master of Business Administration *(degree of INSEAD, q.v.)*; Member of the British Arts Association

MBAE Member of the British Association of Electrolysis

MBAOT Member of the British Association of Occupational Therapists

MBASW Member of the British Association of Social Workers

MBBCh Bachelor of Medicine, Bachelor of Surgery

MBBChir(Cam) Bachelor of Medicine, Bachelor of Surgery, University of Cambridge

MBBS Bachelor of Medicine, Bachelor of Surgery

MBC Metropolitan Borough Council

MBChB Bachelor of Medicine, Bachelor of Surgery

MBCO Member of the British College of Ophthalmic Opticians

MBCS Member of the British Computer Society

MBE Member of the Order of the British Empire

MBEI Member of the Institution of Body Engineers

MBES Member of the Bureau of Engineer Surveyors

MBF Musicians' Benevolent Fund

MBFR Mutual Balanced Force Reductions *(NATO, q.v.)*

MBHA Member of the British Hypnotherapy Association

MBHI Member of the British Horological Institute

MBID Member of the British Institute of Interior Design

MBIE Member of the British Institute of Embalmers

MBIM Member of the British Institute of Management

MBKS Member of the British Kinematograph Sound and Television Society

MBNOA Member of the British Naturopathic and Osteopathic Association

MBOU Member of the British Ornithologists' Union

MBS *(USA)* Mutual Broadcasting System

MBSc Master in Business Science

MBSSG Master Glassblower, British Society of Scientific Glassblowers

MBT Member of the Association of Beauty Teachers

MC Military Cross; Master of Ceremonies; Medical Corps; *(USA)* Member of Congress; 1100 *(Roman numeral)*; Monaco International Motor Vehicle Registration Letters

Mc/s Megacycles per second

MCA Monetary Compensation Accounts *(EEC, q.v.)*; Medical Council on Alcoholism; Middle Class Association *(British Conservative Group)*

MCAM Member of the CAM, *q.v.*, Foundation

MCB Master in Clinical Biochemistry

mcb miniature circuit breaker *(electricity)*

MCBA Member of the Certified Bailiffs Association

MCC Marylebone Cricket Club *(ruling body of English cricket)*; *(USA)* Mennonite Central Committee; 1200 *(Roman numeral)*

MCCC 1300 *(Roman numeral)*

MCD Doctor of Comparative Medicine; Master of Civic Design

MCDH Master of Community Dental Health

MCCEd Member of the College of Craft Education

MCCEdHons Member with Honours of the College of Craft Education

MCF Fluorescent Tube *(electric light)*

MCH Maternal and Child Welfare

MCh Master of Surgery

MChD Master of Dental Surgery

MChE Master of Chemical Engineering

MChir Master of Surgery

MChOrth Master of Orthopaedic Surgery

MChS Member of the Society of Chiropodists

MCIBS Member of the Chartered Institution of Building Services

MCIOB Member of the Chartered Institute of Building

MCIT Member of the Chartered Institute of Transport

MCL Master of Civil Law

MCM 1900 *(Roman numeral)*

MCMA Milk Carton Manufacturers' Association

MCMES Member of the Civil and Mechanical Engineers' Society

MCMV Mine Counter and Measure Vessels

MCom Master of Commerce

MCommH Master of Community Health

MConsE Member of the Association of Consulting Engineers

MCP Member of the College of Preceptors; *(USA)* Master of City Planning; Male Chauvinist Pig

MCPA *(Australia)* Master of the College of Pathologists

MCPS Member of the College of Physicians and Surgeons; Mechanical Copyright Protection Society

MCR Mass Communications Research

MCS Missile Control System

MCSEE Member of the Canadian Society of Electrical Engineers

MCSI Member of the Construction Surveyors' Institute

MCSP Member of the Chartered Society of Physiotherapy

MCST Member of the College of Speech Therapists

MD Doctor of Medicine; Managing Director; Mentally Deficient; 1500 *(Roman numeral)*

Md Maryland *(USA State)*; Mendelevium

MDB *(Brazil)* Movimento Democratico Brasileiro *(Democratic Movement)*

MDC 1600 *(Roman numeral)*

MDCC 1700 *(Roman numeral)*

MDCCC 1800 *(Roman numeral)*

MDes(RCA) Master of Design (Royal College of Arts)

MDP *(Brazil)* Movimento Democratico Popular *(Popular Democratic Movement)*

MDP/CDE *(Portugal)* Movimento Democrático Português/Convergência Democrática Electoral *(Portuguese Democratic Movement/Electoral Democratic Convergence)*

MDS Master of Dental Surgery

MDSc Master of Dental Science

MDSF Mission for Deep Sea Fishermen

ME Mining Engineer; Marine Engineer; Mechanical Engineer

Me Maine *(USA State)*; Methyl

MEA Member of the European Assembly; Middle East Airlines/Lebanese Airlines

MEC Member of the Executive Council; Medical Executive Committee *(NHS, q.v.)*

MECAS Middle East Centre for Arab Studies

MECC Middle East Council of Churches

mech mechanics; mechanical

MECI Member of the Institute of Employment Consultants

MECILic Licentiate Member of the Institute of Employment Consultants

MEd Master of Education

med medium; medical

MEd(EdPsych) Master of Education (Educational Psychology)

MEdPsych Master of Educational Psychology

MEdStud Master of Educational Studies

MEES Middle East Economic Survey *(Cyprus-based)*

MEF Middle East Force

MEGS Market Entry Guarantee Scheme *(Board of Trade)*

MEIC Member of the Engineering Institute of Canada

Mem Member

Memo Memorandum

MENA Middle East News Agency

MENCAP National Society for Mentally Handicapped Children and Adults

MEND Member of EQUITY *(q.v.)* for Nuclear Disarmament

MEng Master of Engineering

MEP Member of the European Parliament *(see also EMP)*; Microelectronics in Education Programme

MERB Mechanical Engineering Research Board *(of SSIR, q.v.)*

MES *(Portugal)* Movimento da Esquerda Socialista *(Socialist Leftist Movement)*

M ès A *(France)* Maître ès Arts *(Master of Arts)*

MESAN Mouvement d'Evolution Sociale en Afrique Noire *(Movement for the Social Evolution of Black Africa)*

Met Meteorological; Metropolitan

M-et-M Meurthe-et-Moselle *(Department of France)*

MetSoc Metals Society

METU Middle East Technical University

MEX Mexican International Motor Vehicle Registration Letters

Mex Mexico; Mexican

mez *(music)* mezzo *(half, medium)*

MF Medium Frequency

mf *(music)* mezzo forte *(fairly loud)*

MFA Master of Fine Art; *(Portugal)* Movimento das Forças Armadas *(Armed Forces Movement)*

MFC Mastership in Food Control; *(USA-*

Israeli) Tanker-owning group
MFCM Member of the Faculty of Community Medicine
MFCS Missile Fire Control System
MFDO Member of the Faculty of Dispensing Opticians
MFGB Miners' Federation of Great Britain
MFH Master of the Foxhounds
MFHom Member of the Faculty of Homeopathy
MFOM Member of the Faculty of Occupational Medicine
MFP Monofluorphosphate
MFPA Mouth and Foot Painting Artists
MFTCom Member of the Faculty of Teachers in Commerce
MG Machine Gun; Myasthenia Gravis *(rare muscle disease)*
Mg Magnesium
mg milligram
MGA Major-General in charge of Administration
MGB Motor Gun Boat
MGC Machine Gun Corps
MGDSRCSEng Membership in General Dental Surgery, Royal College of Surgeons England
MGGS Major-General General Staff
MGI Member of the Institute of Certificated Grocers
MGP Managerial, Professional and Staff Liaison Group
Mgr Monsignor
MH Master of the Horse; Military Hospital; Master of Hounds; Malignant Hyperexia
mH millihenry
MHA Methodist Homes for the Aged; Member of the House of Assembly
MHC Mentally Handicapped Children
MHCIMA Member of the Hotel, Catering and Institutional Management Association
MHD Magnetohydrodynamic *(electricity generating system)*
MHF Medium High Frequency
MHK Member of the House of Keys *(Manx)*
MHR *(USA)* Member of the House of Representatives
MHRA Member of the Humanities Research Association
MHRF Mental Health Research Fund
MHTTA Member of the Highway and Traffic Technicians' Association
MHZ Megahertz
MI Military Intelligence
MI5/Mi5 Military Intelligence Department
MI6 Secret Intelligence Service *(see also SIS)*
MI9 *(Colombia)* Marxist-Leninist Guerrilla Group
MIAA Member of the Institute of Automobile Assessors; Member of the Incorporated Association of Architects and Surveyors *(Architects)*
MIAE Member of the Institution of Automobile Engineers
MIAeE Member of the Institute of Aeronautical Engineers
MIAgrE Member of the Institution of Agricultural Engineers
MIAM Member of the Institute of Advanced Motorists
MIArb Member of the Institute of Arbitrators
MIAS Member of the Incorporated Association of Architects and Surveyors *(Surveyors)*
MIAT Member of the Institute of Asphalt Technology
MIBCO Member of the Institution of Building Control Officers
MIBE Member of the Institution of British Engineers
MIBF Member of the Institute of British Foundrymen
MIBiol Member of the Institute of Biology
MIBritE Member of the Institution of British Engineers.
MIBS Member of the Institute of Bankers in Scotland
MIC Mountain Instructor's Certificate
MICE Member of the Institution of Civil Engineers
MICEI Member of the Institution of Civil Engineers of Ireland
Mich Michigan *(USA State)*
MIChemE Member of the Institution of Chemical Engineers
MICM Associate Member of the Institute of Credit Management
MICO Member of the Institute of Careers Officers
MICorrT Member of the Institution of Corrosion Science and Technology
MICR Magnetic Ink Character Reader *(Computer Terminology)*
MICW Member of the Institute of Clerks of Works of Great Britain Incorporated
MID Mediation in Divorce
Mid Midshipman
MIDAS Missile Defence Alarm System
Middx Middlesex
MIDTA Member of the International Dance Teachers' Association
MIEAust Member of the Institution of Engineers, Australia
MIED Member of the Institution of Engineering Designers
MIEE Member of the Institution of Electrical Engineers
MIEEE *(USA)* Member of the Institution of Electrical & Electronic Engineers
MIEI Member of the Institution of Engineering Inspection

MIE(Ind) Member of the Institution of Engineers, India

MIEM Master Member of the Institute of Executives and Managers

MIERE Member of the Institution of Electronic & Radio Engineers

MIES Member of the Institution of Engineers & Shipbuilders, Scotland

MIEx Member of the Institute of Export

MIExE Member of the Institute of Executive Engineers and Officers

MIExpE Member of the Institute of Explosives Engineers

MIFED *(Italy)* International Television and Documentary Market

MIFF Member of the Institute of Freight Forwarders

MIFireE Member of the Institution of Fire Engineers

MIGasE Member of the Institution of Gas Engineers

MIGD Member of the Institute of Grocery Distribution

MIGeol Member of the Institute of Geologists

MIH Member of the Institute of Housing; Member of the Institute of Hygiene

MIHE Member of the Institute of Health Education; Member of the Institution of Highway Engineers

MIIE Member of the Institution of Industrial Engineers

MIIM Member of the Institution of Industrial Managers

MIInfSc Member of the Institute of Information Scientists

MIISE Member of the International Institute of Social Economics

MIISec Member of the Institute of Industrial Security

MIL Member of the Institute of Linguists

Mil Military

mil/ml millilitre

MILGA Member of the Institute of Local Government Administrators

MILocoE Member of the Institution of Locomotive Engineers

MIM Member of the Institution of Metallurgists

MIManf Member of the Institute of Manufacturing

MIMarE Member of the Institute of Marine Engineers

MIMC Member of the Institute of Management Consultants

MIMechE Member of the Institution of Mechnical Engineers

MIMF Member of the Institute of Metal Finishing

MIMGTechE Member of the Institution of Mechanical and General Technician Engineers

MIMH Member of the Institute of Materials Handling

MIMI Member of the Institute of the Motor Industry

MIMinE Member of the Institution of Mining Engineers

MIMIT Member of the Institute of Municipal Instrument Technology

MIMM Member of the Institution of Mining and Metallurgy; Member of the Institute of Male Masseurs

MIMS Member of the Institute of Management Specialists

MIMunE Member of the Institution of Municipal Engineers

MIN Member of the Institute of Navigation

Min Ministry

min minute; minimum

MIND National Association for Mental Health

MINIS Management Information System for Ministers *(Government)*

Minn Minnesota *(USA State)*

MINOS Mine Operating System *(microcomputer)*

MInstAM(Dip) Member of the Institute of Administrative Management

MInstBB Member of the Institute of British Bakers

MInstBCA Member of the Institute of Burial and Cremation Administration

MInstBE Member of the Institution of British Engineers

MInstBRM Member of the Institute of Baths and Recreation Management

MInstBRMDip Diploma Member of the Institute of Baths and Recreation Management

MInstCM Member of the Institute of Commercial Management

MInstD Member of the Institute of Directors

MInstE Member of the Institute of Energy

MInstF Member of the Institute of Fuel

MInstFF Member of the Institute of Freight Forwarders

MInstHE Member of the Institution of Highway Engineers

MInstM Member of the Institute of Marketing

MInstMC Member of the Institute of Measurement and Control

MInstMO Member of the Institute of Market Officers

MInstNDT Member of the British Institute of Non-Destructive Testing

MInstP Member of the Institute of Physics

MInstPet Member of the Institute of Petroleum

MInstPkg Member of the Institute of Packaging

MInstPI Member of the Institute of Patentees and Inventors

MInstPS Member of the Institute of Purchasing and Supply

MInstR Member of the Institute of Refrigeration

MInstRM Member of the Institute of Recreation Management

MInstSM Member of the Institute of Sales Management

MInstSP Member of the Institute of Sales Promotion

MInstSWM Member of the Institute of Solid Wastes Management

MInstT Member of the Institute of Technology *(see also MIT)*

MInstTA Member of the Institute of Traffic Administration

MInstWHS Member of the Institute of Works and Highways Superintendents

MInstWPC Member of the Institution of Water Pollution Control

M-INTEL Manpower Intelligence

MINucE Member of the Institution of Nuclear Engineers

MIOA Maternity and Infant Care Association

MIOD Member of the Institute of Directors

MIO(E) Ministerial Information Officers *(Government)*

MIOP Member of the Institute of Printing

MIP Member of the Institute of Plumbing; Maximum Investment Plan

MIPA Member of the Institute of Practitioners in Advertising

MIPC Member of the Institute of Production Control

MIPHE Member of the Institution of Public Health Engineers

MIPI Member of the Institute of Professional Investigators

MIPlantE Member of the Institution of Plant Engineers

MIPM Member of the Institute of Personnel Management

MIPR Member of the Institute of Public Relations

MIPRE Member of the Incorporated Practitioners in Radio and Electronics

MIProdE Member of the Institution of Production Engineers

MIPTC Men's International Professional Tennis Council

MIPTV *(France)* Marché International des Programmes de Télévision *(Cannes Film Festival)*

MIQ Member of the Institute of Quarrying

MIQA Member of the Institute of Quality Assurance

MIQPS Member of the Institute of Qualified Private Secretaries

MIR Member of the Institute of Population Registration; *(Bolivia and Chile)* Movimiento de la Izquierda Revolucionaria *(Revolutionary Left Movement)*

MIRA Motor Industry Research Association; Member of the Institute of Registered Architects

MIRAS Mortgage Interest Relief at Source

MIREE (Aust) *(Australia)* Member of the Institution of Radio & Electronics Engineers

MIRO Mineral Industries Research Organisation

MIRSE Member of the Institution of Railway Signal Engineers

MIRTE Member of the Institute of Road Transport Engineers

MIRV Multiple Independently-Targeted Re-entry Vehicle

MIS Member of the Institute of Statisticians

MISA *(India)* Maintenance of International Security Act

Misc Miscellaneous

MISEP Mutual Information System on Employment Policies *(EEC, q.v.)*

MISER Militant Society for the Eradication of Rounds *(public-house custom of "treating" drinks)*

MISEREOR *(West Germany) (Latin)* to have compassion *(Church Relief Agency)*

MISM Member of the Institute of Supervisory Management

MISOB Member of the Incorporated Society of Organ Builders

MISP Member of the Institute of Sales Promotion

Miss Mississippi *(USA State)*

MIST Member of the Institute of Science Technology

MISTC Member of the Institute of Scientific and Technical Communicators

MISTM Member of the Institute of Sales Technology and Management

MIStructE Member of the Institution of Structural Engineers

MISW Member of the Institute of Social Welfare

MIT Member of the Institute of Technology *(see also MInstT)*; Massachusetts Institute of Technology; Mandatory Independent Taxation

MITA Member of the Industrial Transport Association

MITD Member of the Institute of Training and Development

MITE Member of the Institution of Electrical and Electronics Technician Engineers

MITI *(Japan)* Ministry of International Trade and Industry

MITMA Member of the Institute of Trade Mark Agents

MITO Member of the Institute of Training Officers *(of the IISE, q.v.)*

MITSA Member of the Institute of Trading Standards Administration

MIWES Member of the Institution of Water Engineers and Scientists

MIWHTE Member of the Institution of Works and Highways Technician Engineers

MIWPC Member of the Institute of Water Pollution Control

MIWSOM Member of the Institute of Practitioners in Work Study, Organisation and Methods

MIWO Member of the Institute of Welfare Officers

MJF *(France)* Mouvement Jeunes Femmes *(Young Women's Movement)*

MJI Member of the Institute of Journalists

MJIE Member of the Junior Institute of Engineers

MJS Member of the Japan Society

MJur Master of Jurisprudence

Mk Mark *(Monetary unit of Germany)*

Mkk Markka *(Monetary unit of Finland)*

MKS Meter Kilogram Second

MKW Military Knight of Windsor

ML Master of Laws; Licentiate in Medicine

MLA Master in Landscape Architecture; Modern Language Association; Member of the Legislative Assembly

MLAC *(France)* Mouvement de Libération de l'Avortment et de la Contraception *(Movement for the Liberation of Abortion and Contraception)*

MLC Member of the Legislative Council; Meat & Livestock Commission; Mountain Leadership Certificate

MLCO Member of the London College of Osteopathy

MLD Minimum Lethal Dose

MLF *(France)* Mouvement pour la Libération Féminine *(Women's Liberation Movement)*

MLib Master of Librarianship

MLitt Master of Letters

Mlle *(France)* Mademoiselle *(Miss)*

MLO Military Liaison Officer

MLP Malta Labour Party

MLR Minimum Lending Rate *(Banks)*

MLS Microwave Landing Systems; Member of the Linnean Society; Master of Library Science

MM Military Medal *(also France, Médaille Militaire)*; Mercantile Marine; Master Mason; 2000 *(Roman numeral)*

mm millimetre

MMA Master of Management and Administration

MMB Milk Marketing Board

MMC Monopolies and Mergers Commission

Mme *(France)* Madame *(Mrs.)*

MMedSci Master of Medical Science

Mmes *(France)* Mesdames *(Mrs. in the plural)*

MMet Master of Metallurgy

mmf magnetomotive force

MMGI Member of the Mining, Geological & Metallurgical Institute of India

MMIGD Master Member of the Institute of Grocery Distribution

MMIM Master Member of the Institute of Executive Managers

MMM Mouvement Militant Mauricien *(Socialist Militant Movement of Mauritius)*; 3000 *(Roman numeral)*

MMMM 4000 *(Roman numeral)*

MMPA Qualified Member of the Master Photographers' Association

MMRBM Mobile Medium Range Ballistic Missile

MMS Methodist Missionary Society; Member of the Institute of Management Services

MMSA Merchant Marine Service Association; Master of Midwifery, Society of Apothecaries

MMSc Master of Medical Sciences

MMus Master of Music

MN Merchant Navy

Mn Manganese

MNAEA Member of the National Association of Estate Agents

MNAOA Merchant Navy and Airline Officers' Association

MNAS *(USA)* Member of the National Academy of Sciences

MNC Multi National Company; *(Congo)* Mouvement National Congolais *(National Movement)*

MNC-K *(Congo)* Mouvement National Congolais *(Kalongi Wing of the National Movement)*

MNF *(France)* Mouvement National Féminin *(National Women's Movement)*

MNI Member of the Nautical Institute

MNIH Member of the National Institute of Hardware

MNIMH Member of the National Institute of Medical Herbalists

MNLF *(Philippines)* Moro National Liberation Front

MNR *(Bolivia)* Movimiento Nacionalista Revolucionario *(National Revolutionary Movement)*; Mozambique National Resistance

MNR-I *(Bolivia)* Movimiento Nacionalista Revolucionario de Izquierda *(Left-Wing of MNR, q.v.)*

MO Medical Officer; Meteorological Office; Municipal Officer; Money Order

Mo Missouri *(USA State)*; Molybdenum

mo moment *(slang)*

MOC Mother of the Chapel *(Unions)*

MOD Method of Delivery

MoD Ministry of Defence

mod *(music)* moderato *(moderate time)*

Mod Con/s Modern Convenience/s

MODS Manned Orbital Defence System *(USAF, q.v., project)*

Mods Moderations *(Oxford examinations for Bachelor of Arts degree)*

M of A Ministry of Agriculture *(Fisher-*

ies & Food)

M of E Ministry of Education *(now DES, q.v.)*

M of RAF Marshall of the Royal Air Force

MOH Medical Officer of Health; Master of Otter Hounds

MoH Ministry of Health *(now DHSS, q.v.)*; Ministry of Housing *(and Local Government)*

Mol Molecule

MoMA Museum of Modern Art

MOMS Member of the Organisation and Methods Society

Mon Monday; Monmouthshire

Mons *(France)* Monsieur *(Mr.)*

Mont Montgomeryshire; Montana *(USA State)*

MOO Money Order Office

MOR Middle of the Road *(music)*

MORI Market and Opinion Research Institute

MOS Metal Oxide Semi-conductor *(Computer Terminology)*

MoT Ministry of Transport *(now Departments of the Environment and Transport)*

MOW Movement for the Ordination of Women

MP Member of Parliament; Metropolitan Police; Military Police; Managerial, Production and Editorial *(BBC, q.v., Staff Grade)*

mp melting point; *(music)* mezzo piano *(fairly soft)*

MPA Music Publishers' Association; Master Photographers' Association; Master of Public Administration

MPAIAC *(Canaries)* Movement for the Self-Determination and Independence of the Canary Archipelago

MPBB Maximum Permissible Body Burden *(in relation to plutonium danger to humans)*

MPBW Ministry of Public Buildings and Works *(now DOE, q.v.)*

MPC Member of Parliament, Canada; Multi-Project Chip *(Australian Silicon Chip)*

mpd minutes per day *(European typing formula)*

MPG Miles Per Gallon; Management and Professional Liaison Group *(TUC, q.v.)*

mpg miles per gallon

MPH Miles Per Hour; Master of Public Health

mph miles per hour

MPharm Master of Pharmacy

MPhil Master of Philosophy

MPLA *(Kenya)* National Movement *(Zaire-backed, see also FNLA and UNITA)*; *(Angola)* Marxist Popular Liberation Movement

MPLC *(Mexico)* Cinchonero Popular

Liberation Movement

MPO Management and Personnel Office *(Government)*

MPP Member of Provincial Parliament; Multi Plasmid Pseudomas *(bacterial)*

MPR Member of the Institute of Public Relations

MPRP *(Iran)* Main Azerbaijani Political Party

MPS Medical Protection Society; Member of the Philological Society; Member of the Pharmaceutical Society

MPsychol Master of Psychology

MPsychMED Master of Psychological Medicine

MPU Medical Practitioners Union; Mental Patients' Unit

MQB Mining Qualifications Board

MR Master of the Rolls; Municipal Reform; Moisture Resistant *(plywood)*

Mr Mister

MRA Moral Rearmament *(Oxford Group/Buchmanite)*; Multiple Regression Analysis

MRAC Member of the Royal Agricultural College

MRACP Member of the Royal Australasian College of Physicians

MRad Master of Radiology

MRAeS Member of the Royal Aeronautical Society

MRAIC Member of the Royal Architectural Institute of Canada

MRAS Member of the Royal Academy of Science; Member of the Royal Astronomical Society; Member of the Royal Asiatic Society

MRBF Mutual Reduction of Balanced Forces

MRBM Medium Range Ballistic Missile

MRC Medical Research Council

MRCA Multi-Role Combat Aircraft *(developed by Britain/West Germany/Italy)*

MRCGP Member of the Royal College of General Practitioners

MRCO Member of the Royal College of Organists

MRCOG Member of the Royal College of Obstetricians and Gynaecologists

MRCP Member of the Royal College of Physicians

MRCPA Member of the Royal College of Pathologists of Australia

MRCPath Member of the Royal College of Pathologists

MRCPEdin Member of the Royal College of Physicians, Edinburgh *(now MRCP, UK, q.v.)*

MRCP (Glas) Member of the Royal College of Physicians, Glasgow *(now MRCP, UK, q.v.)*

MRCPI Member of the Royal College of Physicians, Ireland

MRCPsych Member of the Royal College of Psychiatrists

MRCP(UK) Member of the Royal College of Physicians of the United Kingdom

MRCS Member of the Royal College of Surgeons

MRCSEd Member of the Royal College of Surgeons, Edinburgh

MRCSI Member of the Royal College of Surgeons, Ireland

MRCVS Member of the Royal College of Veterinary Surgeons

MRDE Mining Research & Development Establishment *(EEC, q.v.)*

MRE Microbiological Research Establishment; Market Research Enterprises

MREmps Member of the Royal Empire Society

MRFlight Meteorological Research Flight

MRG Minority Rights Group; *(Corsica)* Mouvement des Radicaux de Gauche *(Left-Wing Radical Political Party)*

MRGS Member of the Royal Geographical Society

MRI Meat Research Institute; Member of the Royal Institution

MRIA Member of the Royal Irish Academy

MRIAI Member of the Royal Institute of Architects of Ireland

MRIC Member of the Royal Institute of Chemistry, *(now MRSC, q.v.)*

MRICS Member of the Royal Institution of Chartered Surveyors

MRIN Member of the Royal Institute of Navigation

MRINA Member of the Royal Institution of Naval Architects

MRIPHH Member of the Royal Institute of Public Health and Hygiene

MRMA(Dip) Diploma of Membership of the Recreation Managers' Association of Great Britain

MRO Member of the Register of Osteopaths

MRP Manufacturers' Recommended Price; *(France)* Mouvement Républicain Populaire *(Popular Republican Movement)*

Mrs Mistress

MRSanA Member of the Royal Sanitary Association of Scotland

MRSC Member of the Royal Society of Chemistry

MRSH Member of the Royal Society of Health

MRSM Member of the Royal Society of Medicine; Member of the Royal Society of Musicians

MRSMA Member of the Royal Society of Marine Artists

MRSMP Member of the Royal Society of Miniature Painters

MRSPE Member of the Royal Society of Painters & Etchers

MRSPP Member of the Royal Society of Portrait Painters

MRST Member of the Royal Society of Teachers

MRTPI Member of the Royal Town Planning Institute

MRU Medical Rehabilitation Unit

MRUSI Member of the Royal United Service Institution

MRVA Member of the Rating and Valuation Association

MS Master of Surgery; Medical Staff; *(USA)* Master of Science; Multiple Sclerosis; Metals Society; Mauritius International Motor Vehicle Registration Letters

MS & MSS/Ms & Mss Manuscript/s

MSA Member of the Society of Apothecaries; *(USA)* Master of Science, Agriculture; Mineralogical Society of America

MSAAT Member of the Society of Architectural and Allied Technicians

MSAE *(USA)* Member of the Society of Automotive Engineers

MSAICE Member of the South African Institution of Civil Engineers

MSAInstMM Member of the South African Institute of Mining and Metallurgy

MSAutE Member of the Society of Automobile Engineers

MSBTh Member of the Society of Health and Beauty Therapists

MSC Manpower Services Commission

MSc Master of Science

MSCA Member of the Society of Company and Commercial Accountants

MScD Master of Dental Science; *(USA)* Doctor of Medical Science

msec millisecond

MScEcon Master in the Faculty of Economic and Social Studies

MSc(Econ) Master of Science in Economics

MSc(Social Sciences) Master of Science in the Social Sciences

MSCT Member of the Society of Cardiological Technicians

MScTech Master of Technical Science

MSE Member of the Society of Engineers; *(USA)* Master of Science in Engineering

MSERT Member of the Society of Electronic and Radio Technicians

MSF Member of the Society of Floristry

MSG Monosodium Glutamate *(food flavouring)*

Msgr Monsigneur; Monsignor

MSH Master of Staghounds

MSHAA Member of the Society of Hearing Aid Audiologists

MSI or MSI-DN *(Italy)* Neo-Fascist Political Party

MSIA Member of the Society of Industrial Artists

MSIAD Member of the Society of Industrial Artists and Designers

MSIE Member of the Society of Industrial Engineers

MSINZ Member of the Surveyors' Institute of New Zealand

MSIT Member of the Society of Instrument Technology *(Now MInst MC, q.v.)*

MSJ Member of the Society of Jesus

MSLAET Member of the Society of Licensed Aircraft Engineers and Technologists

MSM Meritorious Service Medal

MSMA Member of the Sales Managers' Association

MSocSc Master of Social Science

MSR Member of the Society of Radiographers

MSRG Member of the Society of Remedial Gymnasts

MSS Multiple Sclerosis Society; Manuscripts; Member of the Finnish Sauna Society

MSSc Master of Social Science; Master of Surgical Science

MSSF Member of the Society of Shoe Fitters

MSSG Multiple Sclerosis Susceptibility Gene

MSTA Member of the Swimming Teachers' Association

MSTD Member of the Society of Typographical Designers

MSU *(Portugal)* Movimento Socialista Unificado *(Unified Socialist Movement)*

MSW Master in Social Work

MSY Maximum Sustainable Yields *(EEC, q.v., fishing regulations)*

MT Mechanical Transport; Motor Transport

Mt Mount; Mountain

MTA Music Trades' Association; Minimum Time Ashore

MTB Motor Torpedo Boat

MTC Member of Technical College; Music Teacher's Certificate

MTCA Ministry of Transport & Civil Aviation

MTD Master of Transport Design

MTDE Maintenance Technique Development Establishment

MTech Master of Technology

MTFS Medium Term Financial Strategy

MTh/MTheol Master of Theology

MTI *(Hungary)* Megyiar Tivirat Iroda *(News Agency)*

MTM Methods-Time Measurement *(Time and Motion Study)*

MTN *(USA)* Multi-National Trade Negotiations

MTP Master of Town and Country Planning

MTTA Machine Tools Trades Association

MU Mothers' Union; Musicians' Union; Monetary Unit; Maintenance Unit

MUA Mail Users' Association

MUF Materials Unaccounted For *(atomic energy)*

MUFTI Minimum Use of Force For Tactical Intervention *(by police)*

Mun Municipal

MUniv Honorary Master of the University of Surrey

Mus Museum

MusB Bachelor of Music

MusD Doctor of Music

MUSE Mini-Microcomputer Users in Education *(Government-sponsored education group)*

MusM Master of Music

MUSTARD Multi-racial Union of Squatters to Alleviate Racial Discrimination

MV The Virgin Mary; Motor Vessel; Merchant Vessel

M$\bar{\text{V}}$ 4000 *(Roman numeral)*

mV millivolt

mv/mV *(music)* mezza voce *(half the power of voice or instrument)*

MVM Master of Veterinary Medicine

MVO Member of the Royal Victorian Order

MVSc Master of Veterinary Science

MW Medium Wave; Megawatt; Malawi International Motor Vehicle Registration Letters

mW milliwatt

MWA Married Women's Association

MWASA Media Workers' Association of South Africa *(Black Journalists Union)*

MWB Metropolitan Water Board

MWD Military Works Department

MWeldI Member of the Welding Institute

MWES Member of the Women's Engineering Society

MWF Medical Women's Federation

MWIA Medical Women's International Association

MWSOM Member of the Institute of Practitioners in Work Study Organisation and Methods

myth mythological

MX *(USA)* Missile Experimental *(mobile intercontinental missile system)*

MYBP Millions of Years Before the Present

MYOB Mind-Your-Own-Business

N

N North; Nitrogen; Norway International Motor Vehicle Registration Letter

n note; noon

NA Naval Attaché; North America; National Assembly; (USA) National Academician; Netherlands Antilles International Motor Vehicle Registration Letters

Na (Latin) Nitrum (Sodium)

NAAC National Alcohol Affairs Commission

NAACP (USA) National Association for the Advancement of Colored People

NAADC North America Air Defence Command

NAAFI Navy, Army and Air Force Institutes

NAB National Assistance Board; National Advisory Board for Higher Education

NABC National Association of Boys' Clubs

NABM National Association of British Manufacturers

NABS National Advertising Benevolent Society; Nuclear-Armed Bombardment Satellite (USA Space Research)

NAC National Advisory Council; National Abortion Campaign; National Association of Carers; National Association for the Childless; Noise Advisory Council

NACAAA National Advisory Council on Alcohol Abuse and Alcoholism

NACAB National Association of Citizen's Advice Bureaux

NACODS National Association of Colliery Overmen, Deputies and Shot-firers

NACRO National Association for the Care and Resettlement of Offenders and the Prevention of Crime

NACT National Association of Cycle Traders; National Association of Career Teachers

NAD Nothing Abnormal Detected

NADC Naval Aide-de-Camp

NADFAS National Association of Decorative and Fine Arts Societies

NADP National Association of Doctors in Practice

NADPAS National Association of Discharged Prisoners' Aid Societies

NAFD National Association of Funeral Directors

NAFE National Association for Film in Education; National Association of Further Education

NAFF National Association for Freedom (Right-Wing Pressure Group)

NAFO National Association of Fire Officers

NAG National Association of Grooms; National Association of Groundsmen; National Advisory Group (Television Voluntary Action Through Community Service)

NAGC National Association for Gifted Children

NAGM National Association of Governors & Managers (of Schools)

NAHA National Association of Health Authorities

NAHT National Association of Head Teachers

NAI Non-Accidental Injury (social work)

NAIDEX National Aids for the Disabled Exhibition (1981)

NALC National Association of Local Councils

NALGO National and Local Government Officers' Association

NALHF National Association of Leagues of Hospital Friends

NALHM National Association of Licensed House Managers

NALIC National Association of Loft Insulation Contractors

NALS National Association of Labour Students

NAM New Architectural Movement

NAMB National Association of Master Bakers

NAMCW National Association for Maternal and Child Welfare

NAME National Association for Multiracial Education

NAMH National Association for Mental Health

NAOS North Atlantic Ocean Stations

NAP (Italy) Nucleo Armato Proletario (Armed Proletarian Nuclei, urban guerrilla organisation); (Turkey) Nationalist Action Party (ultra right-wing)

NAPE National Association of Port Employers

NAPF National Association of Pension Funds

NAPO National Association of Prison Officers; National Association of Probation Officers

NAPT National Association for the Prevention of Tuberculosis

NARA National Association for the Rescue of Animals

NARACC National Association for Research and Action in Community Care

NARAG National Association of Ratepayers' Action Groups

NARAL *(USA)* National Abortion Rights Action League

NARE National Association for Remedial Education

NAS National Adoption Society; Noise Abatement Society; National Association of Schoolmasters

NASA *(USA)* National Aeronautics and Space Administration

NASC National Association of Solo Clubs; National Society for Autistic Children

NASDIM National Association of Security Dealers and Investment Managers *(formerly ALDS, q.v.)*

NASDU National Amalgamated Stevedores and Dockers Union

NASL North Atlantic Soccer League

NASO National Adult School Organisation

NASS National Association for Small Schools

NASUWT ⎫National Association of
NAS/UWT ⎭Schoolmasters and Union of Women Teachers

Nat National

NATCS National Air Traffic Control Services

NATESLA National Association for Teaching English as a Secondary Language to Adults

NATFHE National Association of Teachers in Further and Higher Education *(amalgamation of ATTCDE and ATTI, q.v.)*

NATKE National Association of Theatrical and Kine Employees

NATO North Atlantic Treaty Organisation *(French equivalent OTAN, q.v.)*

NATpro North American Treaties and population rights organisation

NATSOPA National Society of Operative Printers Graphical and Media Personnel

Naut Nautical

NAV Net Annual Value

NAVAR Combined Navigation and Radar System

NAVS National Anti-Vivisection Society

NAW National Association of Widows

NAWC National Association of Women's Clubs

NAWCH National Association for the Welfare of Children in Hospitals

NAYC National Association of Youth Clubs

NAYCEO National Association of Youth and Community Education Officers

NAYPCAS National Association of Young People's Counselling and Advisory Service

NB *(Latin)* Nota Bene *(mark well)*; North Britain *(old-fashioned reference to Scotland); (Canada)* New Brunswick

Nb Niobium

NBA National Building Agency; North British Academy

NBB *(Netherlands)* Nederlandse Boksbond a.o. *(Boxing Association)*

NBC National Broadcasting Councils; *(USA)* National Broadcasting Company

NBCW National Board of Catholic Women

NBG No Bloody Good

NBHS National Bureau for Handicapped Students

NBL National Book League

NBPA National Bookmakers' Protection Association

NBPI National Board for Prices and Incomes *(see also PIB)*

NBS *(USA)* National Bureau of Standards

NBTPS National Book Trade Provident Society

NBWTAU National British Women's Total Abstinence Union

NC National Certificate; North Carolina *(USA State)*

NCA National Council for Alcoholism; National Childminders' Association; National Certificate in Agriculture

NCAE *(USA)* National Centre for Alcohol Education

NCAL National Committee for Adult Literacy

NCB National Coal Board; National Children's Bureau

NCC National Consumer Council; Nature Conservancy Council; National Computing Centre; *(USA)* National Control Centre

NCCC National Child Care Campaign

NCCL National Council for Civil Liberties

NCD Naval Construction Department

NCDL National Canine Defence League

NCER National Committee for Electoral Reform

NCES National Council for Educational Standards

NCH National Children's Home

NCILT National Centre for Industrial Language Training

NCIP Non-Contributory Invalid Pension *(DIG, q.v.)*

NCLC National Council of Labour Colleges

NCM National College of Music

NCN National Council of Nurses

NCNA New China News Agency

NCNE National Campaign for Nursery Education

NCO Non-Commissioned Officer

NCOPF National Council for One-Parent Families

NCP National Car Parks; National Certificate in Poultry Practice

NCPS Non-Contributory Pension Scheme

NCPTA National Conference of Parent Teachers' Associations

NCQR National Council for Quality and Reliability *(in commerce)*

NCROPA National Campaign for the Reform of the Obscene Publications Acts

NCRT National College of Rubber Technology

NCSS National Council of Social Services

NCSWD National Council for the Single Woman and her Dependants

NCT National Childbirth Trust; National Chamber of Trade

NCTA National Council for Technological Awards *(now CNAA, q.v.)*

NCTEC Northern Counties Technical Examination Council

NCTJ National Council for the Training of Journalists

NCTYP National Council of Theatre for Young People

NCU National Cyclists' Union

NCVO National Council for Voluntary Organisations

NCVYS National Council for Voluntary Youth Services

NCW National Council of Women *(see also CNF)*

NCWA National Council of Women of Australia; National Council of Women of Austria

NCWC National Council of Women of Canada

NCWGB National Council of Women of Great Britain

NCWI National Council of Women of India

NCWK National Council of Women of Kenya

NCWNZ National Council of Women of New Zealand

NCWOM National Council of Women's Organisation of Malaysia

NCWPA National Council for the Welfare of Prisoners Abroad

NCWS National Council of Women's Societies of Nigeria

NCWSA National Council of Women of South Africa

NCWT National Council of Women of Thailand

NCWUSA National Council of Women of the United States of America

ND Diploma in Naturopathy

Nd Neodymium

NDA National Diploma in Agriculture

NDAgrE National Diploma in Agricultural Engineering

NDak North Dakota *(USA State)*

NDCS National Deaf Children's Society

NDD National Diploma in Design; National Diploma in Dairying

NDF *(Iran)* National Democratic Front

NDH National Diploma in Horticulture

NDP *(Canada)* New Democratic Party; National Diploma in Poultry Husbandry; *(Egypt)* National Democratic Party

NDT National Diploma in the Science and Practice of Turf-culture and Sports-ground Management

NDU *(USA)* National Democratic Union

NE North East

Ne Neon

NEA National Economic Assessment

NEAC New English Art Club

NEAF Near East Air Force

NEB National Enterprise Board; New English Bible

Neb Nebraska *(USA State)*

NEBSS National Examinations Board for Supervisory Studies

NEC National Executive Committee *(Labour Party)*; National Exhibition Centre; National Executive Centre *(Birmingham)*; National Extension College

NECCCRW *(Gaza)* Near East Council of Churches Committee for Refugee Work

NECCTA National Educational Closed Circuit Television Association

NECInst North East Coast Institution of Engineers and Shipbuilders

NED Non-Executive Director; New English Dictionary

NEDC/NEDDY National Economic Development Council

NEDO National Economic Development Office

NEECPR *(Cyprus)* Near East Ecumenical Committee for Palestine Refugees

Neg Negative; Negotiable

nem con *(Latin)* nemine contradiscente *(no-one against)*

nem diss *(Latin)* nemine dissentente *(no-one dissenting)*

NEPRA National Egg Producers' Retail Association

NERC Natural Environment Research Council

Neth Netherlands

Neut Neuter

Nev Nevada *(USA State)*

New M New Mexico *(USA State)*

NF National Front; Newfoundland

NFA National Film Archives

NFAC National First Aid Council

NFBTE National Federation of Building Trades Employers

NFC National Freight Corporation

NFCA National Federation of Community Associations; National Foster Care Association

NFCC National Family Conciliation Council

NFCG National Federation of Consumer Groups

NFCO National Federation of Community Organisations

NFCWC National Free Church Women's Council *(see also FCFC)*

NFEPG National Federation of 18-Plus Groups

NFER National Foundation for Educational Research

NFFC National Film Finance Corporation

NFFF National Federation of Fish Fryers

NFHA National Federation of Housing Associations

NFIB National Federation of Independent Businesses

NFKPA National Federation of Kidney Patients' Association

NFOL National Festival of Light

NFP Natural Family Planning

NFPW National Federation of Professional Workers

NFRCD National Fund for Research into Crippling Diseases

NFRN National Federation of Retail Newsagents

NFS National Fire Service; National Film School

NFSA National Federation of Sea Anglers; National Fire Services Association

NFSE National Federation of the Self-Employed

NFT National Film Theatre

NFTU National Federation of Trade Unions

NFU National Farmers' Union

NFVLS National Federation of Voluntary Literacy Schemes

NFWI National Federation of Women's Institutes

NFYFC National Federation of Young Farmers' Clubs

NG National Gallery

NGA National Graphical Association

NGEC National Gypsy Education Council

NGO Non-Governmental Organisation *(see also WINGO, QUANGO and ONG)*

NGRC National Greyhound Racing Club

NGUT National Group of Unit Trusts

NH National Hunt; New Hampshire *(USA State)*

NHA National Horse Association

NHBC National House Building Council

NHBPM National Housebuilders' and Plumbers' Merchants

NHBR *See NHBRC*

NHBRA National Housebuilders' Registration Association

NHBRC National Housebuilders' Registration Council

NHC National Hunt Committee

NHEB National Home Enlargement Bureau

NHK *(Japan)* Nippon Hoso Kyokai *(National Broadcasting Service)*; *(South Korea)* Radio and Television

NHI National Health Insurance

NHLBI *(USA)* The National Heart Lung and Blood Institute

NHMRC National Health and Medical Research Council

NHN National Homes Network

NHR National Housewives' Register

NHRP *(USA)* National Hurricanes Research Project

NHS National Health Service

NI National Insurance; Northern Ireland; Naval Instructor; Nuclear Institute; Northern Ireland Law Reports

Ni Nickel

NIAAA *(USA)* National Institute on Alcohol Abuse and Alcoholism

NIAB National Institute of Agricultural Botany

NIACRO Northern Ireland Association for the Care and Resettlement of Offenders

NIACE National Institute of Adult Continuing Education; National Institute of Agricultural Engineering

NIBMAR No Independence Before Majority Rule

NIC National Incomes Commission; Newly Industrialised Countries; Nicaraguan International Motor Vehicle Registration Letters

NICC Nationalised Industries Consumer Councils; Northern Ireland Consumer Council

NICE Nationally Integrated Caring Employees *(Union)*

NICEC National Institute for Careers Education and Counselling

NICEIC National Inspection Council for Electrical Installation Contracting

NICS Northern Ireland Civil Service

NID Naval Intelligence Division; National Institute for the Deaf

NIEO New International Economic Order *(UN, q.v.)*

NIESR National Institute of Economic and Social Research

NIH *(USA)* National Institute of Health

NII Nuclear Installations Inspectorate

NIIP National Institute of Industrial Psychology

NILP Northern Ireland Labour Party

NIMR National Institute for Medical Research

NIO Northern Ireland Office

NIOC *(Iran)* National Iranian Oil Company

NIOSH *(USA)* National Institute for Occupational Safety and Health

NIS National Insurance Surcharge

(Employers' Contribution)

NIT *(USA)* Negative Income Tax

NJ New Jersey *(USA State)*

NJAC National Joint Advisory Council; National Joint Action Committee

NJB National Joint Board

NJC National Joint Committee; National Joint Council

NJCC National Joint Consultative Council

NJIC National Joint Industrial Council

NJNC National Joint Negotiating Committee/Council

NKN *(Norway)* Norske Kvinners Nasjonalrad *(NCW, q.v.)*

NL National Liberal; Navy League; Netherlands International Motor Vehicle Registration Letters

NLC National Liberal Club

NLF National Liberal Federation; *(Vietnam)* National Liberation Front; National Land Fund

NLGOA National Local Government Officers' Association

NLP *(Lebanon)* National Liberal Party

NLS National Library of Scotland

NMCC National Mass Communication Councils

NMGC National Marriage Guidance Council

NMI National Maritime Institute

NMR Nuclear Magnetic Resonance *(diagnostic measuring machine)*

NNC Namibia National Convention

NNE North North East

NNEB National Nursery Examination Board

NNHT Nuffield Nursing Home Trust

NNI Noise and Number Index *(measurement of aircraft nuisance)*

NNLC *(Swaziland)* Ngwane National Liberation Congress

NNP Net National Product

NNPT Nuclear Non-Proliferation Treaty

NNW North North West

NO Naval Officer; Naval Operation; Navigation Officer *(RN, q.v.)*; Nursing Officer

No Number; Nobelium

NOAA *(USA)* National Oceanic and Atmospheric Administration

NODA National Opera Drama Association

nol pros *(Latin)* nolle prosequi *(stay, relinquishment of legal proceedings)*

NOLS National Organisation of Labour Students

Nom Nominal

NON *(USA)* National Association for Non-Parents

non seq *(Latin)* non sequitur *(it does not follow)*

NOP National Opinion Poll

NORAD *(USA)* North American Air Defense; *(Norway)* Agency for Development

NorAID Illegal American organisation exporting arms to Ireland

NORMAL *(USA/Calif)* National Organisation for the Reform of Marijuana Laws

Northants Northamptonshire

North'ld Northumberland

NOS *(Netherlands)* Nederlandse Omroep Stichting *(Broadcasting Foundation)*

Nos Numbers

NOTB National Ophthalmic Treatment Board

Notts Nottinghamshire

Nov November

NOVIB *(Netherlands)* Nederlandse Organisatie voor Ontwikkelingssamenwerking *(Ecumenical Organisation for Co-operation with International Development)*

NOW Negotiable Order of Withdrawal; *(USA)* National Organisation for Women

NOWME National Organisation for Women's Management Education

NP Notary Public; Nursing Procedure; New Paragraph; Net Proceeds; Nobel Prize; *(South Africa and Malta)* National Party; Naval Patrol *(RN, q.v.)*

Np Neptunium

NPA National Playbus Association; National Pharmaceutical Association; Newspaper Publishers' Association; New People's Army; National Pistol Association

NPC National Ports Council; National Press Club; National Pony Club

NPD *(West Germany)* National Demokratische Partei *(National Democratic Party)*

NPF Newspaper Press Fund

NPFA National Playing Fields Association

NPL National Physical Laboratory

NPMSC National Professional and Management Staffs Council *(TUC, q.v.)*

NPN National Party of Nigeria

NPO New Philharmonic Orchestra

NPP Nigerian People's Party

NPR *(USA)* National Public Radio

NPS National Pony Society

NPT Non-Proliferation Treaty; Normal Pressure and Temperature

NRA National Rifle Association; *(USA)* National Recovery Administration

NRC Nuclear Research Council; *(USA)* Nuclear Regularity Commission

NRD National Registered Designer

NRDC National Research Development Corporation; National Retail Distribution Certificate; *(USA)* Natural Resources Defense Council *(nuclear)*

NRP *(South Africa)* New Republic Party *(remnant of the old United Party)*; *(Israel)* National Religious Party

NRZ National Railway of Zimbabwe

NS Newspaper Society; National Service; National Society; *(Canada)* Nova Scotia

NSA National Skating Association of Great Britain; *(USA)* National Security Agency

NSB National Savings Bank; *(Netherlands)* Nationaal Socialistiche Beweging *(Dutch Nazi Movement before World War 2)*

NSC National Savings Committee; National Sporting Club

NSCA National Society for Clean Air

NSCIA National Supervisory Council for Intruder Alarms

NSCT *(Thailand)* National Student Centre

NSG Nuclear Suppliers' Group *(Association of Nations)*

NSL National Sporting League

NSM National Savings Movement; National Socialist Movement; New Smoking Material *(tobacco substitute)*

NSMHC National Society for the Mentally Handicapped Child

NSMM National Society of Metal Mechanics

NSN-S National Society for Non-Smokers

NSO Naval Staff Officer

NSOPA See *NATSOPA*

NSP *(Turkey)* National Salvation Party

NSPCC National Society for the Prevention of Cruelty to Children

NSPSE National Society of Painters, Sculptors and Engravers

NSRA National Small-Bore Rifle Association; National Society for Research in Allergy

NSRC National Space Research Consortium

NSS National Secular Society

NSSU National Sunday School Union

NSUK Nichiren Shoshu of the UK, *q.v.* *(The Buddhist Society)*

NSW New South Wales

NSY New Scotland Yard

NT National Trust; National Theatre; New Testament; *(Australia)* Northern Territory; *(Canada)* Northwest Territories

NTB *(Norway)* Norske Telegrambyrå *(News Agency)*

NTD Neural-Tube Defects

NTDA National Trade Development Association

NTDS Naval Tactical Data System

NTP Normal Temperature and Pressure

N-Trust Naval Dependants' Assurance Trust

NTS National Trust for Scotland; Nevada *(nuclear)* Test Site; Polish Anti-Communist emigré organisation

NTVLRO National TV, *(q.v.)* Licence Record Office

NU National Union; Nations Unies *(United Nations)*

NUAAW National Union of Agricultural and Allied Workers

NUB National Union of Blastfurnacemen

NUBE National Union of Bank Employees

NUBSO National Union of Boot and Shoe Operatives

NUC *(USA)* National Union Catalog *(pre-1976 imprints)*

NUCUA National Union of Conservative and Unionist Associations

NUDBTW National Union of Dyers Bleachers and Textile Workers

NUF *(Zimbabwe)* National Unifying Force

NUFLAT National Union of Footwear Leather and Allied Trades

NUFSO National Union of Funeral Service Operatives

NUHKW National Union of Hosiery and Knitwear Workers

NUI National University of Ireland

NUIS National Union of Iraqi Students

NUIW National Union of Insurance Workers

NUJ National Union of Journalists

NULC National Union of Labour Clubs

NULO National Union of Labour Organisers

NULV National Union of Licensed Victuallers

NUM National Union of Mineworkers

NUPE National Union of Public Employees; National Union of Post Office Employees

NUR National Union of Railwaymen

NURA National Union of Ratepayers' Associations

NURC National Union of Research Councils

NUS National Union of Seamen; National Union of Students

NUSAS National Union of South African Students

NUSEC National Union of Societies for Equal Citizenship

NUSMWCHDE National Union of Sheet Metal Workers Coppersmiths Heating and Domestic Engineers

NUSS National Union of School Students

NUT National Union of Teachers

NUTG National Union of Townswomen's Guilds

NUTGW National Union of Tailors and Garment Workers

NUTN National Union of Trained Nurses

NUU New University of Ulster

NUVB National Union of Vehicle Builders *(now amalgamated with TGWU, q.v.)*

NUWSS National Union of Women's Suffrage Societies

NUWW National Union of Women Workers

NV *(Netherlands)* Naamloze Venootschap *(Limited Company)*; New Version *(Bible)*

NVA National Video Association; *(East Germany)* Nationale Volksarmee *(People's Army)*

NVAES *(USSR)* Novo-Voronezhskaya Atomnaya Energeticheskaya Stantisiya *(atomic power station)*

NVLA National Viewers and Listeners Association

NVRS National Vegetable Research Station

NW North West

NWAF National Women's Aid Federation

NWICO New World Information and Communication Order *(UN, q.v.)*

NWPC *(USA)* National Women's Political Caucus *(see also WPC)*

NWRAC North Western Regional Advisory Council for Further Education

NY New York *(USA State)*

NYB National Youth Bureau

NYC New York City

NYCB *(USA)* New York City Ballet

NYK *(Japan)* Nippon Yusen Kaisha *(Shipping Company)*

NYO National Youth Orchestra

NYSA New York State Assembly

NYSE New York Stock Exchange

NYT National Youth Theatre

NZ New Zealand; New Zealand International Motor Vehicle Registration Letters

NZBS New Zealand Broadcasting Service

NZIA New Zealand Institute of Architects

NZS *(Poland)* Niezalézny Zwiazek Studenton *(Independent Student Union)*

O

O Oxygen; Ohio *(USA State)*

OA Officier d'Académie *(French Academy Officer)*

OAC *(USA)* Orbiting Astronomical Observatory

OALC African Liberation Committee *(see also ALC)*

O and E *(USA)* Operations and Engineering

O and G Obstetrics and Gynaecology

O and M Organisation and Method

OAP Old Age Pensioner/Pension

OAPEC Organisation of Arab Petroleum Exporting Countries *(see also OPEC)*

OAS On Active Service; Organisation of American States; *(Algeria)* Organisation d'Algérie Secrète *(Secret organisation)*

OASDI *(USA)* Old Age, Survivors and Disability Insurance

OAU Organisation for African Unity; *(Israel)* Radio

OB Out-of-Body *(psychic research)*

ob *(Latin)* obiit *(died)*

obb *(music)* obbligato *(obligatory part of composition)*

OBA Open Broadcasting Authority *(proposed by Annan Committee)*; Overpowering Body Assault

OBC Old Boys' Club *(usually preceded by the name of the Club)*

OBCT Outside Broadcast Camera Team

OBE Officer of the Order of the British Empire

OBI Order of British India

OBLI Oxford and Bucks Light Infantry

OBU Oriental Boxing Union

OC Officer Commanding; Old Comrades; Observer Corps

o/c overcharge

OCA Old Comrades' Association

OCarm Order of the Carmelites

OCart Order of the Carthusians

OCC Ocean Cruising Club

OCDE *(France)* Organisation de Coopération et de Développement Economique *(Organisation for Economic Cooperation and Development)*

OCE Office for Co-operation in Education *(EEC, q.v.)*

OCF Officiating Chaplain to the Forces

OCFR Oxford Committee for Famine Relief *(see also OXFAM)*

OCHE *See CHE*

OCPCA Oil and Chemical Plant Construction Association

OCPU Outer Circle Policy Unit

OCR Order of the Cistercians *(Reformed)*; Optical Character Reader *(computer terminology)*

OCSO Order of the Cistercians of Strict Observance

Oct October

OCTU Officer Cadet Training Unit

OD *(Latin)* Opus Dei *(Work of God,*

section of the Catholic Church); Over-draft; Overseas and Defence (Cabinet Committee); Overdose

OD(E) Overseas Defence (Europe)

ODA Overseas Doctors' Association; Official Development Assistance, UN, q.v.; Overseas Development Administration

ODE One Day Event (horse-riding)

ODI Overseas Development Institute; Open Door International (Women's Organisation)

ODM Overseas Development Ministry

ODS/OSD (Lebanon) Office de Développement Social/Office of Social Development

OE Old English

OECD Organisation for Economic Co-operation and Development

OECE Organisation Européenne de Coopération Economique (European Organisation for Economic Co-operation)

OED Oxford English Dictionary

OEEC Organisation for European Economic Co-operation (see also OECD)

OEM Original Equipment Manufacturers

OEPP Organisation Européenne et Méditeranéenne pour la Protection des Plantes (FAO, q.v., see also EPPO)

OETB Offshore Energy Technology Board

OF Old French

OFM Order of Friars Minor (Franciscans)

OFS Orange Free State

OFT Office of Fair Trading

OFUNC Organisation des Femmes de l'Union Nationale Camerounaise (NCW, q.v., of the Cameroons)

OG Olympic Games

OGM Ordinary General Meeting

OGO Orbiting Geophysical Observatory (see also EGO and POGO)

OGPU (USSR) Otdelenie Gasudarstvenni Politcheskoi Ypravi (Special Secret Police, see also GPU)

OHBMS On Her/His Britannic Majesty's Service

OHE Office of Health Economics

OHMS On Her/His Majesty's Service

OHNC Occupational Health Nursing Certificate

OIC Organisation Internationale du Commerce (International Organisation for Commerce)

OIE Office International des Epizootics (International Office for Epidemic Diseases Among Animals, FAO, q.v.)

OIML Organisation Internationale pour la Métrologie Légale (International Weights and Measures Organisation)

OIRT Organisation Internationale de Radiodiffusion et Télévision (International Radio and Television Organisation)

OIV Office International de la Vigne et du Vin (International Vine and Wine Office, FAO, q.v., see also IWO)

OK Orl Korrect (All Correct)

Okla Oklahoma (USA State)

OL Ordnance Lieutenant; Officer of the Order of Leopold

OLevel Ordinary Level (GCE, q.v.)

OLF Open Learning Federation

OM Order of Merit

OME Office of Manpower Economics

OMEP Organisation Mondiale pour l'Education Préscolaire (World Organisation for Pre-School Education)

OMI Oblate of Mary Immaculate

OMM L'Organisation Météorologique Mondiale (World Meteorological Organisation, see also WMO)

OMO One-Man-Operated

OMS Organisation and Methods Society; Organisation Mondiale de la Santé (World Health Organisation, see also WHO)

ONA (Australia) Office of National Assessments (Intelligence Agency)

ONC Ordinary National Certificate

OND Ordinary National Diploma

ONG (France) Organisation Non-Gouvernementale (see also NGO, WINGO and QUANGO)

ONI Office of Naval Intelligence

ONISEP (France) L'Office National pour l'Information Scolaire et Professionelle (National Student and Professional Information Office)

ONO/ono Or Near Offer

ONR (USA) Office of Naval Research; (Trinidad) Organisation for National Reconstruction

Ont Ontario (Canada)

ONU Organisation des Nations Unies (Organisation of the United Nations)

OP Operational (BBC, q.v., Staff Grade); (Latin) Ordinis Praedicatorum (of the Order of Preachers); Observation Post; Out of Print

OPA (USA) Office of Price Administration

OPB Occupational Pensions Board

op cit (Latin) opere citato (in the work quoted)

OPCS Office of Population Censuses and Surveys

OPD Out-Patients' Department

OPDC Overseas Policy Defence Committee

OPEC Organisation of Petroleum Exporting Countries (see also OAPEC)

OPEX Operational, Executive and Administrative Personnel (UN, q.v.)

OPI Office of Public Information

OPM Optically Projected Map

OPS Obscene Publications Squad

OPT Orthopantomogram *(X-ray machine)*

OPUS Organisation for Promoting Understanding in Society; Orbital Power Unit Steam; Organisation for Parents Under Stress

OR Official Receiver

or operational research; at owner's risk

ORACLE Optional Reception of Announcements by Coded Line Electronics *(ITV Television newspaper)*

ORC Opinion Research Centre

Orch Orchestra

Oreg Oregon *(USA State)*

ORF Obesity Research Foundation; *(Austria)* Oesterreischer Rundfunk *(Austrian Broadcasting Corporation)*

ORN *(France)* Organisation pour la Recherche Nucléaire; *(Lebanon)* Extreme Right-Wing Organisation

Ornith Ornithology

ORPA *(Guatemala)* Organización Revolucionaria del Pueblo Armado *(Organisation of People in Arms)*

ORT Organisation for Rehabilitation by Training *(Jewish Social Welfare Organisation)*; *(Spain)* Workers' Revolutionary Party

ORTF *(France)* Office de la Radiodiffusion et Télévision Française *(Broadcasting Authority)*

ORTO *(Canada)* Television

OS Ordnance Survey; Ordinary Seaman; Outsize

Os Osmium

OSA Official Secrets Act; Order of St. Augustine; Ontario Society of Artists

OSB Order of St. Benedict

OSD Order of St. Dominic; *(See also ODS/OSD (Lebanon))*

OSF Order of St. Francis

OSFC Franciscan *(Capuchin)* Order

OSHA *(USA)* Occupational Safety and Health Administration

OSO *(USA)* Orbiting Solar Observatory

OSP Order of St. Paul

OSRD Office of Scientific Research and Development

OSS Office of Strategic Studies

OStJ Officer of the Order of the Hospital of St. John of Jerusalem

OSUK Ophthalmological Society of the UK, *q.v.*

OT Old Testament; Occupational Therapist; Over-Time

OTAN Organisation du Traité de l'Atlantique Nord *(North Atlantic Treaty Organisation, see also NATO)*

OTASE Organisation du Traité de Défense Collective pour l'Asie du Sud *(South East Asia Treaty Organisation)*

OTC Officers' Training Corps *(see also CCF)*

OTI *(South America)* Television

OTLS Overseas Traders Lists Service

OTS Orbital Test Satellite *(European Space Agency)*

OU Oxford University; Open University

OUA Organisation de l'Unité Africaine *(Organisation for African Unity)*

OUAC Oxford University Athletic Club

OUAFC Oxford University Association Football Club

OUAS Oxford University Air Squadron

OUBC Oxford University Boat Club

OUCC Oxford University Cricket Club

OUDS Oxford University Dramatic Society

OUGC Oxford University Golf Club

OUHC Oxford University Hockey Club

OULC Oxford University Lacrosse Club

OULTC Oxford University Lawn Tennis Club

OUP *(Ulster)* Official Unionist Party; Oxford University Press; Oklahoma University Press

OURC Oxford University Rifle Club

OURFC Oxford University Rugby Football Club

OUSA Open University Students' Association

OUSC Oxford University Swimming Club

OVP *(Austria)* Oesterreichische Volkspartei *(People's Party)*

OW Office of Works

OWAAD Organisation of Women of Asian and African Descent

OWI *(USA)* Office of War Information

OWLS Oxford *(University Press)* Language Service

OWS Ocean Weathership Service

OXFAM Oxford Committee for Famine Relief *(see also OCFR)*

OXON Oxonian *(of Oxford University)*

O/y *(Finland)* Osakeytiö *(Limited Company)*

oz ounce

ozt ounce troy

P

P President of the Family Division *(of the High Court)*; Portuguese International Motor Vehicle Registration Letter; President; Paragraph; Parking; Phosphorous

p penny; peseta *(Monetary unit of Spain)*; peso *(Monetary unit of South America, Mexico, Paraguay and the Philippines)*

PA Power of Attorney; Press Agent; Press Association; Press Attaché; Public Address; Public Accountant; Personal Assistant; Panama International Motor Vehicle Registration Letters

Pa Pennsylvania *(USA State)*; Protactinium

pa *(Latin)* per annum *(yearly)*

PAA Pan American Airways

PABX Private Automatic Branch Exchange

PAC Public Administration Committee *(Western European Union)*; Pan Africanist Congress; *(USA)* Political Action Committee; Professional Advisory Committee *(NHS, q.v.)*; La Politique Agricole Commune *(Common Agricultural Policy, see also CAP)*

PACE Polytechnic Association for Continuing Education; Protestant and Catholic Encounter Movement

PACH Publishers' Accounts Clearing House

PAD *(Spain)* Partido de Acción Democratica *(Democratic Action Party)*

PAF *(Ulster)* Protest/Protestant Action Force

PAK Pakistan International Motor Vehicle Registration Letters

Pak Pakistan

PAL Parents Anonymous Lifeline *(organisation to help potential child-batterers)*; Progressive Alliance of Liberia; Television Line Definition; Philippine Air Lines

PALS People Against Loneliness *(self-help group)*

PAM *(Trinidad)* People's National Movement

PAMAD Parents Against Middle-Aged Discrimination

PAN *(Mexico)* Partido de Acción Nacionalista *(National Action Party)*; Pagans Against Nukes

Pan Pan-American World Air Lines

P and L Profit and Loss

P and O Peninsular and Oriental Steamship Company

p and p postage and packing

PAP *(Poland)* Polska Agencja Prasowa *(Press Agency)*; *(Singapore)* People's Action Party

PAR Programme Analysis and Review *(of the DES, q.v.)*

PAR38/PAR56 Parabolic Aluminium Reflector *(electric lightbulbs)*

par paragraph

Para Paraguay, South America

Parl Parliament/Parliamentary

PARS Pedestrians Association for Road Safety

PAS Port Auxiliary Service; Public Address System; Probation and After-Care Service; Pregnancy Advisory Service *(sometimes preceded by initial of Town or County)*

PASOK *(Greece)* Panellimios Socialistiko Kinima *(Pan Hellenic Socialist Movement)*

PASS Promoting-A-Sober-Society

PASSIM *(USA)* Presidential Advisory Staff on Scientific Management

PAT Professional Association of Teachers; Patents Appeal Tribunal

PAU Public Appointments Unit *(Civil Service)*; Pan American Union

PAWS Pet Animal Welfare Scheme

PAYE Pay-As-You-Earn; Pay-As-You-Enter

PAYG Pay-As-You-Go

PB Prayer Book; Premium Bond

Pb *(Latin)* Plumbum *(Lead)*

PBFA Provincial Booksellers Fairs Association

PBMA Plastic Bath Manufacturers Association

PBR Payment By Results

PBS *(USA)* Public Broadcasting System

PBU Premature Baby Unit

PC Police Constable; Press Council; Press Club; Privy Council/Councillor; Prison Commission/er; Post Card; Pony Club; Perpetual Curate; Parish Council/Councillor; Pioneer Corps; *(France)* Parti Communiste *(Communist Party)*; *(Portugal)* Partido Communista *(Communist Party)*

pc *(Latin)* per centum *(per hundred)*; *(Latin)* post cibum *(after meals)*

p/c petty cash

PCB Polychlorinated biphenyl *(a pesticide)*

PCC Parochial Church Council; *(Cuba)* Partido Communista Cubano *(Communist Party)*

PCE *(Spain)* Partido Communista de España *(Communist Party)*

PCI *(Italy)* Partito Communisto Italiano *(Communist Party)*

PCL Polytechnic of Central London; *(Spain)* Communist Party

PCMO Principal Colonial Medical Officer

PCN *(Nicaragua)* Partido Conservador Nicaraguense *(Conservative Party)*; *(El Salvador)* Partido de Conciliacão Nacional *(National Conciliation Party)*

PCP Portugal Communist Party

PCR Programme to Combat Racism

PCS Private Counselling Service

PCSPS Principal Civil Service Pension Scheme

PCT Printers' Charitable Trust

PCV *(France)* Payé Contre Valeur *(reverse telephone charges)*

PD Position Doubtful *(on old charts and maps, see also ED); (Latin)* Per Diem *(daily)*

Pd Paid; Palladium

PDAD Probate, Divorce and Admiralty Division *(now FD, q.v.)*

Pdb Paradichlorobenzene

PDG *(France)* Président Directeur-Général *(Managing Director)*

PDGF Platelet Derived Growth Factor

PDI Pre-Delivery Inspection *(of motor cars)*

PDL Poverty Datum Line

PDPA People's Democratic Party of Afghanistan

PDQ Pretty-Damn-Quick

PDRY People's Democratic Republic of Yemen

PDS Pure-Dàmn-Swank

PDSA People's Dispensary for Sick Animals

PE Peruvian International Motor Vehicle Registration Letters; Physical Education/Exercise; Parlement Européen *(European Parliament, see also EP);* Parlamento Europeo *(European Parliament, see also EP);* Protestant Episcopalian

PEBB Public Enquiry Board for Broadcasting

PEI Prince Edward Island

PEL Paid Educational Leave; Protected Expenditure Limits *(Government)*

Pemb Pembrokeshire

PEN Poets, Playwrights, Editors, Essayists, Novelists *(International Club)*

PEng *(Canada)* Registered Professional Engineer

Penn Pennsylvania *(USA State)*

PEP Political and Economic Planning *(now PSI, q.v.)*

PER Professional Executive Register

per cent *(Latin)* per centum *(for every hundred)*

Perm Permanent *(hairdressing)*

per pro *(Latin)* per procurationem *(for and on behalf of)*

PERT Programme Evaluation & Review Technique *(computers)*

PESC Public Expenditure Scrutiny/Survey Committee

PEST Pressure for Economic and Social Toryism *(now part of TRG, q.v.)*

PF Police Federation; Procurator Fiscal; *(Zimbabwe)* Patriotic Front

pf *(music)* piano forte *(soft, then loud); (music)* piu forte *(a little louder)*

PFA Professional Footballers' Association

PFC Parents for Children *(Organisation)*

pfg pfennig *(Monetary unit of Germany)*

PFLOAG *(Iran)* Left-Wing Popular Front for the Liberation of the Arabian Gulf

PFLP Palestine Fatah Liberation Party *(Arab)*

PFLP-GC Popular Front for the Liberation of Palestine – General Command *(Arab)*

PFP *(South Africa)* Progressive Federal Party

PFR Prototype Fast Reactor

PFU *(Belgium)* Parti Féministe Unifié *(United Feminist Party)*

PG Please God!; Procurator General; Paying Guest; Post Graduate; Parental Guidance *(film censorship category, formerly "A")*

PGA Professional Golfers' Association

PGCE Post Graduate Certificate of Education

PGM Past Grand Master *(Masonic)*

PH Public Health; Purple Heart *(drug)*

pH Hydrogen ion concentration

PHAB Physically-Handicapped and Able-Bodied

PHAS Public Health Advisory Service

PhC Pharmaceutical Chemist

PhD Doctor of Philosophy

PhD(RCA) Doctor of Philosophy (RCA, q.v.)

PHG Postman Higher Grade

PHI Public Health Inspector *(NHS, q.v.);* Public Health Insurance

Phil Philharmonic; Philosophy; Philology; *(USA)* Philadelphia

PhM *(USA)* Master of Philosophy

Phon Phonetics

PhysEd Physical Education

PhysSc Physical Science

PIA Pakistan International Airlines

PIB Prices and Incomes Board *(see NBPI)*

PIDE Portugal's *(former)* Secret Police

PIE Paedophile Information Exchange

PIME Pontifical Foreign Mission Institute

PIMS Purchase and Improvement Mortgage Scheme *(Birmingham Housing Venture, see also AIMS)*

PIN Personal Identification Number *(credit card)*

PINX/Pinx *(Latin)* Pinxit *(he/she painted it)*

PIRA Paper Industries Research Organisation; Packaging Industries Research Association *(see also IOP, INCPEN and) EAT)*

PIRC Public Interest Research Centre

PIStructE President of the Institution of Structural Engineers

PIW Period of Incapacity for Work

pizz *(music)* pizzicato *(plucking with fingers)*

PK Indonesia Airline

PL Poet Laureate; Primrose League; Patrol Leader; Polish International Motor Vehicle Registration Letters; Paymaster Lieutenant *(RN, q.v.)*

Pl Place

P/L Profit and Loss

PLA Port of London Authority; Palestine Liberation Army; Passenger Luggage in Advance *(British Rail Service)*; *(China)* People's Liberation Army

PLAN Prostitution Laws Are Nonsense

PLC/plc Public Limited Company

Plen Plenipotentiary

PLF *(San Salvador)* Popular Liberation Force

PLI Public Local Inquiry

PLM Paris - Lyons - Méditerranée *(French Railway to Riviera)*

PLN *(Costa Rica)* Partido Liberacion Nacional *(National Liberation Army)*

PLO Palestine Liberation Organisation

PLP Parliamentary Labour Party; *(Bermuda)* Progressive Labour Party; *(Bahamas)* Progressive Liberal Party

PLR Public Lending Right

PLUTO Pipe-Line-Under-The-Ocean

PM Prime Minister; Past Master; Postmaster; Provost Marshall; Paymaster; *(Latin)* Post Meridiem *(afternoon)*; *(Latin)* Post Mortem *(after death)*

Pm Promethium

pm *(Latin)* post meridiem *(afternoon)*

PMA Positive Mental Attitude

PMB Potato Marketing Board

PMC Professional and Managerial Class; *(Association of)* Parents of Murdered Children

PMG Postmaster General; Paymaster General

pmh production per man hour

PMI Indonesian Red Cross

PMO Principal Medical Officer

PMRAFNS Princess Mary's Royal Air Force Nursing Service

PMS President of the Miniature Society; Pre-Menstrual Syndrome

PMT Pre-Menstrual Tension

PMTS Pre-Determined Motion Time System *(work study)*

PMU *(Botswana)* Para-Military Mobile Police Unit; *(France)* Paris Mutuel *(betting organisation)*

PN Pupil Nurse

PNA Pakistan National Alliance

PNC *(Guyana)* People's National Congress

PNDC *(Ghana)* Provisional National Defence Council

PNEU Parents' National Educational Union; *(France)* Pneumatique *(tyre)*

PNG Papua New Guinea International Motor Vehicle Registration Letters

PNM *(Trinidad)* People's National Movement

PNO Principal Nursing Officer

PNP *(Jamaica)* People's National Party; *(Puerto Rico)* Partido Progresista Nacional *(New Progressive Party)*; *(Ghana)* People's National Party

PNV *(Spain)* Partido Nacionalista Vasco *(Basque Nationalist Party)*

PO Philharmonic Orchestra; Petty Officer; Post Office; Postal Order; Patent Office; Personnel Officer; Pilot Officer; Parcels Office

Po Polonium

POA Prison Officers' Association

POAC Post Office Ambulance Centres

POB Post Office Box; Ponies of Britain

POBF Post Office (Clerks) Benevolent Fund

PoCo Procedures for Political Co-operation *(EEC, q.v., Council of Ministers)*

POD Post Office Department; Pay on Delivery

POETSDay! Push - Off - Early - Tomorrow's - Saturday!

POEU Post Office Engineers' Union

POFR Post Office Fellowship of Remembrance

POGO Polar Orbiting Geophysical Observatory *(see also EGO and OGO)*

POID Post Office Investigation/Intelligence Department

POIS Post Office Insurance Society

Polio Poliomyelitis

Poly Polytechnic

POMSA Post Office Management Staff Association

POO Post Office Order

Pop Population

POPA Property Owners' Protection Association

POPE People Opposing Papal Edicts

POQO *(Azania)* National Liberation Army *(see also ANLA)*

POR Professional and Office Recruitment

PORCH Parish of Richmond *(Surrey)* Community Help

PORIS Post Office Radio Interference Service

Porn Pornography

POSB Post Office Savings Bank *(now NSB, q.v.)*

POSE Promotion of Social Education

POSH Port Cabin Outward Starboard Home *(sea booking)*

POSSF Post Office Staff Superannuation Fund

POSSUM Patient Operated Selector Mechanism *(see PUA)*

POU *(Zimbabwe)* Psychological Operators Unit

POUNC Post Office Users' National Council

POW Prince of Wales; Prisoner of War; Pictures of Women *(a collective)*

POWAR Place of Work Accredited Representatives *(of BMA, q.v.)*

POWU Post Office Workers' Union

PP Past President; *(South Africa)* Progressive Party; *(Ghana)* Progress Party; *(Burundi)* Parti du Peuple *(People's Party)*; Polypropylene; Parish Priest

pp *(Latin)* per procurationem *(on behalf of)*; pages; *(Latin)* post prandium *(after lunch)*; *(music)* pianissimo *(very soft)*

PPA Planned Parenthood Association; Pre-school Playgroup Association; Prescription Pricing Authority *(NHS, q.v.)*; Periodical Proprietors' Association; Phenylpropanolamine

PPB Party Political Broadcasts *(TV and Radio)*

PPC Parochial Parish Council; *(Peru)* Partido Popular Cristiano *(Christian Popular Party)*; Prospective Parliamentary Candidate.

PPD *(Corsica)* Parti du Peuple Corse *(People's Party)*; *(Portugal)* Partido Popular Democratico *(Popular Democratic Party)*

ppd post paid; pre-paid; pages per day *(European Typing Formula)*

PPD/PSD *(Portugal)* Partido Popular Democrático/Partido Social Democrata *(now combined in PSD, q.v., Social Democratic Party)*

PPE Philosophy, Politics and Economics *(Oxford University)*

PPGA Pre-school Playgroup Association

PPIAS Parent-to-Parent Information on Adoption Services

PPInstHE Past President of the Institution of Highway Engineers

PPIStructE Past President of the Institution of Structural Engineers

PPL Private Pilot's Licence

PPM *(Portugal)* Partido Popular Monárquico *(Popular Monarchist Party)*

PPP Private Patients Plan; Purchasing Power Parity; Pakistan People's Party; *(Liberia)* Progressive People's Party; *(Jakarta)* Muslim United Development Party

ppp *(music)* pianissimo *(as softly as possible)*

PPPS People's Press Printing Society

PPR *(Poland)* Polska Partja Robotnicza *(Workers' Party)*

PPRA Past President of the Royal Academy

PPRBA Past President of the Royal Society of British Artists

PPRBS Past President of the Royal Society of British Sculptors

PPRE Past President of the Royal Society of Painters Etchers and Engravers

PPRSA Past President of the Royal Society of Arts

PPRTPI Past President of the Royal Town Planning Institute

PPRNCM Professional Performance of the Royal Northern College of Music

PPS Parliamentary Private Secretary; *(Latin)* Post Post Scriptum *(additional PS, q.v.)*

PPSEAWA Pan-Pacific and South East Asia Women's Association

PPSIAD Past President of the Society of Industrial Artists and Designers

PPU Peace Pledge Union

PQ Province of Quebec *(Canada)*

PR Public Relations; Proportional Representation; Puerto Rico; Postal Regulations; Pre-Raphaelite

Pr Praseodymium

PRA President of the Royal Academy; Pre-Retirement Association; *(Bolivia)* Partido Revolucionario Auténtico *(Authentic Revolutionary Party)*

PRBS President of the Royal Society of British Sculptors

PRCA Public Relations Consultants' Association; President of the Royal Cambrian Academy

PRCP President of the Royal College of Physicians

PRCS President of the Royal College of Surgeons; Palestinian Red Crescent Society *(equivalent to the Red Cross)*

PRD *(Dominican Republic)* Partido Revolucionario Dominicano *(Revolutionary Party)*

PRE President of the Royal Society of Painters,Etchers and Engravers

Preb Prebendary

Prec Precentor

Prefab Prefabricated

Prelim Preliminary

Prep Preparation *(school homework)*

Pres President

PRHA President of the Royal Hibernian Academy.

PRI President of the Royal Institute of Painters in Water Colours; Plastics and Rubber Institute; *(Mexico)* Partido Revolucionario Institucional *(Institutional Revolutionary Party)*

PRIA President of the Royal Irish Academy

PRIBA President of the Royal Institute of British Architects

PRIDE Parents' Rights to Insist on Decent Education *(Norfolk)*

Prin Principal

PRISE Programme for Reform in Secondary Schools

PRO Press Officer; Public Relations Officer; Public Records Office; Professional Actor/Boxer/Athlete; Prostitute

Pro Province; Provincial

Prob Probate

Proc Proctor

Prof Professor

PROI President of the Royal Institute of Oil Painters

PROM Programmable ROM, *q.v. (Computer Terminology)*

Proms Promenade Concerts

PRON *(Poland)* Patriotic Movement for National Re-birth *(Organisation created to replace Solidarity)*

PROP Prisoners' Right of Privacy/ Preservation of the Rights of Prisoners

Prop Proprietor

PROS Programme for Reform of the Laws on Soliciting *(see also PUSSI)*

pro tem *(Latin)* pro tempore *(for the time being)*

Prov Provosts

prox *(Latin)* proximo *(next)*

prox acc *(Latin)* proxime accessit *(next in order of merit to the first, i.e. a very close second)*

PRP *(Portugal)* Partido Revolucionário do Proletariado *(Workers' Revolutionary Party)*

PRP-BR *(Portugal)* Partido Revolucionário do Proletariado - Brigadas Revolucionárias *(PRP, q.v. - Revolutionary Brigades)*

PRRA Principal Race Relations Adviser

PRS Performing Rights Society; President of the Royal Society

PRSA President of the Royal Scottish Academy

PRSE President of the Royal Society of Edinburgh

PRSH President of the Royal Society for the Promotion of Health

PRSW President of the Royal Scottish Water Colour Society

PRT *(USA)* Petroleum Revenue Tax *(see also APRT)*

PRU Pay Research Unit

PRUAA President of the Royal Ulster Academy of Arts

PRWS President of the Royal Society of Painters in Watercolours

PS Parliamentary Secretary; Permanent Secretary; Pharmaceutical Society; Police Sergeant; Private Secretary; Primary School; Penal Servitude; Pastel Society; Philological Society; *(Portugal)* Partido Socialista *(Socialist Party)*; *(Latin)* Post Scriptum *(postscript)*; Physical Society; Philosophical Society

PSA Public Service Announcements *(TV, q.v.)*; Property Services Agency; *(Spain)* Partida Socialista de Andalucia *(Andalusian Socialist Party)*; President of the Society of Antiquaries

PSAB Public School Appointments Bureau

PSBO Premium Savings Bond Office

PSBR Public Sector Borrowing Requirement

PSC Private Secretary's Certificate; Polish Solidarity Campaign

PSD Private Secretary's Diploma; *(Tunis)* Parti Socialiste Destourien *(Destourien Socialist Party)*; *(Portugal)* Partido Social Democrata *(Social Democratic Party)*

PSDE *(Spain)* Partido Socialista de Euzkadi *(Social Democratic Party, splinter group of USDE, q.v.)*

Pseud Pseudonym

PSI Policy Studies Institute; Pharmaceutical Society of Ireland

PSIAD President of the Society of Industrial Artists and Designers

PSM *(Mauritius)* Parti Socialiste Mauricien *(Socialist Party)*

PSMA President of the Society of Marine Artists

PSO Personnel Staff Officer

PSOE *(Spain)* Partido Socialista Obrero Español *(Socialist Party)*

PSP *(Spain)* Popular Socialist Party

PSPS Posh Sunday Paper Syndrome

PSSC Personal Social Services Council

PST Pacific Summer Time

PSU *(France)* Parti Socialiste Unifié *(United Socialist Party)*

PSUC *(Spain)* Partido Socialista Unificat de Catalunya *(Unified Socialist Party of Catalan)*

PSUM *(Mexico)* Partido Socialista Unificat de Méjico *(United Socialist Party)*

PSV Public Service Vehicle

PSW President of the Society of Marine Artists

PT Physical Training; Pupil Teacher; Brazil Airline

Pt Pint; Platinium; Punt *(Monetary unit of the IFS, q.v.)*

PTA Parent-Teachers' Association

PTBT Partial Test-Ban Treaty

PTE Passenger Transport Executive; *(Spain)* Partido Trabajadores Españoles *(Labour Party)*

Pte Private *(Army)*

PTFE Polytetrafluorethylene

PTI Physical Training Instructor

PTO Please Turn Over; Public Trustee Office; Professional and Technical Officers *(Civil Service)*

PTT *(France and Switzerland)* Postes, Télégraphes Telephones *(Post, Telegraph and Telephones)*

Pty/pty Proprietary *(of a company)*

PU Public Utilities

Pu Plutonium

PUA POSSUM *(q.v.)* Users' Association

Pub Public House *(licensed premises for alcohol consumption)*
PUC Post Office Users' Committee
PUK *(Iran/Kurdistan)* Patriotic Union of Kurdistans
PULSAR Pulsating Radio Star
PUO Pyrexia Unknown Origin
PUP *(Belize)* People's United Party
PUSH People's Unity to Save Humanity
PUSSI Prostitutes United for Social and Sexual Integration *(see also PRO and PROS)*
PUWP Polish United Workers' Party
Puy-de-D Puy-de-Dome *(Department of France)*
PV Positive Vetting; Planned Volume
PVA Polyvinyl Acetate; Polyvinyl Alcohol
PVC Polyvinyl-chloride *(plastic)*

PVDA *(Netherlands)* Partij Van De Arbeid *(Labour Party)*
PVO Project Vietnam Orphans
PVOA Public Vehicle Operators' Association *(superseded by CBRPT, q.v.)*
PW Police Woman
pw per week
PWA Prince of Wales Committee
PWLB Public Works Loan Board
PWP Parents Without Partners; Polish Workers Party
PWR *(USA)* Pressurised Water Reactor
PX Part Exchange
PY Paraguay International Motor Vehicle Registration Letters
PYO Pick-Your-Own
Pyr-Or Pyrénées-Orient *(Department of France)*
PZ Netherlands Surinam Airline

Q

Q Queen; Question
QAB Queen Anne's Bounty
QAIMNS Queen Alexandra's Imperial Military Nursing Service
QALAS Qualified Associate of the Chartered Land Agents' Society *(now ARICS, q.v.)*
QANTAS Queensland and Northern Territory Airline Service
QARANC Queen Alexandra's Royal Army Nursing Corps
QARNNS Queen Alexandra's Royal Naval Nursing Service
QB Queen's Bench *(Law Reports)*
QBD Queen's Bench Division *(of the High Court)*
QC Queen's Counsel
QD Quarter Deck *(RN, q.v.)*
QDG Queen's Dragoon Guards
QED *(Latin)* Quod Erat Demonstrandum *(which was to be proved)*
QF Quick Firing
QFSM Queen's Fire Service Medal
QGM Queen's Gallantry Medal
QHA Quaker Homeless Action
QHC Honorary Chaplain to the Queen
QHDS Honorary Dental Surgeon to the Queen
QHM Queen's Harbour Master *(RN, q.v.)*
QHNS Honorary Nursing Sister to the Queen
QHP Honorary Physician to the Queen
QHS Honorary Surgeon to the Queen

QID *(Latin)* Quater in Die *(four times daily)*
QIDN Queen's Institute of District Nursing
Qld Queensland *(Australia)*
Qly Quarterly
QM Quartermaster *(RN, q.v.)*
qm *(Latin)* quoque mane *(every morning)*
QMAAC Queen Mary's Army Auxiliary Corps
QMC Queen Mary College London
QMG Quartermaster-General
qn *(Latin)* quoque nocte *(every evening)*
QOCH Queen's Own Cameron Highlanders
QOH Queen's Own Hussars
QPM Queen's Police Medal
QPR Queen's Park Rangers
Qr Quarter/Quarterly
QRA Quick Reactor Alert
QS Quantity Surveyor; Quarter Sessions
QSJM Queen's Silver Jubilee Medal
qt quart
qty quantity
QUALGO Quasi-Autonomous Local Government Organisation
QUANGO Quasi-Autonomous Non-Governmental Organisation *(see also NGO, ONG and WINGO)*
QUB Queen's University Belfast
Que Quebec
qv *(Latin)* quod vide *(which see)*

R

R *(Latin)* Regina *(Queen)*; *(Latin)* Rex *(King)*; Rector; Republican; Resistance/ Resistor; Romania International Motor Vehicle Registration Letter

r Rouble/ruble *(Monetary unit of the USSR)*; rupee *(Monetary unit of India)*

RA Regional Administrator *(NHS, q.v.)*; Academician of the Royal Academy of Arts; Royal Artillery; Regional Architect *(NHS, q.v.)*; Ratepayers' Association; Royal Academy; Ramblers' Association *(usually preceded by the name of the Association)*; Argentina International Motor Vehicle Registration Letters

Ra Radium

RA (The) The Royal Academy of Arts

RAA Royal Academy of Arts; Royal Artillery Association; Regional Arts Association; Royal Australia Artillery

RAAF Royal Auxiliary Air Force; Royal Australian Air Force

RAAMC Royal Australian Army Medical Corps

RAAs Regional Arts Associations

RABRM Research Associations of British Rubber Manufacturers

RAC Royal Automobile Club; Royal Agricultural College; Royal Armoured Corps; Regional Advisory Councils *(TV/Radio)*

RACGP Royal Australian College of General Practitioners

RACI Royal Australian Chemical Institute

RACMSC Royal Automobile Club Motor Sports Council

RACP Royal Australian College of Physicians

RACS Royal Australian College of Surgeons

RAD Royal Academy of Dancing

RADA Royal Academy of Dramatic Art

RADAR Radio Detection and Ranging; Royal Association for Disability and Rehabilitation

RADC Royal Army Dental Corps

RADD The Royal Association in Aid of the Deaf and Dumb

RAdm Rear Admiral

RAE Royal Aircraft Establishment; Royal Australian Engineers

RAEC Royal Army Educational Corps

RAeS Royal Aeronautical Society

RAF Royal Air Force; *(West Germany)* Red Army Faction *(terrorist group)*

RAFA Royal Air Force Association

RAFBF Royal Air Force Benevolent Fund

RAFRO Royal Air Force Reserve of Officers

RAFS Royal Air Force Staff College

RAFVR Royal Air Force Volunteer Reserve

RAGC Royal and Ancient Golf Club, St. Andrews

RAGE Ratepayers' Action Group Edinburgh

RAI Royal Archaeological Institute; Royal Anthropological Institute; *(Italy)* Radio Audizioni Italiane *(Broadcasting Corporation)*

RAIA Royal Australian Institute of Architects

RAIC Royal Architectural Institute of Canada

RALI *(Portugal)* Regimento de Artilharia Ligeira *(Light Artillery Regiment)*

rall *(music)* rallentando *(becoming slower)*

RAM Member of the Royal Academy of Music; Random Access Memory *(Computer terminology)*; Royal Air Maroc *(Royal Moroccan Airline)*

RAMC Royal Army Medical Corps; Royal Army Medical College

RAMM Radical Association of Methodist Ministers

RAN Royal Australian Navy

RANA Registered Animal Nursing Auxiliary

R and A Royal and Ancient *(Golf Club, St. Andrews)*

R and D Research and Development

R and R Rest and Recuperation

RANR Royal Australian Naval Reserve

RANVR Royal Australian Naval Volunteer Reserve

RAOB Royal Antediluvian Order of Buffaloes

RAOC Royal Army Ordnance Corps

RAP Radical Alternatives to Prison; Rhodesian Action Party

RAPC Royal Army Pay Corps

RAPE Richmond *(on Thames)* Association for the Preservation of the Environment

RAS Royal Astronomical Society; Royal Aeronautical Society; Royal Asiatic Society

RASC Royal Army Service Corps *(now RCT, q.v.)*

RASE Royal Agricultural Society of England

RATP *(France)* Régie Autonome des Transports Parisiens *(Paris municipal transport system)*

RAuxAF Royal Auxiliary Air Force

RAVC Royal Army Veterinary Corps

RAWP Resource Allocation Working Party *(NHS, q.v.)*

RB Rifle Brigade; River Board; Botswana International Motor Vehicle Registration Letters

Rb Rubidium

RBA Member of the Royal Society of

British Artists

RBC Royal British Colonial Society of Artists

RBL Royal British Legion

RBN Registry of Business Names

RBNA Royal British Nurses' Association

RBS Royal Ballet School; Raise-Bottom-Slightly *(comic definition of a gentleman)*; Royal Society of British Sculptors

RBSA Royal Birmingham Society of Artists; Member of the Royal Birmingham Society of Artists

RC Roman Catholic; Red Cross; Research Centre; Royal Commission; Radio Canada; Reformed Church; Resistance-Capacitance; Taiwan International Motor Vehicle Registration Letters

RCA Residential Care Association; Royal College of Arts; Royal Company of Archers; Member of the Royal Canadian Academy; Radio Corporation of America; Central African Empire International Motor Vehicle Registration Letters

RCAA Royal Canadian Academy of Art

RCAC Royal Canadian Armoured Corps

RCAF Royal Canadian Air Force

RCamA Member of the Royal Cambrian Academy

RCB Regular Commissions Board; Congo International Motor Vehicle Registration Letters

RCC Rural Community Council *(usually preceded by initial of County)*; *(Libya)* Revolutionary Command Council; Rape Crisis Centre; *(Iraq)* Revolutionary Command Council

RCD Regional Co-operation of Development *(part of CENTO, q.v.)*

rcd residual current device *(electricity)*

RCDS Royal College of Defence Studies

RCEP Royal Commission on Environmental Pollution

RCGP Royal College of General Practitioners

RCH Chile International Motor Vehicle Registration Letters

RCHA Royal Canadian Horse Artillery

RCI Royal Canadian Institute

RCM Royal College of Music; Royal College of Midwives

RCMP Royal Canadian Mounted Police

RCN Royal Canadian Navy

Rcn Royal College of Nursing

RCNC Royal Corps of Naval Constructors

RCNVR Royal Canadian Naval Volunteer Reserve

RCO Royal College of Organists

RCOG Royal College of Obstetricians and Gynaecologists

RCP Royal College of Physicians; Royal College of Psychiatrists

RCPI Royal College of Physicians of Ireland

RCQ Returned Cheque

RCS Royal College of Surgeons; Royal Commonwealth Society; Royal College of Science; Royal Corps of Signals; Royal Counties Show; Reaction Control System *(astronauts)*

RCSB Royal Commonwealth Society for the Blind

RCSE Royal College of Surgeons of Edinburgh

RCSI Royal College of Surgeons of Ireland

RCT Royal Corps of Transport

RCTA Retail Confectionery and Tobacconists' Association

RCVS Royal College of Veterinary Surgeons

RD Rural Dean; Reserve Decoration *(Royal Navy)*

R/D Refer to Drawer

Rd Road; Rand *(Monetary unit of South Africa)*

RDA Royal Docks Association; Royal Dental Association; Riding for the Disabled Association

RDC Rural District Council *(usually preceded by initial of Council)*; Regional Dental Committee *(NHS, q.v.)*

RDE Research and Development Establishment

RDF Rapid Deployment Force

RDI Royal Designer for Industry *(Royal Society of Arts)*

RDO Regional Dental Officer *(NHS, q.v.)*

RDS Research Defence Society; Royal Drawing Society; Royal Dublin Society

RdTh Radiothorium

RDY Royal Dockyard

RE Royal Engineers; Fellow of the Royal Society of Painters, Etchers and Engravers; Regional Engineer *(NHS, q.v.)*

Re Rupee *(Monetary unit of India, Pakistan and Sri Lanka)*; Rhenium

REACH Retired Executives Action Clearing House

REAL *(USA)* Rape Emergency Assistance League; *(Brazil)* Real Aerovias do Brazil *(airline)*

Rear-Adm Rear Admiral

REB Regional Examining Bodies

recit *(music)* recitativo *(declamatory)*

REconS Royal Economic Society

RECorps Royal Engineers Corps

Rect Rector

REG *(Latin)* Regina *(Queen)*; Random Event Generator *(para-psychology)*

Reg Region; Regional

RegArch Registered Architect

RegProf Regius Professor

Regt Regiment

REHAB Rehabilitation of the Disabled

REM Rapid Eye Movement *(in sleep)*; Radio Electrical Mechanic *(RN, q.v.)*

REME Royal Electrical and Mechanical Engineers

Rep Representative; Repertory

RER *(France)* Réseau Express Régional *(Paris Super Metro)*

RERO Royal Engineers Reserve of Officers

RES Royal Entomological Society of London

RET Road Equivalent Tariff *(ferry financing system)*; Retired

Ret Retired

Rev Reverend

RF Radio Frequency; Royal Fusiliers; Rugby Football; République Française *(French Republic)*; *(Zimbabwe)* White Republican Front

RFA Royal Field Artillery

RFC Rugby Football Club

RFE Radio Free Europe

RFH Royal Festival Hall

RFL Rubgy Football League

RFN Registered Fever Nurse

RFR *(France)* Gaullist Organisation *(replacing UDR, q.v.)*; Former Zimbabwe International Motor Vehicle Registration Letters

RFS Registry of Friendly Societies; Royal Forestry Society.

RFT Regional Film Theatre

RFU Rugby Football Union

RGA Royal Garrison Artillery

Rgd/rgd Registered

R-Genl Registrar-General

RGG Royal Grenadier Guards

RGI Royal Glasgow Institute of the Fine Arts

RGN Registered General Nurse

RGO Royal Greenwich Observatory

RGS Royal Geographical Society

Rgt Regiment

RGTF Royal General Theatrical Fund

RH Royal Highness; Royal Hospital; Royal Highlands; Haiti International Motor Vehicle Registration Letters

Rh Rhodium

RHA Regional Health Authority; Royal Horse Artillery; Royal Hibernian Academy of Arts; Road Haulage Association; Royal Hibernian Academician

RHB Regional Hospitals Board *(NHS, q.v.)*

RHBF Rowland Hill Benevolent Fund

RHC Royal Holloway College

rhd right-hand drive

RHF Royal Highland Fusiliers

RHG Royal Horse Guards

RHistS Royal Historical Society

RHPhC Regional Hospitals Pharmaceutical Committee

RHPLC Royal Hospitals Pharmaceutical Committee *(NHS, q.v.)*

RHR Royal Highland Regiment

RHS Royal Horticultural Society; Royal Humane Society

RHV Registered Health Visitor

RI Rotary International; Member of the Royal Institute of Painters in Water Colours; Rhode Island *(USA State)*; Indonesia International Motor Vehicle Registration Letters

Ri Rial *(Monetary unit of Iran)*

RIA Royal Irish Academy

RIAC Royal Irish Automobile Club

RIAI The Royal Institute of the Architects of Ireland

RIAM Royal Irish Academy of Music

RIAS Royal Incorporation of Architects in Scotland

RIBA Member of the Royal Institute of British Architects

RIBI Rotary International in Great Britain and Ireland

RIC Royal Institute of Chemistry

RICA Research Institute for Consumer Affairs

RICB Research into Child Blindness

RICE Right to Comprehensive Education

RICS Royal Institution of Chartered Surveyors

RIF Royal Irish Fusiliers

RIGB Royal Institution of Great Britain

RIIA Royal Institute of International Affairs

RIM Mauritanian International Motor Vehicle Registration Letters

rin/rinf *(music)* rinforzando *(with additional emphasis)*

RINA Royal Institution of Naval Architects

RIOP Royal Institute of Oil Painters

RIOQ *(Portugal)* Regimento de Infantaria Operacional de Queluz-Operational *(Infantry Regiment of Quelez)*

RIP *(Latin)* Requiescat in Pace *(Rest in Peace)*

RIPA Royal Institute of Public Administration

RIPHH Royal Institute of Public Health and Hygiene

RIRMA Revisers, Ink and Roller Makers' Auxiliaries *(News Printing Union)*

RISD Rural Institutions and Services Division *(of FAO, q.v.)*

rit *(music)* ritardando *(getting gradually slower)*

riten *(music)* ritenuto *(held back)*

RL Rugby League; Lebanon International Motor Vehicle Registration Letters

Rl Riyal *(Monetary unit of Saudi Arabia and the Yemen)*

Rl/s Rouble(s) *(Monetary unit of USSR, q.v.)*

RLO Returned Letter Office

RLSS Royal Life Saving Society

RM Royal Mail; Royal Marines; Registered Midwife; Malagasy Republic International Motor Vehicle Registration Letters

Rm Reichsmark *(Monetary unit of West Germany)*

RMA Royal Military Academy; Royal Marines Association; Royal Marine Artillery

RMC Royal Military College *(now RMA, q.v.)*; Regional Medical Committee *(NHS, q.v.)*; Ready-Mixed Concrete

RMCS Royal Military College of Science

RMetS Royal Meteorological Society

RMFVR Royal Marine Forces Volunteer Reserve

RMM Mali International Motor Vehicle Registration Letters

RMN Registered Mental Nurse

RMND Registered Nurse for Mental Defectives Scotland

RMNS Registered Nurse for the Mentally Sub-normal

RMO Resident Medical Officer; Regional Medical Officer

RMPA Royal Medico-Psychological Association

RMS Royal Medical Society; Royal Meteorological Society; Royal Microscopical Society; Royal Society of Miniature Painters

rms rooms

RMSM Royal Military School of Music

RMSO Regional Management Services Officer *(NHS, q.v.)*

RN Royal Navy; Registered Nurse *(now RGN, q.v.)*; Niger International Motor Vehicle Registration Letters

Rn Radon

RNA Royal Naval Association; Ribonucleic Acid *(in genetic cells, see also DNA)*

RNAS Royal Naval Air Service

RNBT Royal Naval Benevolent Trust

RNC Royal Naval College

RNCM Royal Northern College of Music

RNDQs Royal Naval Detention Quarters

'RNEC Royal Naval Engineering College

RNIB Royal National Institute for the Blind

RNID/RNIFD Royal National Institute for the Deaf

RNLI Royal National Life-boat Institution

RNMC Regional Nursing Midwifery Committee *(NHS, q.v.)*

RNO Registered Nursing Officer *(NHS, q.v.)*

RNR Royal Naval Reserve; Renewable Natural Resources; Zambia International Motor Vehicle Registration Letters

RNS Royal Numismatic Society

RNSC Royal Naval Staff College

RNT Registered Nurse Teacher/Tutor

RNVR Royal Naval Volunteer Reserve

RNVSR Royal Naval Volunteer Supplementary Reserve

RNXS Royal Naval Auxiliary Service

RNZAC Royal New Zealand Armoured Corps

RNZAF Royal New Zealand Air Force

RNZN Royal New Zealand Navy

RNZNVR Royal New Zealand Naval Volunteer Reserve

RO Radio Operator *(RN, q.v.)*; Record Office; Returning Officer; Receiving Officer; Registered Office; Royal Observatory; Reality Orientation *(form of occupational therapy)*

ROA Racehorse Owners' Association

ROC Royal Observer Corps; Regional Optical Committee *(NHS, q.v.)*; Rate of Climb

ROF Royal Ordnance Factories

R of O Reserve of Officers

ROI Member of the Royal Institute of Oil Painters; Return on Investment

ROK Korean International Motor Vehicle Registration Letters

ROM Read-Only-Memory *(Computer Terminology)*

ROP Russian Oil Products

ROPCO *(Polish)* Human and Civil Rights Movement

RORC Royal Ocean Racing Club

ROSL Royal Overseas League

RoSPA Royal Society for the Prevention of Accidents

ROW Rights of Women *(legal feminist group)*

RP Royal Society of Portrait Painters; Regional Pharmacist *(NHS, q.v.)*; Retinitis Pigmentosa *(eye disease, Tunnel Vision)*; Regius Professor; Registered Plumber; Philippines International Motor Vehicle Registration Letters

Rp Rupiah *(Monetary unit of Indonesia)*; Rappen *(Monetary unit of Switzerland)*

rp reply paid; réponse payée *(reply paid)*

RPA Rationals' Press Association

RPC Royal Pioneer Corps; Regional Pharmaceutical Committee *(NHS, q.v.)*

RPD Regius Professor of Divinity; Doctor of Political Science

rph revolutions per hour

RPhilS Royal Philharmonic Society; Royal Philatelic Society

RPhO Regional Pharmaceutical Officer *(NHS, q.v.)*

RPI Retail Price Index

RPM Retail Price Maintenance

rpm revolutions per minute

RPMS Royal Post-graduate Medical School *(NHS, q.v.)*

RPO Royal Philharmonic Orchestra;

Regional Personnel Officer *(NHS, q.v.)*; Railway Post Office

RPP *(Poland)* Republican People's Party; *(Turkey)* Republican People's Party

RPS Royal Philharmonic Society; Royal Photographic Society; Royal Philatelic Society

rps revolutions per second

RPT Recorded Parcel Transit *(British Rail parcel service, discontinued 1980)*

RPTI Royal Town Planning Institute

RPV Pilotless Missile

RQMS Regimental Quartermaster-Sergeant

RQS Regional Quantity Surveyor

RR Research Reactor

RRA Royal Regiment of Artillery

RRB Race Relations Board *(see also CR and CRE)*

RRC Royal Red Cross

RRE Royal Radar Establishment

RRP Recommended Retail Price

RS Royal Society; Research Station

Rs Rupees *(Monetary unit of India, Pakistan and Sri Lanka)*

RSA Royal Society of Arts; Royal Scottish Academy; Republic of South Africa; Royal Scottish Academician; Royal Society of Antiquaries; Response Selection Amplifier; Regular Shift Allowance; Regional Station Assistant

RSAA Royal Society for Asian Affairs

RSAI Royal Society of Antiquaries of Ireland

RSAMD Royal Scottish Academy of Music and Drama

RSAS Royal Surgical Aid Society

RSBEI Registered Student of the Institution of Body Engineers

RSC Royal Society of Canada; Royal Shakespeare Company; Random Security Check; Rules of the Supreme Court; Royal Society of Chemistry

RSCM Royal School of Church Music

RSCN Registered Sick Children's Nurse

RSE Royal Society of Edinburgh

RSF Royal Scots Fusiliers

RSG Rate Support Grant; Regional Seats of Government *(bomb-proof complexes)*

RSGB Radio Society of Great Britain

RSGS Royal Scottish Geographical Society

RSH Royal Society for the Promotion of Health

RSID *(Italy)* Eastern European Counter-Intelligence *(see also SID)*

RSJ Rolled Steel Joist *(now BSB, q.v.)*

RSL Royal Society of Literature

RSM Regimental Sergeant-Major; Royal Society of Medicine; Royal Society of Musicians; Royal School of Mines; Royal Schools of Music; San Marino International Motor Vehicle Registration Letters

RSMA Royal Society of Marine Artists

RSNC Royal Society for Nature Conservation; Railway Staffs' National Committee

RSO Recruiting Staff Officer; Rural Sub-Office; Railway Sub-Office; Resident Surgical Officer

RSPA See RoSPA

RSPB Royal Society for the Protection of Birds

RSPCA Royal Society for the Prevention of Cruelty to Animals

RSPE Royal Society of Painter-Etchers and Engravers

RSPP Royal Society of Portrait Painters

RSR Zimbabwe International Motor Vehicle Registration Letters

RSS Royal Shakespeare Society; Royal Statistical Society; Richmond Shakespeare Society; Registered Shoeing Smith

RSSPCC Royal Scottish Society for the Prevention of Cruelty to Children

RSV Respiratory Synctial Virus

RSVP Répondez s'il vous plaît *(please reply)*

RSW Member of the Royal Society of Painters in Water Colours

RT Regional Treasurer *(NHS, q.v.)*; Return Ticket; Radio Telegraphy/Telephony

RTA Road Traffic Accident

RTB *(Belgium)* French-speaking Radio and Television

RTE Radio and Television Eire *(Radio Telefis Eireann)*

Rt Hon Right Honourable

RTO Railway Transport Officer; Regional Team of Officers *(NHS, q.v.)*

RTPI Royal Town Planning Institute

RTR Royal Tank Regiment

RTRA Radio and Television Retailers' Association

Rt Rev The Right Reverend

RTS Religious Tract Society; Royal Television Society; Royal Toxophilite *(Archery)* Society

RTSA Retail Standards Association

RTU Renal Transplant Unit *(NHS, q.v.)*

RTVE *(Spain)* Radio-Televisión Española *(Radio and Television)*

RTYC Royal Thames Yacht Club

RU Rugby Union *(the senior body, all others are preceded by initial letter of County or Town)*; Burundi International Motor Vehicle Registration Letters

Ru Ruthenium

RUA Royal Ulster Academy

RUC Royal Ulster Constabulary

RUKBA Royal United Kingdom Beneficent Association

RUR Universal Robots; Royal Ulster Regiment

RUSI Royal United Services Institute

for Defence Studies
RV Revised Version *(Bible)*
RVA Returned Volunteer Action
RVC Royal Veterinary College
RVO Royal Victorian Order
RVR Runway Visual Range *(aviation)*
RW Royal Warrant; Right Worshipful
RWA Member of the Royal West of England Academy; Regional Water Authority; Rwanda International Motor Vehicle Registration Letters
RWAFF Royal West African Frontier Force
RWF Royal Welsh Fusiliers

RWGT Right Worthy Grand Templar *(freemasonry)*
RWS Royal Water-colours Society; Member of the Royal Society of Painters in Water Colours
RWT Rutland Weekend Television
RYA Royal Yachting Association
RYE Radical Youth for Europe
RYS Royal Yacht Squadron
RZS Royal Zoological Society
RZSI The Royal Zoological Society of Ireland
RZSS Royal Zoological Society of Scotland

S

S South; Ship; Sulphur; Swedish International Motor Vehicle Registration Letter
s sign; section; silver; shilling
S4C *(Television)* Siance Pedwar Cymru *(Welsh Fourth Channel)*
SA Salvation Army; Society of Authors; Small Arms; South Africa; South Australia; *(USA)* State Assembly; Sex Appeal; Soil Association; Society of Antiquaries; *(France)* Société Anonyme *(Limited Company)*; *(Spain, South America, etc.)* Sociedad Anonima *(Limited Company)*
SAA Surface Active Agents; South African Airways; Small Arms Ammunition
SAAB *(Sweden)* Svenska Aeroplan Aktie Bolaget *(airline)*; *(Sweden)* Svenska Automobil Aktie Bolaget *(motor car manufacturing company)*
SAAD Society for the Advancement of Anaesthesia in Dentistry
SAAF South African Air Force
SAAN South African Associated Newspapers
SAAWU South African Allied Workers' Union
SABA South Africa Booksellers' Association
SABC South African Broadcasting Corporation
SABENA *(Belgium)* Société Anonyme Belge d'Exploitation de la Navigation Aérienne *(Airline)*
SABRA South Africa Bureau of Racial Affairs
SAC Scottish Automobile Club; Scottish Arts Council; Senior Aircraftsman; *(USA)* State Athletic Commission; *(France)* Service d'Action Civique *(Civil Action Service, Gaullist Private Police)*
SACA/SACLANT Supreme Allied Command Atlantic *(NATO, q.v.)*

SACEUR Supreme Allied Commander Europe
SACOS South African Council On Sport
SACP South African Conservative Party
SACSEA Supreme Allied Commander South East Asia
SACU Society for Anglo-Chinese Understanding
SACW Senior Aircraftswoman
SADC Scottish Agricultural Development Council
SADCC South African Development Co-ordination Conference
SADF South African Defence Force
SADG *(France)* Société des Architectes Diplômés par le Gouvernement *(Society of Government Certified Architects)*
SADR Saharan Arab Democratic Republic
SAE/sae Stamped Addressed Envelope
SAF Scottish Air Force; South African Foundation; Swedish Employers' Confederation
SAG Salaried Artists Ginger Group
SAGA Social Amenity and Golden Age Club *(for elderly)*
SAIC South African Indian Council
SAIDA *(South Africa)* The Southern African Inherited Disorders Association
SALA Secret Army for the Liberation of Armenia; South African Library Association
SALC Secret Army for the Liberation of Corsica
SALDRU South African Labour and Development Research Unit
Salop Shropshire
SALP South African Labour Party
SALRC Society for the Assistance of Ladies in Reduced Circumstances

SALT Strategic Arms Limitation Treaty

SAM Social Accounting Matrix *(National Economy)*; Sort and Merge *(DHSS, q.v.)*; *(USSR)* Surface to Air Missile

SAm South America

SAMC South African Medical Corps

SAMI Students Against Mass Indoctrination *(Cambridge University)*

SANA Scientists Against Nuclear Arms; South African News Agency; Syrian Official News Agency

SANC South African National Congress

SANCAD Scottish Association of National Certificates and Diplomas

s and m sausage and mash

SANROC South African Non-Racial Olympic Committee

SANU South African National Union

SAO *(Algeria)* Secret Army Organisation *(see also OAS)*

SAP South Africa Party; *(Thailand)* Social Action Party

SAPA South African Press Association

SAR South African Republic; Special Administrative Region; *(USA)* Sexual Attitude Restructuring

SARAH Search and Rescue and Homing *(aircraft radio beacon)*

SARL *(France)* Société à Responsabilité Limitée *(Limited Company)*

SARUM Salisbury; *(also Bishop of)*

SAS Special Army Squadron; Stop Animals Suffering; Special Air Service; Security Advisory Services; Scandinavian Airlines System

SASJ South African Society of Journalists

Sask Saskatchewan *(Canada)*

SASO Senior Air Staff Officer; South African Students' Organisation

SASU South African Students' Union

SAT *(USA)* Scholastic Achievement Test; *(France)* Société Anonyme de Télécommunications *(Telecommunications Company)*

Sat Saturday

SATAF *(West Germany)* Second Allied Tactical Air Force

SATCO *(Netherlands)* Automatic Air Traffic Control

SATRA Shoe and Allied Trades Research Association

SATV South Africa Television

SAus South Australia

sav stock at valuation

SAVAK *(Iran)* Secret Police

SAVE Save Britain's Heritage

SAVOS *(South Africa)* Suidanke Afrikaanse Vereniging vir Oorgeërfde Sektes *(SAIDA, q.v.)*

SAVS Scottish Anti-Vivisection Society

SAWVA South African War Veterans' Association

SAYE Save-As-You-Earn

SB Supplementary Benefit; *(USA)* Bachelor of Science

Sb *(Latin)* Stibium *(Antimony)*

SBA School Bookshop Association; Sick Bay Attendant

SBAC Society of British Aerospace Companies

SBAT Supplementary Benefits Appeal Tribunal

SBC Supplementary Benefits Commission; Swiss Broadcasting Corporation

SBH Save Britain's Heritage

SBI *(Brazil)* Sociedade Brasileira dos Indios *(Indian Society)*

SBIC Small Businesses Investment Companies

SBS Special Boat Squadron

SC School Certificate; Special Constable; Special Constabulary; Staff Captain; Staff Chaplain; Staff College; Standing Committee; Statutory Committee; Salvage Corps; Short Course; *(Eire and South Africa)* Senior Counsel; South Carolina *(USA State)*; Sailing/ Shooting / Skating / Ski-ing / Social / Sports/Swimming Club *(usually preceded by the name of the club)*; Secretarial *(BBC, q.v., Staff Grade)*

Sc Scottish; Science; Scandium

sc self-contained

SC(HL) Court of Sessions Cases (House of Lords) Scotland

SC (J) Court of Sessions Cases *(Scotland)*

SCA Scottish Council on Alcoholism

SCALA Society of Chief Architects of Local Authorities

SCAO Senior Civil Affairs Officer

SCAPA Society for Checking the Abuses of Public Advertising

SCAR Schools Campaign Against Racism

ScB Bachelor of Science

SCC Specialist Claims Control

SCCA Society of Company and Commercial Accountants

SCCL Scottish Council for Civil Liberties

ScD Doctor of Science

SCDI Scottish Council of Development and Industry

SCE Scottish Certificate of Education

SCEP Steering Committee on Economic Policy *(Senior Treasury Officials)*

SCF Save the Children Fund; Senior Chaplain to the Forces

SCGB Ski Club of Great Britain

Scherz *(music)* Scherzando *(in playful manner)*

SCHR *(USA, New York)* State Commission on Human Rights

SCI Society of the Chemical Industry

SCK Belgian Research Foundation

SCLC *(USA)* Southern Christian

Leadership Conference

SCLI Somerset and Cornwall Light Infantry

SCM State Certified Midwife *(now RM, q.v.)*; Specialist in Community Medicine *(NHS, q.v.)*; Student Christian Movement

SCODA Standing Conference On Drug Abuse

SCOLA Sutton College of Liberal Arts

SCONUL Standing Conference of National and University Libraries

SCOPG *(Hong Kong)* Standing Committee On Pressure Groups

SCOTBEC Scottish Business Education Council

SCOTEC Scottish Technical Education Council

SCOW Scottish Convention of Women

SCPL Senior Commercial Pilot's Licence

SCPR Social and Community Planning Research

SCPS Society of Civil and Public Servants

SCR Senior Common Room

SCRAA Standing Conference of Regional Arts Associations

SCRAM Scottish Campaign to Resist the Atomic Menace

SCRE Scottish Council for Research in Education

SCS Society of Civil Servants; Space Communications System

SCSA Supreme Council for Sport in South Africa

SCSS Scottish Council of Social Service

SCT Society of Cardiological Technicians

SCU Scottish Cycling Union

SCUBA Self-Contained Undersea Breathing Apparatus

SCUE Standing Conference on University Entrance

SCUM *(USA)* Society for Cutting Up Men *(Women's Movement)*

SCUTREA Standing Conference on University Teaching and Research in the Education of Adults

SCV Vatican City

SCWO Standing Conference of Women's Organisations

SD State Department; Supply Depot; Supply Department; Senior Deacon; Special Duty; Sight Draft *(financial)*; Staff Duties; Swaziland International Motor Vehicle Registration Letters

sd *(Latin)* sine die *(indefinitely)*

s/d semi-detached

SDA Sex Discrimination Act; Social Democratic Alliance; Seventh Day Adventist; Scottish Development Agency

SDak South Dakota *(USA State)*

SDAW Shop, Distributive and Allied Workers' Union

SDBL Sight Draft Bill of Lading

SDC Society of Dyers and Colourists; Society of Designer Craftsmen; Single Data Converter

SDF Seychelles Democratic Party; Social Democratic Federation; Sudan Defence Force

SDI Selective Discrimination of Information

SDLP *(Ulster)* Social Democratic and Labour Party

SDN Société des Nations *(United Nations Association)*

SDP Social Democratic Party; *(West Germany)* Sozial Demokratische Partei *(Social Democratic Party)*; Society of Disgruntled Politicians *(nickname for the Social Democratic Party)*

SDR Special Drawing Rights *(IMF, q.v.)*

SDT *(Spain)* Sociedad Democrática de Toreros *(Democratic Bullfighting Union)*

SE Stock Exchange; Staff Engineer; South East; Society of Engineers; *(France)* Son Eminence *(His Eminence)*

Se Selenium

SEAC South East Asia Command

SEAFARER *(USA Submarine Project)* Surface Extremely Low Frequency Antennae for Addressing Remotely Employed Receivers

SEAT *(Spain)* Largest industrial plant

SEATO South East Asia Treaty Organisation

Sec Secretary; Section

SECL Scottish Council for Civil Liberty

SecLeg Secretary of Legation

SED *(East Germany)* Sozialistische Einheitspartei *(Communist Party)*

SEE Society of Environmental Engineers

SEEB South Eastern Electricity Board

SEECC South Eastern Electricity Consultative Council

SEeO *(Latin)* Salois erroribus et omissis *(errors and omissions excepted, usually E & OE, q.v.)*

SEFIC Spoken English For Industry and Commerce *(London Chamber of Commerce and Industry Examination)*

SEFT Society for Education in Film and Television

SEGAS South Eastern Gas Board

SELA *(Venezuela)* Sistema Economico Latino Americano *(Latin American Economic System)*

SELMOUS Special English Language Materials for Overseas University Students

SELTEC South East London Technical College

SEMIP *(France)* Service de Maintenance des Installations Postales *(Maintenance Service of Postal Installations)*

SEN State Enrolled Nurse *(now ENG,*

q.v.)

Sen Senator; Senior

SEng Qualified Sales Engineer

SEN (M) State Enrolled Nurse *(mental nursing (now ENG(M), q.v.))*

SEN (MS) State Enrolled Nurse *(mental sub-normal nursing (now ENG (MS), q.v.))*

SENSE Society for Ending Needless and Silly Expenditure

SenTechWeldI Senior Technician of the Welding Institute

SenWO Senior Warrant Officer

SEO Society of Education Officers

Seo See SEeO

seoo sauf erreur ou omission *(French for E & OE, q.v.)*

SEPM Société à l'Etude du Pont de la Manche *(Society to Study Channel Tunnel)*

Sept September

seq *(Latin)* sequitur *(it follows)*

SERA Self-Employed Retirement Annuity; Socialist Environmental Resource Association

SERC Science and Engineering Research Council

SERFACE South East Regional Forum for Adult and Continuing Education

Sergt Sergeant

Serj Serjeant

SERL Services Electronics Research Laboratory

SES Social Economic Studies

SESO Senior Equipment Staff Officers

Sess Session

SET Selective Employment Tax

SETAG Social Effects Television Advisory Group

S et M Seine et Marne *(Department of France)*

S et O Seine et Oise *(Department of France)*

SETI Search for Extra-Terrestrial Intelligence

SEWO Senior Educational Welfare Officer

SEZ *(China)* Special Economic Zones

SF Society of Friends *(Quakers)*; Shipping Federation; Science Fiction; San Francisco; Sinn Fein; Furniture Timber and Allied Trades Union; Finland International Motor Vehicle Registration Letters

Sf Science fiction

sf *(Latin)* sub finem *(towards the end)*

sf/sfz *(music)* sforzando *(emphasis on note or chord)*

SFA Scottish Football Association; Sweet Fanny Adams *(nothing at all)*

SFAC Solid Fuel Advisory Council

SFD Society of Film Distributors *(formerly KRS)*

SFDip Society of Floristry Diploma

SFEEC Social Fund of EEC, *q.v.*

SFInstE Senior Fellow of the Institute of Energy

SFInstF Senior Fellow of the Institute of Fuel

SFM Sinai Field Mission

S4C *(Television)* Siance Pedwar Cymru *(Welsh Fourth Channel)*

SFTA Society of Film and Television Arts *(now with BAFTA, q.v.)*

SFWP Sinn Fein Workers' Party

SG Solicitor General; Surgeon-General; Society of Genealogists; Scots Guards; *(France)* Sa Grace *(His Grace)*

Sgn Surgeon

SGA Member of the Society of Graphic Art

SGB Scaffolding Great Britain

SGHWR Steam Generating Heavy Water Reactor

SGM Sea Gallantry Medal

SGP Singapore International Motor Vehicle Registration Letters

Sgt Sergeant

SgVA Surgeon Vice-Admiral

SGW Senior Grand Warden *(Freemasonry)*

SH Staghounds

S/H Shorthand

SHA Secondary Heads' Association *(amalgamation of Association of Headmasters and Headmistresses)*

SHAC Shelter Housing Aid Centre

SHAEF Supreme Headquarters Allied Expeditionary Force

SHAK St. Helier Artificial Kidney Holiday and Amenity Fund *(member of NFKPA, q.v.)*

SHAPE Supreme Headquarters Allied Powers, Europe

SHARE Self Help Association for Rehabilitation and Employment; Shelter Housing Aid Renewal Experiment

SHAS Self Help Association for Stammerers

SHBTh Society of Health and Beauty Therapists

SHE Self Help Endowment *(for blind women and girls)*

SHEG Scottish Health Education Group

SHNC Scottish Higher National Certificate

SHND Scottish Higher National Diploma

SHOC *(USA)* Self-Help Opportunity Center

SHS Shire Horse Society

SI Socialist International; Order of the Star of India; Society of Indexers; Système International d'Unités *(International Unified System, i.e. metric)*

Si Silicon

SIA Soroptomist International Association

SIAD Society of Industrial Artists and

Designers

SIAE Scottish Institute of Adult Education

SIB Special Investigation Branch; Shipbuilding Industry Board

SIBCM Small Inter-continental Ballistic Missile

SIC Special Inductive Capacity *(electricity)*

sic *(Latin)*thus *(in this manner)*

SID Society for International Development; *(Italy)* Counter-Intelligence Service *(see also RSID)*

SIDS Sudden Infant Death Syndrome

SIFO *(Sweden)* Svenska Institutet för Opinions Undersökningar *(Research Institute of Public Opinion)*

SIGINT Signals Intelligence *(Army)*

SIGMA Science in General Management

SIIAEC Secretariat International des Ingénieurs et des Agronomes et des Cadres Economiques Catholiques *(International Secretariat of Catholic Technologists, Agriculturists and Economists, FAO, q.v.)*

SIMA Steel Industry Management Association

SIMG *(Latin)* Societas Internationalis Medicinae Generalis *(International Society of General Medicine)*

SInstBB Student of the Institute of British Bakers

SIP Society for Infant Protection

SIPRI Stockholm International Peace Research Institute

SIRA Scientific Instruments Research Association

SIRM *(USA)* Sterile Insect Release Method *(anti-insect)*

SIS Secret Intelligence Service *(see also MI6)*; Special Industrial Services *(UN, q.v.)*

SISIR Singapore Institute of Standards and Industrial Research

SIT Society of Industrial Tutors

SITA Société Internationale de Télécommunications Aéronautiques *(International Society for Aeronautical Telecommunications)*

SITE Satellite Instructional Television Experiment; Summer Institute of Theological Education *(Baptist Seminar, Switzerland)*

SITPRO Simplification of International Trade Procedures Organisation

SIU *(Hong Kong)* Special Investigation Unit

SJ Society of Jesus *(Jesuits)*; Show Jumper/Jumping *(horsemanship)*

SJAA St. John Ambulance Association

SJAB St. John Ambulance Brigade

SJD Director of Juridical Science

SJF *(Sweden)* Svenska Journalistförbundet *(Journalists' Union)*

SKC Scottish Kennel Club

Skr Skipper

Skt Sanskrit

SL Serjeant-at-Law; Sub-Lieutenant; Supplementary List

SLA Small Landlords Association; Special Libraries Association; *(USA)* Symbionese Liberation Army

SLAD Society of London Art Dealers

SLADE Society of Lithographic Artists Designers Engravers and Process Workers

SLAET Society of Licensed Aircraft Engineers and Technologists

SLAG Save London Action Group

SLANG South London Anti-Nuclear Group

SLAS Society for Latin-American Studies

SLBM Submarine-Launched Ballistic Missile

SLC Secretarial Language Certificate

SLD Secretarial Language Diploma

SLE Systematic Lupus Erythrinatosus *(arthritic-like disease)*

SLFP Sri Lanka Freedom Party

SLL Socialist Labour League

SLP Scottish Labour Party

SLR Self-Loading Rifle

SM Master of Science; Sergeant Major; Stipendiary Magistrate; Submarine Duty Officer; Stage Manager; Sa Majesté *(His/Her Majesty –The same initials are also used in Spain, Italy and West Germany)*

Sm Samarium

SMA Science Masters' Association

SMC (Disp) Spectacle Makers Company (Dispenser)

SME School of Military Engineering; *(Latin)* Sancta Mater Ecclesia *(Holy Mother Church)*

SMI Scientific and Medical Instruments

SMIC *(France)* Salaire Minimum Interprofessional de Croissance *(minimum wage)*; Study of Man's Impact on Climate

SMIEEE *(USA)* Senior Member of the Institute of Electrical and Electronics Engineers

SMIRE *(USA)* Senior Member of the Institution of Radio Engineers

SMLC Scottish Mountain Leadership Certificate

SMMB Scottish Milk Marketing Board

SMMT Society of Motor Manufacturers and Traders

SMO Senior Medical Officer; Sovereign Military Order

SMPTE *(USA)* Society of Motion Picture and Television Engineers

SMR Statutory Minimum Remuneration

SMSA Senior Award of the Worshipful Company of Spectacle Makers

SMSAS *(USA)* Standard Metropolitan

Statistical Areas

SMT Scottish Motor Transport; Society of Metropolitan Treasurers

SMTRB Ship and Marine Technology Requirements

SN Staff Nurse *(NHS, q.v.)*; Student Nurse *(NHS, q.v.)*; Senegal International Motor Vehicle Registration Letters

Sn *(Latin)* Stannum *(Tin)*

SN (Sabina) Belgian Air Line

SNAME *(USA)* Society of Naval Architects and Marine Engineers

SNC Scottish National Certificate

SNCF *(France)* Société Nationale des Chemins de Fer Français *(National Railways)*

SND Scottish National Diploma

SNESUP *(France)* Higher Education Unit

SNG Substitute Natural Gas

SNLA Scottish National Liberation Army

SNLF *(Nicaragua)* Sandinista National Liberation Front

SNLR Services No Longer Required

SNM Somali National Movement

SNNEB Scottish Nursery Nurses Examination Board

SNO Scottish National Orchestra

SNP Scottish National Party

SNTS Society for New Testament Studies

SNU Safe Neighbourhoods Unit *(Part of NACRO, q.v.)*

SO Standing Order; Stationery Office; Symphony Orchestra; Sub-Office; Sorting Office; Senior/Staff/Supply/Signals Officer

SOAP Society of Access Petitioners *(to children from broken marriages)*

SOAS School of Oriental and African Studies

SOB Silly-Old-Blighter; Son-Of-a-Bitch

SOC *(Spain)* Sociedad Obrera de Campesinos *(Farm Labourers' Union)*

Soc/Socy Society

SOCELEX Society Against Elephant Exploitation

SOD/SOED Shorter Oxford Dictionary/Shorter Oxford English Dictionary

SOFA Stockport Odd Feet Association *(for people with feet of unequal size)*

SOGAT Society of Graphical and Allied Trades

SOLACE Society of Local Authority Chief Executives

SolGen Solicitor-General

Sols Solicitors

Som Somerset

SONAR Sound Navigation and Ranging *(Radar & Electrocoustics)*

SOPA See NATSOPA

SOR Sale Or Return

SOS Save Our Souls; Stars' Organisation for Spastics; Save Our *(Transport)* Services

Sos/sost *(music)* sostenuto *(prolonging the tone for the indicated period)*

SOV/Sov Sovereign

SOVA Society of Voluntary Associates

SP Special Branch; Staff Paymaster; Stop Press; Polish Airline; *(Belgium)* Flemish Socialist Party; Self-Propelled; *(Italy)* Santo Padre *(Holy Father)*

SPA Schools' Poetry Association; *(France)* Société Protectrice des Animaux *(animal protection society)*; *(Italy)* Societa per Azione *(Limited Company)*

spA *(Italy)* Societa per Azione *(Limited Company)*

SPAB Society for the Protection of Ancient Buildings

SPAC Single Parent And Child

SPAID Society for the Prevention of Asbestosis and Industrial Diseases

SPAN *(USA)* Single Parent Action Network

SPARKS Sportsmen Pledged to Aid Research into Crippling Diseases

SPARTA System for Private Access for Reservations and Travel Agents

SPAT Supplementary Pay Appeals Tribunal

SPC South Pacific Commission

SPCK Society for Promoting Christian Knowledge

SPD Supplementary Petroleum Duty; *(West Germany)* Sozialdemokratische Partei *(Socialist Party)*

Spec Speculate; Speculation

SPES South Place Ethical Society

SPEX Small and Specialist Publishers' Exhibition

SPF Set-the-Party-Free Charter Movement *(Tory Dissident group)*

SPG Special Patrol Group *(police)*; Society for the Propagation of the Gospel *(now USPG, q.v.)*

spgr specific gravity

SPIC Special Projects In Christian Missionary Areas

SPIDOT Self-Propelled Immersible Drive-Off Trolley

spir *(music)* spiritoso *(in lively manner)*

SPLATT Single Pedestrians League Against Taxes and Traffic

spm strokes per minute *(European Community typing formula)*

SPMO Senior Principal Medical Officer

SPNC Society for the Promotion of Nature Conservation

SPO *(Austria)* Sozialistische Partei Oesterreich *(Socialist Party)*

SPOD Sexual Problems of the Disabled

SPOE Society of Post Office Executives

SPR Society for Psychical Research

SPRC Society for the Prevention and Relief of Cancer

SPRL *(Belgium)* Société de Personnes à Responsibilité Limitée *(Limited Company)*

SPRU Science Policy Research Unit

SPSE   Structure Plan for the South East

SPSP   St. Peter and St. Paul *(Papal Seal)*

SPT   Socialist Party of Thailand

SPTL   Society of Public Teachers of Law

SPUC   Society for the Protection of the Unborn Child

Spurs   Tottenham Hotspur Football Club

SQ   Sick Quarters

Sq   Square

Sqdn   Squadron

Sqdn-Ldr   Squadron-Leader

Sq Ft   Square Foot/Feet

Sq In   Square Inch/Inches

SQUID   Superconducting Quantum Interference Device

SR   Special Reserve; Southern Railway; Southern Region

Sr   Senior; *(Spain)* Señor *(Mr.)*; Strontium

SRA   Sea Rangers' Association; Scottish Rifle Association

Sra   *(Spain)* Señora *(Mrs.)*

SRBM   Short Range Ballistic Missile

SRC   Social Research Council *(now SSRC, q.v., expected to revert to SRC)*; Strathclyde Regional Council

SRCh/SRegCh   State Registered Chiropodist

SRD   State Registered Dietician

SRHE   Society for Research into Higher Education

SRI   Stanford Research Institute

SRN   State Registered Nurse *(now RGN, q.v.)*

SRNA   Shipbuilders' and Repairers' National Association

SRO   Supplementary Reserve of Officers

SRP   State Registered Physiotherapist

SRPFU   Society for Religious Peace and Family Unity

SRS   *(Latin)* Societatis Regiae Socices *(Fellow of the Royal Society)*

Srta   *(Spain)* Señorita *(Miss)*

SRTP   *(France)* Service de Recherche Technique des Postes *(Technical Postal Research)*

SRU   Scottish Rugby Union

SS   Secretary of State; Social Security; Staff Surgeon; Straits Settlements; Steamship; Supply and Secretariat; *(Latin)* Sancti *(Saints)*; Sunday School; *(Latin)* Sacra Scriptura *(Holy Writ)*; Sa Sainteté *(His Holiness)*; *(Latin)* Sanctissimus *(most holy)*; *(Italy)* Sante Sede *(the Holy See)*; Schüzstaffel *(Nazi Storm Troops)*

SSA   Society of Scottish Artists

SSAFA/SS and AFA   Soldiers', Sailors' and Airmen's Families Association

SSB   State Sickness Benefit

SSC   Solicitor before the Supreme Court *(Scotland)*; Sculptors' Society of Canada; Species Survival Commission *(part of IUCN, q.v.)*; Secretarial Studies Certificate, London Chamber of Commerce

SSCF   Swedish Save the Children Fund

SSDF   Somali Salvation Democratic Front

SSE   South South East

SSEB   South of Scotland Electricity Board

SSFA   See SSAFA/SS and AFA

SSgt   Staff Sergeant

SSJE   Society of St. John the Evangelist

SSL   *(South Africa)* Soweto Students' League

SSM   Surface to Surface Missile; Society of the Sacred Mission

SSN   Severely Sub-Normal *(educationally)*

SSO   Scottish Symphony Orchestra; Senior Supply Officer; Station Staff Officer

SSP   Statutory Sick Pay

SSPCA   Scottish Society for the Prevention of Cruelty to Animals

SSR   Soviet Socialist Republic *(see also USSR)*

SSRC   Social Science Research Council *(expected to become SRC, q.v.)*; Soweto South African Students' Representatives Council

SSSI   Sites of Special Scientific Interest

SSSR   *(USSR, q.v.)* Soyuz Sovietskikh Sotsialisticheskikh Respublik *(Union of Soviet Socialist Republics, see also CCCP)*

SST   Super Sonic Transport

SSTA   Scottish Secondary Teachers' Association

SSU   Sunday School Union

SSW   South South West

ST   Standard Time; Sudan Airline; Summer Time

St   Saint; Street

STA   Swimming Teachers' Association

STABEX   Stabilisation of Exports

Staffs   Staffordshire

STAG   Social Tory Action Group

START   *(USA)* Strategic Arms Reduction Talks

STB   *(Latin)* Sacrae Theologiae Bachelor *(Bachelor of Sacred Theology)*

STC   Senior Training Corps

STD   Subscriber Trunk Dialling; Sexually Transmitted Disease; *(Latin)* Sacrae Theologiae Doctor *(Doctor of Sacred Theology)*

Ste   *(France)* Sainte *(female Saint)*

STEP   Schools Traffic Education Programme; Stop the 11-plus Examination; Special Temporary Employment Programme

STh   Scholar in Theology

STI   Sexually Transmitted Infection

Stip   Stipendiary

Stir   Stirlingshire

STL   *(Latin)* Sacrae Theologiae Lector *(Reader of Sacred Theology)*

STM *(Latin)* Sacrae Theologiae Magister *(Master of Sacred Theology)*

STO Soft Target of Opportunity *(description of defenceless victim, murdered by terrorists in order to disrupt normal life)*

STOL Short-Take-Off-and-Landing *(aircraft, see also VTOL)*

STOP Stop Selling Our Past *(campaign against sale of British antiquities abroad)*

STOPP Society of Teachers Opposed to Physical Punishment

S to S Ship-to-Shore; Station-to-Station

STP Standard Temperature and Pressure; *(Latin)* Sacrae Theologiae Professor *(Professor of Divinity)*; Czechoslovakian State Police

STRAD Signal Transmitting Receiving and Distribution; Stradivarius *(violin maker)*

STRICOM Strike Command *(USA Air Force)*

STRIVE Society for the Preservation of Rural Industries and Village Enterprises

STSO Senior Technical Staff Officer

STUC Scottish Trade Union Council

StudIManf Student Member of the Institute of Manufacturing

StudIMS Student of the Institute of Management Specialists

StudITE Student Member of the Institution of Electrical and Electronics Engineers

StudIWHTE Student of the Institution of Works and Highways Technician Engineers

Stud SE Student of the Society of Engineers

Stud SLAET Student of the Society of Licensed Aircraft Engineers and Technologists

Stud Weld I Student of the Welding Institute

STV Scottish Television; Southern Television; Single Transferable Vote; *(Spain)* Solidaridad de Trabajadores Vascos *(Basque General Workers' Union)*

STW Sewage Treatment Works

SU Union of Soviet Socialist Republics International Motor Vehicle Registration Letters; Egyptian Airline

Sub Subaltern; Submarine; Substitute; Subscription

SUBAW Scottish Union of Bakers and Allied Workers

Sub-L Sub-Lieutenant

Suc Sucré *(Monetary unit of Ecuador)*

SUE Students for United Europe

Suff Suffolk

SUM Save Uganda Movement; Surface to Underwater Missile

Sun Sunday

SUNFED Special United Nations Fund for Economic Development

Super Superintendent

SUPERMAN *(France)* Super Manifestation Anti-Nucléaire *(Anti-nuclear Environmental Protection Organisation)*

Supp Res Supplementary Reserve

Supt Superintendent

Surg Surgeon

Surv Survey/Surveyor

SUS "Suspicion" *(law to arrest on suspicion of intent to commit a felony)*

SVO Scottish Variety Orchestra

SVP *(Netherlands)* Stuf Vrij Partij *(Legalise Cannabis Party)*

svp s'il vous plaît *(please)*

SW South West; Short Wave

SWALK Sealed-With-A-Loving-Kiss

SWANK Sealed-With-A-Nice-Kiss

SWANU South West African National Union

SWAPAC South Wales Anti-Poverty Action Group

SWAPO *(Namibia)* South West Africa People's Organisation

SWB South Wales Borderers; Summary of World Broadcasts

SWC Status of Women Commission *(UN, q.v.)*

SWE Society of Wood Engravers and Relief Printers

SWET Society of West End Theatres

SWETM Society of West End Theatre Managers

swg standard wire gauge

SWP Socialist Workers' Party *(formerly IS, q.v.)*

SWPA South West Pacific Area

SWRI Scottish Women's Rural Institutes

SY Steam Yacht; Seychelles International Motor Vehicle Registration Letters

Syll Syllabus

Sym Symmetrical

Syn Synonymous

SYNCOPAC *(France)* Fédération Nationale des Coopératives de Production et d'Alimentation Animales *(National Federation of Cooperatives of Production of Animal Foods, FAO, q.v.)*

SYR Syria International Motor Vehicle Registration Letters

T

T Time; Thailand International Motor Vehicle Registration Letter

t ton; transit

TA Telegraphic Address; Territorial Army; Typographical Association; Tithe Annuity; Transactional Analysis

Ta Tantalum

TAA Territorial Army Association

TA and AVRA Territorial Auxiliary and Army Volunteer Reserve Association

TAB Technical Assistance Board *(UN, q.v.)*

Tab Tablet

TAC Trades Advisory Council; Technical and Agricultural College; Telecommunications Advisory Committee; Tobacco Advisory Committee; Total Allowable Catches *(fishing rights)*

TACADE Teachers' Advisory Council on Alcohol and Drug Addiction

TACE Transport and Chemical Engineering

TACT Tories against Cruise and Trident *(Missiles)*

TAF Tactical Air Force

TAFF Take-Away-Food Federation

TAFTA *(Durban, South Africa)* The Association For the Aged

Tai Taiwan

TAM Television Audience Measurement

T and AFA Territorial and Auxiliary Forces Association

T and SWG Television and Screen Writers' Guild

TANS Territorial Army Nursing Service

TANU Tanganyika African National Union

TAP *(Portugal)* Transportes Aeros Portugueses *(Airline)*

TAPS Trans-Air Protective Services

TARA Territorial Army Rifle Association

TARDIS Time and Relative Dimension In Space

TARO Territorial Army Reserve of Officers

TAS Torpedo Anti-Submarine *(RN, q.v.)*

TAS (UK) Traditional Acupuncture Society (United Kingdom)

TASS Official Russian News Agency; Technical, Administrative and Supervisory Section of the Engineering Union *(white-collar workers)*; Transport Aircraft Servicing Specialist *(RAF, q.v.)*

TAVR Territorial Army Volunteer Reserve

TAVRA Territorial Army Volunteer Reserve Association

TB Treasury Bill; Tuberculosis; Trial Balance; Torpedo Boat; Thoroughbred *(of horses)*

Tb Terbium

TBC Tokyo Broadcasting Company

TBID Technician, British Institute of Interior Design

TBS Teachers' Benevolent Society

tbsp tablespoon

TC Technical College; Technician's Certificate; Training Corps; Traveller's Cheques; Tennis Club *(usually preceded by name)*; Tax Cases *(Law Reports)*; Treatment Centre *(NHS, q.v.)*; Touring Club *(usually preceded by the name of the Club)*

Tc Technetium

TCA Technician in Costing and Accounting; Trans-Canada Airline; Travellers Cheque Associates

TCB Thames Conservancy Board

TCBM Trans-Continental Ballistic Missile

TCCB Test and County Cricket Board

TCD Trinity College Dublin

TCDC Technical Co-operation between Developing Countries

TCDD Tetrachlorodioxin *(poison)*

TCDG Technical Co-ordination and Defence of Independent Groups *(EEC, q.v.)*

TCF To-be-Called-For *(British Rail parcel service, discontinued 1980)*; *(France)* Touring Club de France *(Touring Club)*

TCI *(Italy)* Touring Club Italiano *(Touring Club)*

TCL Trinity College of Music London

TCP Trichlorophenoxyacetic acid *(insecticide)*

TD Technician's Diploma; Touch Down; Territorial Decoration *(see also VDC)*; *(Eire)* Téalta Dail *(Irish Parliament)*

TDA Timber Development Association; Taking-and-Driving-Away *(motoring offence)*

TDCR Teacher's Diploma, College of Radiographers

TDE Three-Day-Event *(horseriding)*

TDF *(France)* Télédiffusion de France *(State-controlled Television)*

TDI Toluene Dilsocyanate

TDN Technical Data Notes

TDS *(Latin)* Tres In Die *(three times daily)*

Te Tellurium

TEA Tunnel-Emission Amplifier

TEAC Technical Education Advisory Council

TEAL Tasman Empire Airline

TEAM The European Atlantic Movement; Top European Advertising Media

TEAR The Evangelical Alliance Relief *(Fund)*

TEC Technician Education Council;

The Entertainment Channel

TechAssociate ITE Technician Associate of the Institution of Electrical and Electronics Technician Engineers

Tech(CEI) Technician (Council of Engineering Institutions)

TechGeol Technical Associate of the Geological Society

TechICeram Technician Institute of Ceramics

TechMIWPC Technician Member of the Institute of Water Pollution Control

TechRMS Technological Qualification in Microscopy, Royal Microspical Society

TechWeldI Technician of the Welding Institute

TEE Trans-Europe Express

Telecom Telecommunications

TELEX Teleprinter Exchange

TELSTAR Television Star *(Satellite)*

TEMA Telecommunications Engineering and Manufacturing Association

Temp Temperature; Temporary

ten *(music)* tenuto *(sustained)*

TEng (CEI) Technical Engineer (Council of Engineering Institutes)

Tenn Tennessee *(USA State)*

TEPSA Trans-European Policy Studies Association *(EEC, q.v.)*

TES Temporary Employment Subsidy; Times Educational Supplement

Test Testament

TETOC Technical Education and Training Organisation for Overseas Countries

TEWT Tactical Exercise Without Troops

Tex Texas *(USA State)*

TEXACO Texas Corporation/Company

TF Iceland Airline; Territorial Forces

TFD *(Philippines)* Task Force Detainees

TFP Tradition, Family, Property *(Brazil-based Catholic anti-socialist organisation of 13 countries, including Britain)*

TFR Territorial Force Reserve

TG Thank God; Townswomen's Guild *(usually preceded by initial of town)*; Togo International Motor Vehicle Registration Letters; Guatemala Airline

TGO Timber Growers' Organisation

TGV *(France)* Train de Grande Vitesse *(high speed train)*

TGWU Transport and General Workers' Union

Th Thursday; Thorium

The RA The Royal Academy

THES Times Higher Education Supplement

ThL Theological Licentiate

THY Turkish Airline

TI Costa Rica Airline; Technical Institute; Textile Industry

Ti Titanium

TIARA There-Is-A-Radical-Alternative *(Parliamentary slang)*

TIB Tuck-In-Back *(meaning sit up straight)*

tic take-into-consideration

TIE Theatre In Education

TIMS The Institute of Management Sciences

TINA There-Is-No-Alternative *(Parliamentary slang)*

TINO There-Is-No-Opposition *(Parliamentary slang)*

TINPOT There-Is-No-Possible-Other-Tactic *(Parliamentary slang for election-winning theory)*

TIR Transport International Routier *(International Road Transport)*

TIROS *(USA)* Television and Infra-Red Observation Satellite

TKK Polish Union *(official successor to Solidarity)*

TKP *(Turkey)* Türkiye Komünist Partisi *(Communist Party)*

Tl Thallium

TLA Toy Libraries Association

TLC Tender Loving Care

TLG Theatrical Ladies' Guild

TLP Turkey Labour Party

TLPWD Tory - Legacy - Plus - World - Depression

TLS Territorial Long Service Medal; Times *(newspaper)* Literary Supplement

TM Tropical Medicine; Transcendental Meditation

Tm Thulium

TMA Theatrical Managers' Association

TMCIOB Technician Member of the Chartered Institute of Building

TMIMGTechE Technician Member of the Institution of Mechanical and General Technician Engineers

TMO Telegraphic Money Order

TMP Thermomechanical *(wood)* Pulp

TN Tunisia International Motor Vehicle Registration Letters

TNC Trans-National Company/Corporation *(see also MNC)*

TnCSI Technician, Construction Surveyors' Institute

TNF Theatre Nuclear Forces

TNM Tactical Nuclear Missile

TNO *(Netherlands)* Nederlandsche Centrale Organisatie voor Toegepast Natuurwetenschappelijk *(Scientific Research Organisation)*

TNT Trinitrotoluene *(high explosive)*

TO Telegraph Office; Telegraphic *(Money)* Order; Torpedo Officer; Turn Over; Japanese-Spanish spy network

TocH Talbot House *(Soldiers' Club)*

TOKTEN Transfer Of Know-how Through Expatriate Nationals

TOMAC Toroidal Magnetic Chamber

TOPS Training Opportunities Scheme

TOR Treaty of Rome

TOSD Trinity Order of St. Dominic

Tote Totalisator *(calculating device)*

TOTEM Combined Heat/Power Module *(food irradiation)*

TOVALOP Tanker Owners' Voluntary Agreement concerning Liability for Oil Pollution

TOW Transport On Water

TP Tax Payer; *(South Africa)* Transvaal Province

TPC Tyneside Production Council

TPD Television and Promotion Department

TPI Town Planning Institute *(now RTPI, q.v.)*

TPLF Turkish People's Liberation Front; Tigrean People's Liberation Front

TPO Tree Preservation Order

TPS Télégraphie Par le Soleil *(telegraphy via the sun)*

TR Turkey International Motor Vehicle Registration Letters

Trans Translation; Translated; Transfer

TRC Thames Rowing Club

TRD Temporarily Relieved of Duty

TRE Telecommunications Research Establishment *(now RRE, q.v.)*

trem *(music)* tremolando *(trembling/wavering)*

TRF Tuned Radio Frequency

TRF/Trf Transfer

TRG Tory Reform Group

TRH Their Royal Highnesses

TRIGA Trigger *(nuclear)* Reactor

Trin Trinity *(Father, Son and Holy Ghost)*

Trip Tripos *(Cambridge University examination)*

Triple AS See AAAS

TRRL Transport and Road Research Laboratory

TRS Tough Rubber Sheathed

TRUEMID True Industrial Democracy *(Organisation)*

TS Treasury Solicitor; Training Ship; *(music)* Tasto Solo *(one key only)*

TSA Training Service Agency

TSB Trustee Savings Bank

TSD Tertiary of St. Dominick

TSF Télégramme/Téléphone/Télévision sans fils *(wireless communication)*

TSH Their Serene Highnesses

TSLAET Technician of the Society of Licensed Aircraft Engineers and Technologists

TSO Town Sub-Office

tsp teaspoon

TSS Toxic Shock Syndrome

TSSA Transport Salaried Staffs' Association

TSSU Theatre Sterile Supplies Unit *(NHS, q.v.)*

tsvp tournez s'il vous plaît *(please turn over, same as PTO, q.v.)*

TSW Television South West

TT Telegraphic Transfer; Tuberculin Tested; Technical Training; Teetotal/Teetotaller; Tourist Trophy; Trinidad and Tobago International Motor Vehicle Registration Letters; *(Sweden)* Tidningarnas Telegrambyra *(News Agency)*

TTFN Ta-Ta-For-Now

TTT Tyne Tees Television

TU Trades Union

TUA Telecommunications Users' Association

TUC Trades Union Congress/Council

TUCC Transport Users' Consultative Council

Tues Tuesday

TULF *(Sri Lanka)* Tamil United Liberation Front

TULV Trade Unions for a Labour Victory

TUP Trade Union of Prostitutes

TV Television

TVA *(USA)* Tennessee Valley Authority; *(France)* Taxe Valeur Ajoutée *(VAT, q.v.)*

TVAM Breakfast Television

TVP Texturised Vegetable Protein

TVS Television South

TWA Thames Water Authority; Trans World Airlines; Try-walking-Across *(jocular translation of Trans World Airlines)*; Transport Workers' Association *(now TGWU, q.v.)*

TWG Townswomen's Guild *(usually preceded by initial of town, see also TG)*

TWR Trans World Radio

TWTI Two-Wheeler Teach-In

TWUA Transport Workers' Union of America

TWW Television Wales and West

TYC Thames Yacht Club *(now RTYC, q.v.)*

U

U Unionist; Uruguay International Motor Vehicle Registration Letter; Uranium; Universal *(film censorship category)*

UA Unit of Account

UAC Ulster Automobile Club

UACTA United Against Cruelty to Animals

UAE United Arab Emirates

UAM Under-Water to Air Missile

UANC United African National Council

UAR United Arab Republic *(now Republic of Egypt)*

UAS Urban Aid Scheme

UAU Universities Athletic Union

UAW *(USA)* United Automobile Workers

UBCA Universities of Britain and Commonwealth Association

UBI Understanding British Industry

UBJ *(South Africa)* Union of Black Journalists

UBP United Bermuda Party

UC Urban Council; University College

UCA United Chemists' Association

UCAB *(USA)* Civil Aeronautics Board

UCACE Universities Council for Adult and Continuing Education

UCAR Union of Central African Republics

UCATT Union of Construction and Allied Trades Technicians

UCCA Universities Central Council on Admissions

UCCW United Council of Christian Welfare

UCD *(Spain and El Salvador)* Union del Centro Democrático *(Central Democratic Party)*

UCET Universities Council for the Education of Teachers

UCG Underground Coal Gasification

UCH University College Hospital

UCL University College London

UCLA University of California Los Angeles

UCM Union of Catholic Mothers

UCNW University College of North Wales

UCP *(Australia)* United Country Party

UCS Underwater Conservation Society; *(El Salvador)* Unión de Campesinos Salvadorcenos *(Peasant Union)*

UCT Universal Co-ordinated Time

UCTA United Commercial Travellers' Association

UCW University College of Wales

UD/ud *(Latin)* Ut Dictum *(as directed)*

UDA Ulster Defence Army

UDC Urban District Council; Universal Decimal Classification; *(Spain)* Unión Democrátic-Cristiana *(Christian Democratic Union)*

UDE *(Spain)* Unión Democrática Española *(Democratic Union)*

UDF Ulster Defence Force; *(South Africa)* Union Defence Forces; *(India)* United Democratic Front; *(France)* Union pour la Démocratie Française *(Democratic Union)*

UDI Unilateral Declaration of Independence; *(Italy)* Unione delle Donne Italiane *(Left-Wing Women's Organisation)* Union Democratique Internationale *(International Democratic Union, see also IDU)*

UDP *(Belize)* United Democratic Party; *(Bolivia)* Unión Democrática Popular *(Popular Democratic Union)*

UDR Ulster Defence Regiment; Universal Document Reader *(Computer Terminology)*; French Gaullist Political Organisation *(replaced by RFR, q.v.)*

UDSP *(Zaire)* Union for Democracy and Social Progress

UE Underground Evangelism

UEA University of East Anglia

UEFA Union of European Football Associations

UEG Underwater Engineering Group

UEJDC, DEMYC & EDS Three European Conservative and Democratic Student Organisations

UER University Entrance Requirements

UET Universal Expenditure Tax *(suggestion for tax reform)*

UF Urea Formaldehyde

UFA Uganda Freedom Army

UFAW University Federation for Animal Welfare

UFBS *(France)* Union de Français de Bon Sens *(The Commonsense Party – Right Wing)*

UFC United Free Church

UFCS United Free Church of Scotland; *(France)* Union Feminine Civique et Sociale *(Union of Women, Civic and Social)*

UFF Ulster Freedom Fighters; *(France)* Union des Femmes Françaises *(Union of French Women)*

UFO Unidentified Flying Object

UFPA University Film Producers' Association

UFU Ulster Farmers' Union

UFWOC *(USA)* United Farm Workers' Organising Committee

UFWU *(USA)* United Farm Workers' Union

UGC University Grants Committee

UGT *(Spain)* Unión General de Trabajadores *(General Workers' Trade Union)*

UGTP *(Portugal)* União Geral dos Trabajhadores Portugueses *(General Workers' Union)*

UGTT *(Tunis)* Union Générale Tunisienne du Travail *(General Workers' Union)*

UHE *(Spain)* Unión de Homosexuales Españoles *(Union of Homosexuals)*

UHF Ultra High Frequency

UHT Ultra High Temperature; Ultra Heat Treated *(milk)*

UIOF Union Internationale des Organismes Familiaux *(International Union of Family Organisations, see also IUFO, FAO, q.v.)*

UIP Unfair Industrial Practice

UIT Union Internationale des Télécommunications *(French for ITU, q.v.)*

UJD *(Latin)* Ultriusque Juris Doctor *(Doctor of Civil Law and Canon Law)*

UK United Kingdom

UKA United Kingdom Alliance

UKAC United Kingdom Automation Council

UKAEA United Kingdom Atomic Energy Authority

UKAPE United Kingdom Association of Professional Engineers

UKASTA United Kingdom Agricultural Supply Trade Association

UKCOSA United Kingdom Council/Committee for Overseas Students Affairs/Aid

UKCTA United Kingdom Commercial Travellers' Association

UKEA United Kingdom Energy Authority

UKFBPW United Kingdom Federation of Business and Professional Women

UKIAS United Kingdom Immigrants' Advisory Service

UKITO United Kingdom Information Technology Organisation

Ukr Ukraine

UKTA United Kingdom Temperance Association

ULCC Ultra Large Crude *(Oil)* Carriers

ULF *(Trinidad)* United Labour Force/Front

ult *(Latin)* ultimo *(last month or in the end)*

UMCB *(Wales)* Undeb Myfyrwyr Cymraeg Bangor *(Union of Welsh Students, Bangor)*

UMFC United Methodist Free Church

UMIST University of Manchester Institute of Science and Technology

UMN United Mission to Nepal

UN United Nations *(see also ONU)*

UNA United Nations Association

UNAC United Nations Africa Council; United Nations Appeal for Children

UNADA United Nations Atomic Development Authority

UNAG *(Nicaragua)* Unión Nacional Agricultores y Ganaderos *(Union of Agricultural and Livestock Farmers)*

UNARCO United Nations Aid for Refugee Centres Organisation

UNATI *(France)* Union Nationale des Travailleurs Indépendants *(National Union of Self-employed Workers)*

UNCAST United Nations Conference on the Applications of Science and Technology

UNCHS United Nations Centre for Human Settlements

UNCIO United Nations Conference on International Organisation

UNCITRAL United Nations Commission on International Trade Law

UNCNRET United Nations Centre for Natural Resources Energy and Transport

UNCSAT United Nations Conference on the Application of Science and Technology

UNCSTD United Nations Conference on Science and Technology for Development

UNCTAD United Nations Conference on Trade and Development

UNDOF United Nations Disengagement Observer Force

UNDP United Nations Development Programme

UNDRO United Nations Disaster Relief Organisation

UNE *(Spain)* Unión Nacional Español *(National Union)*

UNEC United Nations Education Conference

UNECA United Nations Economic Committee for Africa

UNEF United Nations Emergency Force

UNEP United Nations Environment Programme

UNESCO United Nations Educational, Scientific & Cultural Organisation

UNETAS United Nations Emergency Technical Aid Service

UNFAD United Nations Fund for Agricultural Development

UNFAO United Nations Food and Agricultural Organisation

UNFDAC United Nations Fund for Drug Abuse Control

UNFICYP United Nations Peace-keeping Force In Cyprus

UNFT *(Togo)* Union Nationale des Femmes de Togo *(NCW, q.v.)*

UNGA United Nations General Assembly

UNHCR United Nations High Commission/Commissioner for Refugees

UNHQ United Nations Headquarters *(New York)*

UNI *(Italy)* Ente Nazionale Italiano de Unificazione *(Standards Association)*

UNIC United Nations Information Centre

UNICEF United Nations Children's Fund

UNIDAR United Nations Institute for Disarmament Research

UNIDO United Nations Industrial Development Organisation

UNIFIL United Nations Interim Force In Lebanon

UNIO United Nations Information Organisation

UNIONI Finland Women's Alliance *(affiliated to IAW, q.v.)*

UNIP *(Zambia)* United National Independence Party

UNIPEDE Union Internationale des Producteurs et Distributeurs d'Energie Electrique *(International Union of Producers and Distributors of Electric Power)*

UNISIST Universal System for Information in Science and Technology

UNITA *(Kenya)* National Movement *(see also MPLA and FNLA)*

UNITAR United Nations Institute for Training & Research

UNITAS United Nations International Transition Assistance

Univ University

UNLF Ugandan National Liberation Front

UNMOGIP United Nations Military Observer Group in India and Pakistan

UNO United Nations Organisation

UNP *(Sri Lanka)* United National Party

UNREF United Nations Refugee Emergency Fund

UNRRA United Nations Relief & Rehabilitation Administration

UNRWA United Nations Relief and Works Agency

UNS United News Services

UNSCEAR United Nations Scientific Committee on Effects of Atomic Radiation

UNSCOB United Nations Special Commission on the Balkans

UNSR United Nations Space Registry

UNSSD United Nations Special Sessions on Disarmament

UNTAA United Nations Technical Assistance Administration

UNTAB United Nations Technical Assistance Board

UNTAG United Nations Transition Assistance Group

UNTC United Nations Trusteeship Council

UNTSO United Nations Truce Supervision Organisation *(in Palestine)*

UNTT United Nations Trust Territory

UNU United Nations University

UNWRA United Nations Works and Relief Agency

UOTC University Officers' Training Corps

UP United Press; United Provinces; United Presbyterian

UPAA Ulster Pregnancy Advisory Association

UPC Universal Postal Convention; *(USA)* Universal Product Code; Uganda People's Congress; *(Corsica)* Union du Peuple Corse *(People's Union)*

UPE *(Spain)* Unión de Patriotas Españoles *(Union of Patriots)*

UPI *(USA)* United Press International

UPM Uganda Patriotic Movement

UPN United Party of Nigeria

UPNI Unionist Party of Northern Ireland

UPO Union of Pakistan Organisations

UPU Universal Postal Union

UPW Union of Post Office Workers

URC United Reformed Church

URO Unemployment Review Officer

URSS *(France)* Union des Républiques Socialistes Soviétiques *(USSR, q.v.)*; *(Portugal)* Uniaño das Repúblicas Socialistes Soviéticas *(USSR, q.v.)*

URSSAF Union de Recouvrement de la Sécurité Sociale et des Allocations Familiales *(Union for the recovery of social security and family allowances)*

URY University Radio York

US United States; United States Supreme Court Law Reports; Ulster Society *(for the preservation of the countryside)*

USA United States of America; United States of America International Motor Vehicle Registration Letters

USAAF United States Army and Air Forces

USAD United States Army Dispensary

USAF United States Air Force

USAR United States Army Reserve

USCL United Society for Christian Literature

USDAW Union of Shop Distributive and Allied Workers

USDE *(Spain)* Unión Social Democrática Española *(Social Democratic Union, now part of PSDE, q.v.)*

USEUCOM United States European Command

USM Underwater to Surface Missile; United States Marines; United States Mail

USMA United States Military Academy

USN United States Navy

USNA United States National Army

USNR United States Naval Reserve

USO *(Spain)* Unión Sindical Obrero *(Workers' Trade Union)*

USPA Unique Selling Point In Advertising

USPG United Society for the Propagation of the Gospel

USS United States Ship; Universities' Superannuation Scheme

USSR Union of Soviet Socialist Republics

USW Ultra Sonic Waves

UT Utah *(USA State)*

UTA Unit Trust Association; University of the Third Age

UTC University Training Corps

UTI Urinary Tract Infection

UTV Ulster Television

UU Ulster Unionist

UUUAC Ulster United Unionist Action Council

UUUC United Ulster Unionist Council

UUUP United Ulster Unionist Party

UV Ultra-Violet

UVF *(Ulster)* United Volunteer Force

UW Underwater Weapon *(RN, q.v.)*

UWC United World Colleges

UWIST University of Wales Institute of Science and Technology

UWT Union of Women Teachers

V

V Vicar; Volt; Holy See/Vatican International Motor Vehicle Registration Letter; 5 *(Roman numeral)*; Vanadium

V̄ 5000 *(Roman numeral)*

v velocity; volt/voltage; *(Latin)* versus *(against)*; *(Latin)* vide *(see)*; volume

VA Vicar Apostolic; Vice-Admiral; The Royal Order of Victoria and Albert

Va Virginia *(USA State)*

VABF Variety Artistes' Benevolent Fund

Vac Vacant

VAD Voluntary Aid Detachment

VAdm Vice-Admiral

VAF Variety Artistes' Federation

VAG Vagrancy Action Group

V and A Victoria and Albert *(Museum)*

VAR Visual-Aerial Radio Range

VAS Voluntary Advisory Service

VASCAR Electronic device for timing traffic speed

VAT Value Added Tax *(see also TVA)*

VBRA Vehicle Builders' and Repairers' Association

VC Victoria Cross; Volunteer Centre; Vice Chairman; Vice Consul; Vice Chancellor; Vice Chamberlain; *(Latin)* Vic Coactus *(constrained by force, usually after signature obtained, in the opinion of the signatory, by force)*; 95 *(Roman numeral)*

VCAS Vice-Chief of the Air Staff

VCM Vynyl Chloride Monomer

VCN Véritable Camembert de Normandie *(real Normandy Camembert Cheese)*

VCNS Vice-Chief of the Naval Staff

VCOAD Voluntary Committee on Overseas Aid & Development

VCOD Vertical Carrier Onboard Delivery

VCP Vehicle Check Point

VCR Video Cassette Recorder

VD Victorian Decoration; Volunteer Officer's Decoration; Venereal Disease

VDC Volunteer Defence Corps; Volunteer Decoration *(see also TD)*

VDH Valvular Disease of the Heart

VDQS Vin Délimité Qualité Supérieure *(Wine of Superior Quality and Limited Quantity)*

VDS Association of German Student Unions

VDT Video Display Terminal

VDU Visual Display Unit *(Computer Terminology)*

VE Vocational Education; Victory in Europe

VED Vehicle Excise Duty

VEDC Vitreous Enamel Development Council

Veg Vegetable

Ven Venerable

VERA Vision Electronic Recording Apparatus

Vert Vertical

VET Veterinary Surgeon

Vet Veteran

Vet MB Bachelor of Veterinary Medicine

VFR Visiting Friends & Relatives *(air-reduced fare)*; Visual Flight Rules *(aviation)*

VG Vicar-General

VGE Valery Giscard d'Estaing *(former French President)*

VHF Very High Frequency

VI 6 *(Roman numeral)*; Virgin Islands International Motor Vehicle Registration Letters

Vic and Al Victoria and Albert *(Museum)*

Vice-Adm Vice-Admiral

VII 7 *(Roman numeral)*

VIII 8 *(Roman numeral)*

VIP Very Important Person

VIR Vulcanised India Rubber

Visct Viscount

Visnews See BCINA

Viz *(Latin)* Videlicet *(that is to say)*

VL 45 *(Roman numeral)*

VLCF Victoria League for Commonwealth Friendship

VLF Very Low Frequency

VLSI Very Large Scale Integrated *(Circuit-Australian Silicon Chip)*

VM Victoria Medal; Victory Medal

VMH Victoria Medal of Honour *(Royal Horticultural Society)*

VMO *(Flemish)* Extremist Right-Wing Organisation

VN Vietnam International Motor Vehicle Registration Letters

VO Veterinary Officer; Victorian Order

VOCA Visiting Orchestra Consultative Association

VOF *(Netherlands)* Vennootschap Order Firma *(Company Partnership)*

Vol Volunteer; Volume

vol volume

VOLCUF Voluntary Organisations' Liaison Council for Under-Fives

VONS International Committee for the Defence of the Unjustly Prosecuted

VOSS Voluntary Organisation for Social Services

VP Vice President

VPRO *(Netherlands)* Vrijzinnig Protestantse Radio Omroep *(Combined Protestant Broadcasting Station)*

VPRS Voluntary Price Regulation Scheme *(DHSS, q.v.)*

VPS Visual Programme Systems

VP-T Trinidad & Tobago Airline

VP-U Uganda Airline

VP-V St. Vincent Airline

VP-X Gambia Airline

VP-Z Zanzibar Airline

VQMG Vice-Quartermaster General

VR *(Latin)* Victoria Regina *(Queen Victoria)*; Vicar Rural

VRD Volunteer Reserve Officers' Decoration *(RN, q.v.)*

V Rev Very Reverend

VRI Vulcanised Rubber Insulated

VRS Video Rating System

VS Victorian Society; Veterinary Surgeon

VSO Voluntary Service Overseas

VSOP Vast Surpluses of the Oil Producers; Very Special Old Pale *(brandy classification)*

VSS Victim Support Scheme *(following burglary)*

V/STOL Vertical/Short Take-Off and Landing *(aircraft)*

VSU Voluntary Service Unit

Vt Vermont *(USA State)*

VTA Video Trade Association

VTC Vocational Training Centre

VTOL Vertical Take-Off and Landing

Vte Vicomte *(Viscount)*

VTR Video Tape Recorder

VVD *(Netherlands)* Volkspartij voor Vrijheid en Democratie *(National Democratic Freedom Party)*

VVN *(West Germany)* Vereinigung der Verfolgten der Nazi Regime *(Association of people persecuted by the Nazi regime)*

VVO Very Very Old

VVV *(Netherlands)* Vereniging voor Vreemdelingen Verkeer *(National Tourist Office)*

VWO Vereinigte Wirtschaften Dienst *(German News Agency)*

W

W West; Woman; Watt; Wolfram *(Tungsten)*

WA Western Australia; West Africa; Weapons Armourer *(RN, q.v.)*

WAA Women's Arts Alliance *(formerly WFAA)*; World Assembly on Ageing

WAAA Women's Amateur Athletics Association

WAAC Women's Auxiliary Army Corps *(now WRAC, q.v.)*

WAAF Women's Auxiliary Air Force *(now WRAF, q.v.)*

WACC World Association of Christian Communities

WAC-UNA Women's Advisory Councils-United Nations Association

WAD Women's Action Day *(November 1980)*

WAES Workshop on Alternative Energy Strategy

WAF Women's Aid Federation

WAFA Palestine News Agency *(anti-Israel)*

WAG Writers' Action Group; Writers and Authors Guild; Women's Action Group; Gambia International Motor Vehicle Registration Letters

WAGBI Wildfowl Association of Great Britain and Ireland

WAGFEI Women's Action Group on Female Excision and Infibulation

WAGGS World Association of Girl Guides and Girl Scouts

WAGGGS See WAGGS

WAL Sierra Leone International Motor Vehicle Registration Letters

WAM Working Association of Mothers; United Arab Emirates News Agency

WAN Nigeria International Motor Vehicle Registration Letters

W and M William and Mary

WAP *(USA)* Women Against Pornography

WAR Women Against Rape; Westminster Association of Residents

WARC World Alliance of Reformed Churches; World Administrative Radio Conference

WARC-79 World Administrative Radio Conference 1979

Warks Warwickshire

Wash Washington *(USA State)*

WASP *(USA)* White Anglo-Saxon Protestant

WAVAW Women Against Violence Against Women

WAY World Assembly of Youth

WB Weather Bureau; World Bank *(IBRD, q.v.)*

WBA World Boxing Association

WBC World Boxing Council

WBFL Women's Broadcasting and Film Lobby

WBP Weather and Boil Proof *(plywood)*

WC War Correspondent; Water Closet

WCC World Council of Churches *(see also CCIA)*; Women's Consultative Council *(replaced 1969 by WNC, q.v.)*; Women's Constituency Committee *(Conservative Party)*

W/Cdr Wing Commander

WCG Women's Co-operative Guild

WCMD Advanced Certificate of the Welsh College of Music and Drama

WCOTP World Confederation of Organisations of the Teaching Professions

WCS World Conservation Strategy *(see also UNEP, IUCN and WWF)*

WCT World Championship Tennis

WCTU Women's Christian Temperance Union

WD War Department; Welfare Department; Works Department; Dominican *(Windward Islands)* International Motor Vehicle Registration Letters

WDC World Disarmament Campaign; *(Poland)* Workers' Defence Committee

WDFF *(New Zealand)* Women's Division of Federated Farmers

WDM World Development Movement

WE War Establishment

WEA Workers' Educational Association; West of England Association

WEAL *(USA)* Women's Equality Action League

WEC World Employment Conference

WED World Environment Day

Wed Wednesday

WEEP Work Experience on Employer's Premises *(Manpower Services Commission)*

wef with effect from

WEL Well-Informed *(NSW, q.v., Women's Electoral Lobby)*

WEO Weapons Electrical Officer *(RN, q.v.)*

WES Worldwide Education Services *(of the PNEU, q.v.)*

WETUC Workers' Education and Trade Union Committee

WEU Western European Union

WF Women's Forum

WFA White Fish Authority

WFAA See WAA

WFAW-CMT World Federation of Agricultural Workers *(see also FMTA-CMT)*

WFC World Food Council *(FAO, UN, q.v.)*

WFDY World Federation of Democratic Youth

WFGA Women's Farm and Garden Association

WFH Wages For Housewives

WFI Wait For It

WFP World Food Programme

WFPA World Federation for the Protection of Animals

WFSW World Federation of Scientific Workers

WFTU World Federation of Trade Unions

WFUNA World Federation of United Nations Associations

wg wire gauge

WGA Writers' Guild of America

WHC Women's Health Care/Concern

WHO World Health Organisation

WhSch Whitworth Scholar

WHTSO Welsh Health Technical Services Organisation

WI Women's Institute *(usually preceded by initial of town)*; West Indies

WIB Women In Banking; West Indian Block

WICS Women In the Civil Service

WID West India Docks

WIDF Women's International Democratic Federation

WiE Women in Education

WIF West Indies Federation *(see also FWI)*

WILPF Women's International League for Peace and Freedom

Wilts Wiltshire

WIM Women In Media; Women In Management

WIN Women's International Network

WINGO Women's International Non-Government Organisation *(see also QUANGO)*

WIP Women In Publishing; Women In Printing; *(USA)* Women's Incentive Program; *(USA)* Work Incentive Program

WIPO World Intellectual Property Organisation *(UN, q.v.)*

WIPPL Women In Political and Public Life

WIRA Wool Industry Research Association

WIRES Women's Information Referral and Enquiry Services

WIRF Women's International Religious Fellowship

WiS Women in Science

WISC West Indian Standing Conference

Wisc Wisconsin *(USA State)*

WISP Women's Industrial Savings Plan

Wits Witwatersrand

WIVAB Women's Inter-Varsity Athletics Board

WIZO Women's International Zionist Organisation

WJC World Jewish Congress

WJEC Welsh Joint Education Committee

wkly weekly

WL St. Lucia *(Windward Islands)* International Motor Vehicle Registration Letters; Wave Length

WLA Women's Land Army

WLB *(USA)* War Labor Board

WLF Women's Liberal Federation

WLM Women's Liberation Movement

WLR Weekly Law Reports

WMA World Medical Association

WMAC West Midlands Advisory Council for Further Education; Water Management Advisory Council; Waste Management Advisory Council

WMAG Women's Media Action Group

WMC Working Men's Club

WMCD Advanced Certificate of the Welsh College of Music and Drama

WMCIU Working Men's Club and Institute Union

WMO World Meteorological Organisation

WNAC Women's National Advisory Committee *(Conservative Party)*

WNC Women's National Commission

WNED *(USA)* Wisconsin Non-Commercial Television Station

WNO Welsh National Opera

WNP Welsh Nationalist Party

WNW West North West

WO War Office; Warrant Office/Officer; Welfare Office/Officer

WOASH Women Organised Against Sexual Harassment

WOI Women's Organisation of Iran *(NCW, q.v.)*

Worcs Worcestershire

WORG Women's Organisation *(slang)*

WOR-TV *(USA, New York)* Independent Television Station

WOSB War Office Selection Board

WOW War On Want; Wider Opportunities for Women

WOYL Women of the Year Luncheon

WP Without Prejudice; Word Processor/Processing

WPA Western Provident Association

(for hospital and nursing home services); (Guyana) Working People's Alliance; World Psychiatric Association; World Plan of Action; *(Eire)* Women's Political Association

WPB Waste Paper Basket

WPC Woman Police Constable; *(USA)* Women's Political Caucus

wpm words per minute

WPN World Press News

WPS Wives' Pension Scheme

WR Ward Room; Western Region *(British Rail)*

WRA Water Research Association

WRAC Women's Royal Army Corps

WRAF Women's Royal Air Force

WRC Women's Rights Committee; Women's Research Centre; Water Resource Council

WRENS See WRNS

WRI Women's Rural Institute

WRNR Women's Royal Naval Reserve

WRNS Women's Royal Naval Service

WRP Workers Revolutionary Party

WRRC *(USA)* Water Resources Center

WRSA World Rabbit Science Association

WRVS Women's Royal Voluntary Service

WS Writer to the Signet *(Scottish Solicitor)*; Western Samoa International Motor Vehicle Registration Letters

WSC World Service Cricket *(Packer experiment)*

WSFC Women's Solid Fuel Council

WSL Warren Springs Laboratory

WSLF Western Somali Liberation Front

WSP Women Strike for Peace

WSPU Women's Social and Political Union

WSW West South West

WTS Women's Transport Service *(formerly FANY, q.v.)*

WUCWO World Union of Catholic Women's Organisations

WUS World University Service

WUS(UK) World University Service (United Kingdom)

WV St. Vincent *(Windward Islands)* International Motor Vehicle Registration Letters

WVa West Virginia *(USA State)*

WVF World Veterans' Federation

WVS Women's Voluntary Service

WWAM World-Wide Advent Missions

WWCTU World Women's Christian Temperance Union

WWF World Wildlife Fund

WWOOF Working Weekends On Organic Farms

Wyo Wyoming *(USA State)*

WYS Wildlife Youth Service

WYWCA World Young Women's Christian Association

X

X Adults only *(film censorship classification, now "18")*; Extra; 10 *(Roman numeral)*
XA/B/C Mexico Airline
XC 90 *(Roman numeral)*
XCIX 99 *(Roman numeral)*
XCV 95 *(Roman numeral)*
xd ex-dividend
XD/CO Ex-Directory, Calls Offered *(telephone service)*
XD/NC Ex-Directory, No Connections *(telephone service)*
Xe Xenon
XEROX Formerly Haloid Xerox Incorporated and Haloid Company
XH Honduras Airline
XIX 19 *(Roman numeral)*
XL 40 *(Roman numeral)*
XLIX 49 *(Roman numeral)*
XLV 45 *(Roman numeral)*
Xmas Christmas
XV 15 *(Roman numeral)*; Vietnam Airline
XX 20 *(Roman numeral)*
XXIX 29 *(Roman numeral)*
XXX 30 *(Roman numeral)*
XXXIX 39 *(Roman numeral)*
XY/Z Burma Airline

Y

Y Yttrium
Y/y Yen *(Monetary unit of Japan)*
YA Afghanistan Airline
YACHT Youth And Community Help Trust
YAR Yemen Arab Republic
YARD New Scotland Yard *(police headquarters)*
YAS Yorkshire Agricultural Society
YB Year Book
Yb Ytterbium
YBAW Why-Be-A-Wife *(tax campaign)*
YC Youth Club; Young Conservatives; Yachting Club *(usually preceded by initial of town)*
YCI Young Communist International
YCL Young Communist League
YCNAC Young Conservatives National Advisory Committee
YCW Young Christian Workers *(International)*
YE Yemen Airline
YED Young European Democrats
YEF Young European Federalists
YEL Young European Left
YEO Yeoman
YFC Young Farmers' Club
YHA Youth Hostels Association
YHCFE Yorkshire and Humberside Council for Further Education
YI Iraq Airline
YJ New Hebrides Airline
YK Syria Airline
YL Young Liberal
YLI Yorkshire Light Infantry
YMCA Young Men's Christian Association
YMHA Young Men's Hebrew Association
YOC Youth Opportunities Commission
YOPs Youth Opportunities' Programmes
Yorks Yorkshire
YPF Argentine State Petroleum Company
YPTS Young People's Theatre Scheme
YR Romania Airline
Yr Year
YrB Year Book
YS El Salvador Airline
YT Yukon Territory
YTHF Yours-Till-Hell-Freezes
YTS Youth Training Scheme
YTV Yorkshire Television
YU Yugoslavia International Motor Vehicle Registration Letters; Yugoslavia Airline
YV Venezuela International Motor Vehicle Registration Letters; Venezuela Airline
YWCA Young Women's Christian Association

Z

Z Zero; Zambia International Motor Vehicle Registration Letter; Impedance *(electricity measurement)*

ZA South African International Motor Vehicle Registration Letters; Albanian Airline

Zan Zanzibar

ZANU Zimbabwe African National Union

ZANU-PF Zanu *(q.v.)* – Popular Front

ZAPU Zimbabwe African People's Union

ZAW Zambian Alliance of Women

ZBMM Zenana Bible and Medical Mission

ZC Zionist Congress

ZCT Zinc Citrate Trihydrate

ZDF Zimbabwe Development Fund

ZETA Zero Energy Thermonuclear Apparatus

ZFET Zionist Federation Educational Trust

ZFGBI Zionist Federation of Great Britain & Ireland

Zhr Zero hour

ZI Zone Interdite *(prohibited zone)*

ZIDS Zimbabwe Institute of Development Studies

ZIP *(USA)* Zoning Improvement Plan *(postal)*

ZIPA Zimbabwe People's Army

ZIPRA Zimbabwe People's Revolutionary Army

ZIRIC Zimbabwe Research and Information Centre

ZIRU Zimbabwe Research Unit

Zn Zinc

ZP Paraguay Airline

ZPF Zimbabwe People's Front

ZR Zambian Railways

Zr Zirconium

ZRANC Zimbabwe Reformed African National Council

ZRE Zaire International Motor Vehicle Registration Letters

ZS Zoological Society

ZSI Zoological Society of Ireland

ZST Zone Standard Time

ZS/T/U Union of South Africa Airline

ZU Zollverein *(German Customs Union)*

ZUPO Zimbabwe United People's Organisation

ZW Zimbabwe International Motor Vehicle Registration Letters

ZZ *(Poland)* Zwiazek Zawodowy *(Trade Union)*